D0168975

Food Culture in the Mediterranean

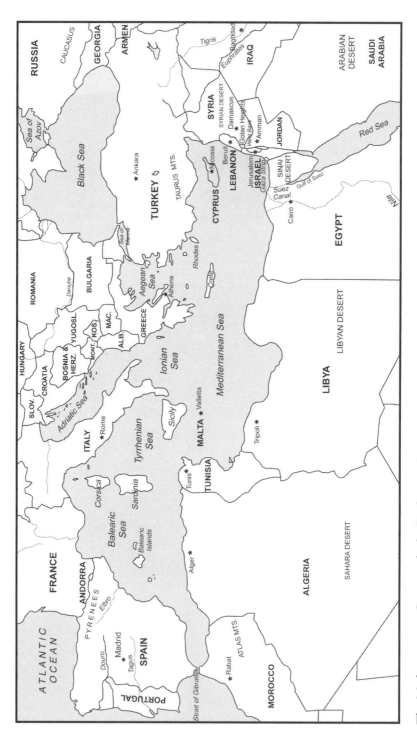

The Mediterranean. Cartography by Bookcomp, Inc.

DISCARD

MAYNARDVILLE PUBLIC LIBRARY
MAYNARDVILLE, TENNESSEE 37807

Food Culture in the
Mediterranean

CAROL HELSTOSKY

Food Culture around the World

Ken Albala, Series Editor

GREENWOOD PRESS
Westport, Connecticut • London

MAYNARDVILLE PUBLIC LIBRARY
MAYNARDVILLE, TENNESSEE 37807

Library of Congress Cataloging-in-Publication Data

Helstosky, Carol.
  Food culture in the Mediterranean / Carol Helstosky.
      p. cm. — (Food culture around the world, ISSN 1545–2638)
  Includes bibliographical references and index.
  ISBN 978–0–313–34626–2 (alk. paper)
  1. Cookery, Mediterranean.   2. Food habits—Mediterranean Region.
I. Title.
  TX725.M35H46   2009
  641.59822—dc22   2008045045

British Library Cataloguing in Publication Data is available.

Copyright © 2009 by Carol Helstosky

All rights reserved. No portion of this book may be
reproduced, by any process or technique, without the
express written consent of the publisher.

Library of Congress Catalog Card Number: 2008045045
ISBN: 978–0–313–34626–2
ISSN: 1545–2638

First published in 2009

Greenwood Press, 88 Post Road West, Westport, CT 06881
An imprint of Greenwood Publishing Group, Inc.
www.greenwood.com

Printed in the United States of America

The paper used in this book complies with the
Permanent Paper Standard issued by the National
Information Standards Organization (Z39.48–1984).

10 9 8 7 6 5 4 3 2 1

The publisher has done its best to make sure the instructions and/or recipes in this book
are correct. However, users should apply judgment and experience when preparing recipes, especially parents and teachers working with young people. The publisher accepts no
responsibility for the outcome of any recipe included in this volume.

Contents

Series Foreword

The appearance of the Food Culture around the World series marks a definitive stage in the maturation of Food Studies as a discipline to reach a wider audience of students, general readers, and foodies alike. In comprehensive interdisciplinary reference volumes, each on the food culture of a country or region for which information is most in demand, a remarkable team of experts from around the world offers a deeper understanding and appreciation of the role of food in shaping human culture for a whole new generation. I am honored to have been associated with this project as series editor.

Each volume follows a series format, with a chronology of food-related dates and narrative chapters entitled Introduction, Historical Overview, Major Foods and Ingredients, Cooking, Typical Meals, Eating Out, Special Occasions, and Diet and Health. (In special cases, these topics are covered by region.) Each also includes a glossary, bibliography, resource guide, and illustrations.

Finding or growing food has of course been the major preoccupation of our species throughout history, but how various peoples around the world learn to exploit their natural resources, come to esteem or shun specific foods, and develop unique cuisines reveals much more about what it is to be human. There is perhaps no better way to understand a culture, its values, preoccupations, and fears, than by examining its attitudes toward food. Food provides the daily sustenance around which families and communities bond. It provides the material basis for rituals through which people celebrate the passage of life stages and their connection to divinity. Food preferences also serve to separate individuals and groups from each other, and as one of the most powerful factors in the construction of identity, we physically, emotionally, and spiritually become what we eat. By studying the foodways of people different from ourselves, we also grow to understand and tolerate the rich diversity of practices around the world. What seems strange or frightening among other people becomes perfectly rational when set in context. It is my hope that readers will gain from these volumes not only an aesthetic appreciation for the glories of the many culinary traditions described, but also ultimately a more profound respect for the peoples who devised them. Whether it is eating New Year's dumplings in China, folding tamales with friends in Mexico, or going out to a famous Michelin-starred restaurant in France, understanding these food traditions helps us to understand the people themselves.

As globalization proceeds apace in the twenty-first century it is also more important than ever to preserve unique local and regional traditions. In many cases these books describe ways of eating that have already begun to disappear or have been seriously transformed by modernity. To know how and why these losses occur today also enables us to decide what traditions, whether from our own heritage or that of others, we wish to keep alive. These books are thus not only about the food and culture of peoples around the world, but also about ourselves and who we hope to be.

Ken Albala
University of the Pacific

Preface

When I agreed to write this book, I found the prospect of writing about Mediterranean food culture very exciting. In the United States and throughout the world, Mediterranean food is incredibly popular: pasta, pizza, gyros, kebab, and falafel can be found just about everywhere. Food experts and cookbook authors adore Mediterranean cuisine and with good reason: it embodies simplicity, variety, quality, and intensity. There are libraries of books and articles about every aspect of the region's food culture. Everyone knows, or thinks they know, something about Mediterranean food. I wondered if I had anything original to add to what was already an enormous body of knowledge and appreciation.

Many people throughout the world have a good idea of what Mediterranean cuisine and diet are all about, but they know less about the entire food culture of the region. Do people eat out or eat at home? How and why do religious rituals differ regarding food preparation? What do Jews, Muslims, and Christians eat on religious holidays? Why is it that the same ingredients can be prepared in so many different ways, even in the same country? Why would cooks take the time to make foods like zucchini, lentils, or figs into dozens of different dishes? Why is hospitality so important to Mediterranean people, and what do they do to demonstrate hospitality and good will through the preparation and serving of meals? Do people in the Mediterranean still eat locally produced food or do they eat more American-style fast food and prepared foods?

In this book, I have answered these questions while emphasizing how the food culture of the region can tell us about the sometimes volatile, but always interesting and dynamic interactions among the peoples of the Mediterranean region. I use the word volatile because for centuries, the Mediterranean region has been a place where different people coexist, live, trade, exchange information, and disagree. The region is home to three of the world's major religions and for centuries, the Mediterranean Sea has been an invitation to trade, travel, conquest, and immigration. Where different cultures, beliefs, and traditions mix there is always tension, but there is also great energy. Understanding food culture is one way readers can see how people of different regions come together and share ideas and information to create new dishes, meals, traditions, and forms of sociability.

To communicate the culinary excitement and dynamism evident throughout the region, I made some choices regarding the scope of this book. In terms of defining the Mediterranean region for the purposes of this study, I stuck closely to the areas that border the Mediterranean Sea: the Mediterranean coasts of Spain, France, and Italy; the islands of Corsica, Sardinia, Sicily, and Malta; Greece and the Greek islands; Cyprus; Turkey; Syria; Lebanon; Israel; Egypt; Libya; Tunisia; Algeria; and Morocco. My intention is to provide readers with the broadest possible understanding of food culture throughout the region. Because of its broad geographical sweep, this book does not cover exhaustively every aspect of food culture for every region that borders the Mediterranean Sea. Rather, I have tried to provide a variety of examples and evidence from across the region to illustrate more general arguments about Mediterranean food culture. Throughout the book, I sometimes think more categorically about the different areas of the region, based primarily on some common culinary characteristics. Thus I refer to the southern Mediterranean or North Africa (Morocco, Algeria, Tunisia, Libya, and Egypt), or to the western Mediterranean or European side of the Mediterranean (Spain, France, Italy, and the French and Italian islands), or the eastern Mediterranean or Levant (Greece, Turkey, Syria, Lebanon, and Israel). Greece and the Greek islands occupy a peculiar position with regard to these categories: many Greek food habits and trends are European-influenced, but much of the food and dishes served there resemble more closely the foods and dishes of the Levant. More often than not, I have placed Greece with other eastern Mediterranean nations when discussing food culture.

In writing this book, I relied on much of the recent scholarship about the Mediterranean region from historians, food experts, cookbook authors, travel writers, anthropologists, environmentalists, doctors, and public health officials. Although writings about the Mediterranean region span several centuries, I chose to focus on the more recently published texts, those that explored the most dynamic aspects of the food culture in the region. Recently published books cover everything from street food served in North Africa, to Sephardic Jewish cooking throughout the region, to food as part of Muslim hospitality. I also relied on many published memoirs that mention food or contain recipes to get a better sense of the recent past (post-1945) in the region. In my research for this book, I found that there were many different opinions about the essential characteristics of Mediterranean cuisine. Although many texts stress the unchanging and timeless qualities of Mediterranean food and food preparation, I relied more on sources and texts that depicted food and its preparation as a dynamic and transformative aspect of culture. In writing this book, I hope to convey some of the enthusiasm and expertise of a growing body of scholarship on this topic. I certainly could not have completed this book without understanding the work of this engaged and engaging community of experts.

Acknowledgments

I could not have completed this book without the help of others. I wish to thank Ken Albala, who provided many excellent suggestions for improving the book manuscript in an encouraging and helpful manner. I would also like to thank Wendi Schnaufer for supporting and seeing this project through and for her patience in dealing with my sometimes erratic working style. My student, Nicole M. Wong, provided important background research for me at critical moments in the writing process; I would like to thank her for her able research skills, her good humor, and her professionalism. Students in my 2007 Freshman Seminar, "We Are What We Eat: Food and Drink Throughout History" helped me explore the many dimensions of Mediterranean food culture. My thanks to all of them and especially to Carrie Gamper, Lauren Letson, Krissy Scommegna, and Shannon Sullivan for their interest and insight. The staff at Penrose Library, including Special Collections, was always courteous, professional, and quick.

And finally, I would like to thank my family who, as always, supported and encouraged me throughout the stages of this book's production. My father, Edward Helstosky, gave me a love for, and curiosity about, food. My children, Helen and Henry, provided much good cheer and enthusiasm for ideas and stories about Mediterranean food culture. And my husband, Martin Gloege, has unfailingly lent his intellectual and personal support to all of my endeavors, including this one. Without his help, this book would not be possible.

Timeline

3100 B.C.E.	Egypt emerges as a centralized state; Egyptians develop agriculture and refine cooking techniques for legumes, vegetables, bread, and beer.
3000 B.C.E.	Wine becomes a popular drink.
350 B.C.E.	Sicilian Greek Archestratus writes *Hedypatheia* (*Life of Luxury*), a guide to the best food in the Mediterranean region.
241 B.C.E.	Start of Roman expansion outside Italian peninsula. Romans under the Roman Empire incorporate foods and preparation techniques from Greeks and others.
200–300 C.E.	Greek librarian Athenaeus writes about food habits of Romans and others around the Mediterranean region.
300–400	Publication of *De Re Coquinaria* (*On the Subject of Cooking*), a collection of recipes and cooking techniques
750–1258	Golden Age of Islam; food and cuisine for the Arab and Arab Mediterranean world develop.
1226	Cookbook from Baghdad, composed by Muhammad ibn al-Hasan ibn Muhammad ibn al-Karim al-Katib al-Baghdadi, mentions kebabs and stews to be served as meze.

1281–1924	Ottoman Empire: Efforts to feed sultans and court develop into a highly refined cuisine that borrows from all surrounding regions and even Asia.
1492	Beginning of the age of exploration and Columbian Exchange. Tomatoes, peppers, potatoes, and chocolate are introduced to the people in the Mediterranean.
1554	The first coffee house is opened in the Mediterranean in Istanbul.
1600	Tea imported to Mediterranean region.
1776	Bekir Effendi sets up a sweet shop in Istanbul, where he sells a confection that comes to be known as Turkish delight.
1799–1815	Rise of Napoleon Bonaparte, who expands and consolidates territories throughout the Mediterranean; beginning of European expansion into North Africa and the Middle East, bringing new foods and food habits to those regions.
1830	France conquers Algeria.
1881	Tunisia placed under French rule.
1889	Queen Margherita of Savoy of Italy tries a pizza topped with tomatoes, basil, and mozzarella cheese while visiting Naples. The pizza margherita is named after her.
1911	Italy conquers Libya.
1912	Morocco becomes a French protectorate after being dominated by the British, French, and Spanish.
1939–45	World War II brings destruction and food shortages to the Mediterranean region. After the war, liberalized trade policies and decolonization affect what and how people eat, mostly by improving nutritional intake and the amount and variety of food available for purchase.
1951	Libya declares independence from Italy.
1954–1962	War for Algerian independence is fought against France.
1956	Morocco and Tunisia achieve independence from France.

1970s   Mediterranean fishing declines; traditional dishes and foods disappear from restaurant menus, leading to fear that Mediterranean way of eating is falling out of favor.

1975   American doctor Ancel Keys publishes *How to Eat Well and Stay Well the Mediterranean Way*, sparking international interest in the Mediterranean diet.

1980s   Expansion of American fast-food restaurants begins in Europe and continues into other parts of the Mediterranean.

1989   Slow Food movement begins, founded in opposition to growth of McDonald's and other fast food restaurants throughout the world.

2008   UN Food and Agriculture Organization finds obesity levels and fat consumption in European countries of the Mediterranean have increased.

2025   Population of Mediterranean region is expected to reach 550 million.

1
Historical Overview

For many centuries, the Mediterranean region's history has been a tale of constant interaction of people, whether through migrations, invasions, colonization, military conquest, trade, immigration, or travel. Such constant activity makes for exciting history; it also makes for exciting cuisine and eating habits. Although the people who live in the countries that border the Mediterranean Sea may differ in terms of their religious beliefs, occupations, or political affiliations, they share an appreciation for similar foods while respecting regional differences in preparation and cooking technique. For example, chickpeas have been a staple food in the Mediterranean region for centuries. In southern France, they are ground into flour and used to make large pancakes called *socca*; in Morocco, they are stewed with spices, lamb, and vegetables to make a tajine; in Lebanon they are ground with tahini (sesame paste), lemon, and garlic to make hummus; and in Syria, they are baked with a spicy tomato sauce, eggplant, and zucchini to make a casserole called *musaqaa*. Each of these recipes uses the same food to create something very different in the end. Mediterranean cuisine has been and continues to be about innovation and variety.

For well over a century, foreign visitors have noticed and commented on the variety of Mediterranean foods and dishes. The smell and color of the food seemed distinctive and appealing to everyone who encountered it. Elizabeth David, a British citizen who lived for a time in Provence, France, the Greek Islands, and Egypt, was so taken by the taste of Mediterranean dishes that she spent years of her life dedicated to writing cookbooks instructing British and American readers in the ways of Mediterranean cooking. For David, it was the simplicity and quality of the ingredients that made Mediterranean food attractive. For others, it was the sheer variety of fresh foods, available year-round, that made Mediterranean food so tasty. British writer D. H. Lawrence visited the Italian island of Sardinia for a time and wrote about his experiences in a diary. He was particularly struck by the smell, color, and abundance of food there, in particular the fruits and vegetables that seemed to glow so lucidly in the market stalls and in the shops. For observers like David and Lawrence, Mediterranean cuisine was about freshness and variety.

Today, there is much talk about the Mediterranean diet, a diet that includes whole grains, vegetables, fruit, olive oil, and fish. This diet does not include much red meat or processed foods like junk foods and frozen food. Doctors, researchers, and nutrition experts around the world have noticed that people in the Mediterranean appear to have fewer problems with coronary heart disease, diabetes, and obesity. Their diet, experts argue, is a determining factor in their overall health and ability to prevent certain diseases and health conditions. There are now many variations on the Mediterranean diet and experts believe that eating the Mediterranean way can reverse certain health problems. For medical and nutritional experts, then, Mediterranean cuisine is about health and well-being.

Variety, freshness, health, quality, simplicity: all have become key words to describe what, and how, people in the Mediterranean region eat. How did Mediterranean cuisine and diet take on these particular characteristics? This chapter explores the history of growing, harvesting, preparing, and eating food in the region around the Mediterranean Sea by examining first ancient food cultures that still influence eating habits today. Next, this chapter looks at the important historical developments in the region that affected what people ate, most notably trade, colonization, and immigration. These events brought diverse populations together, not only to exchange food, but also to exchange ideas about food and its preparation. The chapter also examines the past and present significance of agriculture, which includes not only farming the land, but tending flocks and harvesting food from the sea. Given that the region has been dependent on its own resources for much of its existence, agriculture in all its forms has significant impact on what, and how much, people eat. Finally, this chapter looks at attitudes towards food to show how historical developments, religious beliefs, and demographic factors help shape what people think about food.

THE ANCIENT MEDITERRANEAN

A great deal is known about food habits in ancient Egypt, Greece, and Rome because of the work of historians and classics scholars who use a variety of sources to tell contemporary readers about everyday life. Finding out about food habits and ancient cuisine is not as difficult as one might think. There is a wealth of information in literary sources, from Homer's *Iliad* and the *Odyssey*, both of which record all kinds of information about eating habits, to the elaborate work of the Greek scholar Athenaeus, a librarian who lived in the third century. His job allowed him to compose a 15-volume work called *The Deipnosophists* (*Banquet of the Learned*), which contains detailed notes about ancient Greek food and cookery, as well as what was served and how it was presented at meals and banquets elsewhere in the Mediterranean.[1] In ancient Greece, almost all the authors of the Hellenistic age—storytellers, historians, poets, and comic writers—recorded their observations about food, wine, banquets, and food preparation techniques. Although there are many references to these observations, not all of the works survived. Historians have tried to fill in the knowledge gap with archaeological evidence. For example, there is much evidence to suggest that even the earliest societies in the Mediterranean region made a kind of baked flatbread by pouring dough onto hot rocks. Excavations have revealed where kitchens were set up and how they operated. Through this combination of literary and archaeological sources, historians have been able to determine what people ate, as well as how people prepared food.

Historians have to read literary sources carefully, given that many surviving works chronicle the eating habits of the elite. One would have the impression from this evidence that ancient Romans spent most of their time at elaborate banquets. Hollywood has only embellished these incomplete images, giving the impression that most ancient Romans were gluttons and ancient Egyptians loved to drink out of giant golden goblets. A more accurate understanding of the role of food in ancient Mediterranean societies reveals instead how early populations chose to cultivate, prepare, and eat certain foods, as well as the values they placed on these foods. Many of the foods these populations cultivated, as well as the dishes they prepared, became the basis for Mediterranean cuisine and food habits for centuries. Some ancient habits and dishes are still around today.

Ancient Egypt

Most of the information about food in ancient Egypt comes from the period after Egypt emerged as a centralized state (3100 B.C.E.), which is also known as Pharaonic Egypt. The sources that describe food include artistic depictions on tombs, food offerings, lists in tombs and temples, and archaeological remains. At the core of the Egyptian diet were bread and beer, consumed by rich and poor alike. Bread was produced in the kitchen or was made by professional bakers and was either shaped by hand, or later on, baked in ceramic molds. Emmer, an ancient grain, was most commonly used for bread, but barley and sprouted wheat were also used. Bakers added honey, dates, figs, and other ingredients to the bread to give it different flavors. Beer was brewed at home or in breweries. Testing of ancient beer dregs reveals that both emmer and barley were used to make beer, with barley being the preferred grain for consumers of modest means. Bread and beer were consumed by all but in different quantities. Fruits and vegetables were considered non-necessity foods, out of the reach of most poor Egyptians because of the high cost of watering and tending them. Lower classes may have supplemented their diets with wild plants such as amaranth, wild grasses, and sorrel.

Social status mattered in terms of what one ate on a daily basis. Wealthy Egyptians had access to vegetables, fruits, wine, meat (usually beef), and olive oil, first imported from Palestine. An excavated tomb of a wealthy Egyptian from the third millennium B.C.E. contained barley, porridge, cooked quail, fish, beef, bread, pastries, figs, berries, cheese, wine, and beer.[2] Because meat was expensive even for the wealthy, it was reserved for special occasions. Middle class and upper class Egyptians ate small birds; duck was a delicacy that was served roasted or stuffed with crushed wheat or millet. It was either spit roasted or baked in clay casserole dishes. Wealthy Egyptians ate all kinds of fish and Egyptians figured out how to salt and preserve fish. Because Egyptians did not have sugar, they used honey to sweeten their food, and the marshlands of the Nile yielded lots of celery, lotus root, cucumbers, leeks, peas, okra and beans. Another popular vegetable was called *melokiyah*, used to make a gelatinous soup. If peasants were lucky enough to receive a plot of land to cultivate on their own, they frequently filled the plot with *melokiyah* plants in order to have abundant supplies for soup.

Those who could afford it enjoyed fruit, either as a dessert or as a course in the middle of the meal. Ancient Egyptians ate figs, dates, and pomegranates. Figs, which grew wild, were enjoyed by the rich and poor alike. Fig and date juice were used as sweeteners for dishes, and both fruits were eaten fresh, not dried. There are several dishes that modern Egyptians still share with their ancient ancestors. *Kofta*, or Egyptian meatballs, were made from lamb or beef by ancient Egyptians and grilled. Today, Egyptians enjoy *kofta* in a sandwich, tucked inside pita bread. Also, considered the national dish of Egypt, *ful medames*, or *fuul medammis*, is a fava bean dish that modern Egyptians make at home or buy from a street vendor. Fava beans are slow cooked and then seasoned with olive oil, parsley, onions, and lemon juice. *Ful medames* is a popular breakfast food, eaten with bread. Ancient Egyptians made a similar salad for breakfast, but they probably used a variety of legumes instead of fava beans.

Ancient Greece

Ancient Greeks ate wheat, barley, and lentils as staple foods: lentils as soup, barley as mash or biscuit, and wheat as bread or porridge. Even though wheat was an expensive staple grain, ancient Greeks loved it, making all kinds of bread from wheat flour. The most popular breads were flatbreads with toppings baked on them: *boletus*, rolls shaped like mushrooms; *cubo*, a square bread flavored with anise, cheese, and oil; and *streptikos*, a twisted bread made with milk, pepper, and lard. Bread was eaten with a mint sauce or a vinegar and garum (fermented fish sauce) mixture. Such an astonishing variety of bread types and flavors suggests that the ancient Greeks thought a great deal about preparing food so as to make the ordinary seem more extraordinary, or at least tastier. Greek cooks and consumers also had a wide variety of foods to supplement the staples: vegetables, cheese, eggs, fish, and sometimes meat in the form of lamb, sheep, goat, pig, or game birds. And the Greeks were well known for their fondness for sweets and desserts of all kinds. All of these foods were complemented by wine, which was served watered down.

Literary evidence suggests that ancient Greeks maintained distinctions or divisions between the types of food consumed; these divisions functioned as precursors to courses or distinct types of meals. For example, soldiers were well known for eating a lot of bread, but bread was eaten for a snack or as a meal in itself, but never for dinner. Instead, a soldier's dinner consisted mostly of roasted meat. At the beginning of a meal, ancient Greeks whetted their appetites with a variety of dishes: all kinds of olives, sea urchins, wild hyacinth bulbs (which were also used in love potions), stuffed grape leaves, grasshoppers, and cicadas. Soups were filling, made either with grains like barley or with legumes like lentils. Meat was roasted and Greeks made use of every part of the animal. Feet, ears, heads, hearts, lungs, liver, tongue, and tripe (the stomach lining) were served boiled, or they were made into a kind of gelatinous pudding. And of course Greeks had access to a lot of fish and seafood, including lobster, shrimp, tuna, eel, octopus, squid, and swordfish. Some of the more creative dishes were desserts. Greek cooks made cream desserts, a ricotta and honey mixture, fried

dough balls, pies made with cheese, a sweetened lentil dessert, and a variety of soft cookies and sweet breads. There were also desserts and breads
made for special occasions, like *elaphos*, a dessert in the shape of a deer for
the festival of Elaphebolia, or *kreion*, a flat bread given by a new bride to
her husband. After meals wine was served, a single taste of unmixed wine
followed by wine mixed with water, usually accompanied by cakes, sweets,
nuts, and dried and fresh fruit.

Ancient Greeks were great innovators in the kitchen, so much so that
they are thought to have been the first population to elevate cooking to
an art. They made use of all of ingredients available to them, seasoning
their foods with honey and herbs. They took basic categories of foods, like
bread or desserts, and expanded the culinary offerings in that category
by combining ingredients in new ways or experimenting with cooking
techniques. These innovative approaches to cooking have become the
hallmark of Mediterranean cuisine today, as cooks and chefs continue to
experiment with combining new tastes. According to Greek mythology,
phenomenal appetites spurred the search for new combinations of foods,
as one cookbook author explains:

Darius, king of the Medes and Persians, maintained a staff of gastronomic detec-
tives whose sole function was to search for new and delectable foods to tempt the
appetite of their ruler. Xerxes, Darius' son and successor, demanded such variety
for his table that the countryside, wherever he traveled, was laid bare. "Wherever
Xerxes took two meals, dining as well as supping," wrote Herodotus, "that city
was utterly ruined."[3]

These exaggerated descriptions emphasize how some of the elite understood the world around them as a place that provided new tastes and
stimulated culinary desires. This is not surprising, considering that even
today cookbook authors and travel writers emphasize the diversity, abundance, and vibrancy of food in the Mediterranean region.

Ancient Rome

In the first centuries of Rome's existence, food was quite plain. Most
people ate wheat, olives, pork, and fish. The situation changed dramatically at the end of the third century with Roman conquest. First, Romans
encountered lots of new foods. As one food historian describes the ancient Roman diet, it was enhanced by "exotic spices from Indonesia, pickles imported from Spain, ham from Gaul, wine from the provinces, oysters
from Britain, and pomegranates from Libya. New seasonings, ingredients,
and flavors were imported from all over the Mediterranean, from North

the Greek appetite, the Roman appetite became legendary. The Roman banquet, hosted by wealthy Roman citizens for their fellow male guests (women were admitted during the reign of Augustus) thoroughly ritualized the presentation and consumption of food. Guests would recline on divans or couches, propping themselves on their left side while eating and drinking with their right hand from a table that held platters of food. They were assisted by a large staff of servants and slaves, including a *praegustator*, who tasted everything to see whether it was delicious enough to eat, and a *nomenclature*, who informed diners of the name of each dish. There were also people on hand to cut up the meat, play musical accompaniment, and keep flies away from the guests. And, of course, there was an army of cooks who prepared a sumptuous variety of dishes. There are tales of thousands of dishes being served at a single banquet. Certainly, the banquet host wished to display his hospitality and wealth by having an array of dishes, some exotic, presented to his guests. In addition to more common foods like dates, raisins, seafood, fish, pork, and lamb, foods like peaches, strawberries, and truffles were prized because they were less commonly available. Abundant quantities of wine were also dispensed. Banqueters would start off by drinking wine mixed with honey before the meal, then return to drinking wine mixed with water after the meal. And if one drank too much, servants were available to escort guests home.

Understanding the nature of ancient food cultures provides much insight into understanding Mediterranean food culture today. Although it is interesting to learn what, and how, ancient peoples ate, it is also important to note their influence on food preparation techniques and a broader philosophy toward the enjoyment of food. First, ancient societies experimented a great deal with different seasonings to give the same food a variety of tastes. To do so, ancient cooks used what was available to them, usually a mixture of local herbs and honey with spices and other ingredients from farther away. Whatever fresh local foods were available to them, they used. Also influential was the predominance of grains over meat. Today, the Mediterranean diet (see chapter 7) is internationally praised and recommended because it emphasizes whole grains as the mainstay of diet. Lastly, ancient societies were receptive to culinary change. When conquering armies or inquisitive merchants tasted something different or witnessed a new method of cooking food, they readily embraced and incorporated food and recipes into their own culinary repertoire. As the following chapters of this book argue, this diversity of foods, styles, and approaches makes Mediterranean food culture unique. One finds, for example, North African influence in Sicilian cooking or European influence in Syrian cuisine. To say that the ancients influenced the moderns does not mean, however, that Mediterranean cuisine is essentially unchanged; nothing could be further from the truth. Instead, centuries of trade, conquest, and immigration have shaped and reshaped food preparation and consumption habits, making Mediterranean food culture both diverse and dynamic.

TRADE AND CONQUEST

The entire Mediterranean region consists of coastal communities. There are not a lot of natural barriers such as mountains to divide inhabitants. Instead, the Mediterranean Sea offers a constant invitation for travel, commerce, and adventure. The islands of Corsica, Sardinia, Sicily, Malta, Crete, and Cyprus are hardly isolated. They were easily reached by boat and today are even more accessible by motor boat or airplane. The sea itself is not perilous or particularly difficult to navigate. The Mediterranean Sea acted as a clearinghouse for all sorts of goods, including food, some of which came from farther inland in Europe, the Middle East, or Africa. Interactions and exchanges of populations, whether through trade or conquest, meant that the Mediterranean Sea also acted as a culinary clearinghouse, as people learned about new seasonings, spices, cooking techniques, and styles of eating. The three areas of the world that exchanged information and ingredients were southern Europe, North Africa, and the Middle East.

In ancient times, the sea facilitated both formal and informal exchanges of populations and goods. People would build ships and sail off to settle in new places, bringing with them their mode of life, institutions, and ideas. Settling in to a new area can be formal, as in instances of military invasion and/or colonization, or it can be informal or even unintended, as in the case of travel or immigration. The sea also facilitated the exchange of commodities through trade and commerce and sometimes through piracy. Trade began in the Mediterranean with the Egyptians, who traded with the Minoans in Crete by 2000 B.C.E. and later, the Phoenicians, who founded merchant colonies along the sea. The Greeks later set up trading colonies to rival those of the Phoenicians. These trade rivalries gave way to Roman domination (Rome first took over territory outside the Italian peninsula with Sicily in 241 B.C.E. and expanded throughout the region until the Empire reached Egypt in 30 B.C.E.), which consolidated the area into one political unit under Roman rule. Conquest, trade, and immigration meant that people learned, either by accident or on purpose, about different foods and new ways to combine or prepare foods, as in the case of Romans learning from Greeks.

After the period of Roman domination in the Mediterranean came an extended period of Arab domination, beginning in the seventh century and continuing until the end of the sixteenth century. The Mediterranean Sea became divided between Christians and Muslims; earlier battles for Spain and some of the islands (Cyprus, Crete, Sicily) gave way to confrontations in the eastern Mediterranean between the Turks and the Byzantine Empire. And while the rest of Europe struggled through difficult times during the Middle Ages, trade on the Muslim side of the Mediterranean flourished. Costly spices such as pepper, cardamom, turmeric, and curry were imported from India and China and carried overland by Arabic traders to markets throughout the region. Coffee from Yemen was highly prized as well, and rice, sugar cane, watermelons, and eggplant were brought from China and India and then cultivated in the region. Salt from Mali and Mauritania was traded in North Africa. For Muslims, the Qur'an regarded trade in positive terms and Muslims spent a great deal of time regulating and regularizing trade practices and routes. And from the seventh century forward, Jewish traders were another important means of exchange between east and west. Trade formalized the exchange of commodities through markets, where shoppers could find foods from the region or from far-away China; under the Ottoman Empire, Constantinople's Grand Bazaar had more than 4,000 shops sprawled over 67 streets. The Ottomans adopted a cosmopolitan approach to food, embracing spices from the east, olives and olive oil from Greece, and dates and dried fruits from North Africa, among other foods. Today, Turkish cuisine is a combination of Greek, Middle Eastern, and Central Asian (Chinese and Mongolian) dishes, many of which were sampled, relished, and replicated by the Ottomans.

In addition to increased trade in the region, travel for religious purposes, known as pilgrimages (either to Mecca or to the Holy Land), facilitated the information exchange about food and cooking. As one authority on Sephardic Jewish cuisine described the process, "[t]ravelers, merchants, peddlers, rabbis, preachers, teachers, students, beggars, and pilgrims on their way to and from the Holy Land were vehicles of gastronomic knowledge as they carried news and descriptions of exotic dishes in far off lands."[5] And later, with the age of exploration and European conquest of the New World, a variety of foods entered the Mediterranean through Spain and Italy, foods such as tomatoes, peppers, and potatoes, all of which became central to Mediterranean cooking. It was during this period, then, that Mediterranean cuisine thoroughly integrated the culinary styles of Europe, the Middle East, and Africa.

The cuisine of the island of Sicily provides a good example of how multiethnic and varied Mediterranean cooking has been and still is because of historical circumstances. Contributors to the Sicilian "grocery list" span the globe. From the ancient Greeks came honey, wine, ricotta cheese, and olives. From the ancient Romans came wheat and other grains. From the Arabs came sugar, citrus fruits, couscous, eggplant, and rice; the Greek Byzantines contributed spices and hard cheeses. Normans contributed dried fish and Angevins brought sweet pastries, eel, and spices. The Spanish introduced tomatoes, peppers, squash, potatoes, and chocolate. All of these ingredients form the foundation of Sicilian cooking today. Also important were the cooking techniques that Sicilians learned from successive waves of conquerors and traders. Since ancient times, Sicilian cooks were considered to be the best cooks in the Mediterranean because of their ingenious and sometimes eclectic cooking style. For example, there are many tomato-based dishes that resemble classic southern Italian cuisine (pasta, eggplant dishes, pizza), yet there are lots of sweet-sour taste combinations that resemble North African and Arab cooking (sauces, couscous dishes, stuffed foods). Sicilian cooks were also known for embracing new ingredients such as sugar or chocolate to make the sweetest confections and desserts in the region.

In the eighteenth and nineteenth centuries, European territories consolidated into nation-states that sought to expand their economic and political influence through colonization and imperialism. Parts of the Mediterranean were united, albeit briefly, under Napoleon Bonaparte, a Corsican. As territories, duchies, estates, and small republics came together into nation-states, governments began to play more of a role in the everyday life of citizens. State intervention or involvement in the area of food production and consumption meant controlling food prices and possibly handing out food in times or crisis, monitoring agricultural production and the export trade, and taking care of populations in need of better nutrition (infants, schoolchildren, the poor). State intervention in matters of food and diet was a highly uneven process, dictated not so much by politicians' unwillingness to intervene as much as it was by the absence of economic resources. For example, although Italy unified in 1861, there were tremendous disparities among regions and socioeconomic classes in terms of the amount and kinds of foods consumed. Doctors and scientists argued that low caloric intake and poor nutrition had a dramatic effect on the nation state. The military could not perform well, the economy could not take off, and citizens could not fulfill their obligations on empty stomachs. Yet the government had little money and few resources to address chronic problems such as underproductive agriculture or the subsistence economy in many regions. Not surprisingly, the Italian government could do little to improve the food habits of most of its citizens.

The rise of the nation-state had dramatic impact on the diet and food habits of Mediterranean populations in unanticipated, or less direct, ways through imperialism. France controlled Morocco, Algeria, and Tunisia, and Italy controlled Libya. France and Italy extracted a certain amount of food from their colonies, but the more noticeable impact on food habits came through the exchange of information and populations. Colonial European officials and settlers brought their food habits with them to North Africa and picked up a few new ideas about how to prepare certain foods. Although the exchange of information went both ways, the legacy of European imperialism can be seen more clearly in North African countries, where, for example, a café in Morocco may have a French name or in Libya, where most people drink coffee, not tea, as a pick-me-up. Coffee with milk in Libya is called *mikyaata*, a phonetic spelling of the Italian *"macchiato"* or "stained coffee" popular among Italians living in Libya under the colonial period (1911–1943). Elsewhere in North Africa, people drink tea.

It would not be until the twentieth century that governments would become more involved in monitoring, controlling, and regulating the food habits of citizens. Two world wars necessitated tighter controls over food production and consumption. For many Mediterranean countries, World War II brought devastation and food shortages. In particular, war in North Africa, Italy, and Greece disrupted food production and, in the absence of adequate imports, civilians faced harsh living conditions. In parts of Italy, for example, food available through rations for civilians dropped as low as 800 calories per day, barely enough to support life. In Greece, the devastation of war destroyed crops and disrupted supply lines to urban areas; citizens faced severe shortages. After World War II, governments finally realized the importance of intervening in the food habits of citizens. Whereas state intervention kept populations alive during wartime, in the postwar era, intervention ensured that consumers could buy more food and that populations in need would also have enough to eat. Many governments opened trade to international markets, which had the effect of increasing the standard of living, even if it meant more characteristically Mediterranean foods (olive oil, wine) were being exported from the region. Some governments continued to subsidize popular consumption by controlling the price of necessities. The Egyptian government, for example, lowered prices on wheat and other necessities by law in response to widespread protests and riots. The liberalization of trade, along with increased levels of immigration to the Mediterranean region, had a dramatic effect on Mediterranean food habits. Consumers who were used to buying local produce or growing their own food sampled new foods brought by recent immigrants or manufactured by American corporations. In the latter half of the twentieth century, the Mediterranean palate became global.

A MULTIETHNIC PALATE

For much of the modern era, the population of the Mediterranean remained static. For example, the nineteenth century witnessed few dramatic in-migrations, although Europeans in the region (mostly Italians and Greeks) began leaving for North and South America at the end of the nineteenth century. In the twentieth century, the impact from two major wars and European decolonization in areas like North Africa and the Middle East would not be felt until the last third of the twentieth century. Over the last four decades, there has been a tremendous increase in the overall population of the region. The population of all Mediterranean countries was 350 million in 1985 and will increase to 550 million by 2025. Why? It seems clear that areas around the Mediterranean Sea are becoming attractive to immigrants. Increasing numbers of Africans from the sub-Saharan nations are making their way to North Africa; in Europe, immigrants from former Yugoslavia, Albania, and some Eastern European countries have settled in Greece and Italy. The population of less permanent residents will also increase; the traffic of tourists will increase from 80 million in 1985 to more than 200 million by 2025. There has also been a redistribution of populations in the region. At the outset of the twentieth century, the majority of the region's population resided on the European side of the sea. By 1985, Europeans accounted for half of the total Mediterranean population and by the end of the twentieth century, they accounted for about a third, with the populations of North Africa, Anatolia, and the Levant now accounting for more than two-thirds of the population.[6]

Certainly the Mediterranean region now struggles with a host of problems connected with a rapidly increasing population. And tensions have erupted between native populations and recent immigrants, prompting calls for immigration reform and even provoking threats of violence. Governments throughout the region face a serious challenge in trying to balance population increase with economic growth, sustainability, and social harmony. Frequently overlooked in all the media coverage of the conflicts and problems caused by recent immigration are the ways in which eating habits are changing because of immigration and how these changes are both greeted with enthusiasm and viewed in a mostly positive light.

The food culture of the French port city of Marseille offers a good example of how native and immigrant populations have come together at the dinner table. Marseille is a city where traditional Provencal cuisine (Marseille is famous for the fish stew known as bouillabaisse) mixes with Italian, Algerian, Tunisian, and Moroccan cuisines. Marseille became a multicultural city in the twentieth century. Initially, Italian immigrants were attracted to the work opportunities provided by an economic boom at the beginning of the century. By 1914, one in four people in the city were of Italian origin. Corsican, Greek, and Spanish immigrants also came for work in Marseille. By the 1930s, Marseille became home to a constant flood of political refugees, beleaguered citizens fleeing Franco's Spain or Mussolini's Italy. During World War II, hundreds of Jewish refugees arrived; some eventually left Marseille for the United States, but others were taken away by the German Gestapo and the French Vichy officials. In the decades after the war, France gave up its colonies, sometimes peacefully and other times, under considerable pressure and violence (as was the case with the French Algerian war). Waves of immigrants from Algeria, Morocco, and Tunisia came to Marseille looking for jobs, education, and other opportunity. And after the French Algerian war, a number of French settlers from Algeria (called the *Pied-Noirs*) made Marseille their home. More recently, there have been immigrants from Egypt, Turkey, and Greece, including many Sephardic Jews from these nations, as well as from North Africa. And the most recent immigrants hail from the French West Indies, Indochina, and parts of sub-Saharan Africa.

Such a multiethnic and multicultural mix has meant a dramatic change for the food culture of Marseille. Markets are now full of foods imported from all over the world and not just meat and produce from local farmers. Restaurants and cafés offer a dizzying variety of ethnic specialties, and in people's homes, it is not unusual for families to buy a *bûche de Noël* (a traditional cake) at Christmastime and make *chorba* (a type of soup) for Ramadan, a Muslim holiday. All of the different cuisines have been welcomed by citizens of Marseille with a mixture of curiosity and delight. The presence of ethnic foods in the city does not seem to provoke the same heated reaction that a discussion of citizenship or immigration reform might.[7] This is not to say that there are few tensions and problems as immigrants continue to pour into the Mediterranean region. Rather, the example of Marseille demonstrates the willingness of many people in the Mediterranean to try new tastes, foods, and cooking techniques. This willingness is as much a reflection of their past as it is a symbol for their future.

AGRICULTURE

For thousands of years, people in the Mediterranean have been harvesting foods from both land and sea. It is perhaps most useful to think about Mediterranean agriculture as a multifaceted occupation in which all kinds of foods are cultivated, harvested, or caught. First, there is cultivation of the land, which can range from tending wide open wheat fields to looking after an olive grove perched on a rocky clump of land. Cultivation of grains, fruits, and vegetables means thinking about the best crops to grow on rocky soil, as well as understanding how to make the most from the sun and warm climate. Olive, grape, and grain farms can be small or large enough to produce significant harvests for local and international markets. Fruits and produce, although they tend to be from small producers, can also be large crops. The citrus industry, for example, includes many large farms that export lemons and oranges outside the Mediterranean region. Next, there is pastoral work; shepherds can maintain a flock of sheep or goats just about anywhere, which explains why sheep and goat herding is more popular than cattle ranching in the Mediterranean region, as they make efficient use of sparse amounts of land. Sheep and goat herding provides essential dairy products as well as the main source of red meat for the Mediterranean diet. Farmers and even urban citizens might raise chickens or other birds for eggs and meat. There is also the production of fish, or more accurately, catching or harvesting fish from the Mediterranean Sea, which today has become a global enterprise.

In all three areas of agricultural production, Mediterranean farmers, shepherds, and fishermen are facing issues that their counterparts around the world confront today: the consolidation of agricultural production into large units, declining profitability in the face of international competition and a global market for food, and increasing environmental concerns about the depletion of natural resources. And, as the population begins shifting with immigration and a rural exodus in some areas, there is growing concern over whether the region can continue to feed itself. For example, the country of Egypt has to import about two-thirds of its food supply. A massive exodus from rural to urban areas in recent decades (most of the population lives on about one-tenth of the available land) has meant fewer farms and more urban consumers who need to be fed. The current situation is perhaps ironic, considering that Ancient Egypt was the birthplace of agriculture; Ancient Egyptians cultivated wheat, barley, beans, lentils, onions, dates, grapes, millet, and sesame and later cultivated rice and fruits that came via Arab traders to Egypt from India, China, and Persia. Today, the prospect of importing more and more food to feed the Mediterranean region will, no doubt, change the nature of the popular diet, given that for so long, this diet has been based on locally grown and produced foods.

The history of agricultural production in the Mediterranean closely follows the history of population exchanges in the region, whether through immigration, trade, or conquest. Just as citizens exchanged foods and cooking tips, farmers and fishermen traded seeds, nets, or tips on preserving foods. The Mediterranean region started off as the birthplace of wheat production, sheep farming, and goat herding, all of which were in place in the Near East (Syria, Israel, Turkey) before spreading to Greece and southern Europe. The cultivation of peas, barley, lentils, and other legumes followed the same path. Ancient Greek and Roman farmers honed their skills in olive and grape cultivation as well as honey production. Agricultural production in the western and eastern Mediterranean regions was advanced enough to allow for a variety of staple foods—barley, wheat, legumes—as well as produce and foods such as oil, honey, and wine. Agriculture in the southern Mediterranean, or North Africa, caught up in the fifteenth and sixteenth centuries with the *Reconquista*; Muslims and Jews who were pushed out of Spain resettled in Morocco and Tunisia, bringing knowledge of different agricultural and irrigation techniques that allowed fruits, nuts, and vegetables to flourish.

The fifteenth and sixteenth centuries were also the period of Spanish exploration and conquest. Plants from the New World—tomatoes, peppers, and potatoes—were brought to the Mediterranean region and did well in the sunny climate. New world crops such as peppers and tomatoes changed the nature of Mediterranean cuisine, but the potato did not assume as prominent a role as it did in northern Europe and in countries like Ireland, which made the potato the staple of their diet. And given land limitations, Mediterranean farmers never opted for large-scale meat production as did the United States. Instead, Mediterranean populations continued to exist mostly on grains (wheat and bulgur) prepared in a variety of ways. The dominance of whole grain is what makes the Mediterranean diet (see chapter 7) so distinctive. Another important source of protein for Mediterranean consumers has been fish. Contrary to popular belief, perhaps, the Mediterranean Sea is not an incredibly abundant source for fish, given the high salt content of the water. Still, the sea yields all kinds of fish and seafood: tuna, rock fish, bonita, mackerel, *rascasse*, dory, gurnard, anchovies, sardines, eel, squid, octopus, mussels, lobster, and a host of lesser known species. After World War II, the Mediterranean region's fishing industry boomed. Fishermen had few problems making a living, and hundreds of processing plants sprang up to accommodate the growing international demand for Mediterranean anchovies, sardines, tuna, and other fish. By the 1970s, however, there were problems. Overfishing in many areas led to a marked decline in the size and amount of the average catch; processing plants closed down and fishermen resorted to fishing off season to make ends meet. Today, some fishermen even resort to illegal drift nets for profitable fish such as swordfish. And the United Nations Environmental Program has recently warned of high mercury levels in Mediterranean fish and has declared the ecology of the Mediterranean Sea to be seriously out of balance because of overfishing and other environmental problems.

The fishing industry is struggling to survive an uncertain future, and there is some evidence to suggest that sheep- and goat-herding will also face challenges. Although lamb and goat continue to be popular meats in the region, recent studies of consumer habits indicate that beef, much of it imported, is now popular among Mediterranean consumers. It is still too early to tell how significantly this growing preference for beef will affect these pastoral occupations. The farming industry has fared slightly better; after a slump in the 1970s, agriculture has made a comeback and the small farmer is alive and well throughout the region. Government subsidies have helped farmers stay competitive and in some cases survive, but a host of other factors have also helped. Over the last two decades, there have been many efforts to revive regional culinary traditions through talking about, preparing, and enjoying traditional foods. Consumers tired of fast food and corporate food culture now yearn to go back to the simple traditions of Mediterranean home cooking. Some farms have been able to stay in business because they take in tourists who are curious to understand where their food comes from or who just want to relax in a rural setting and enjoy wholesome, fresh food. Agritourism provides a viable alternative to bankruptcy or consolidation with a larger farm. And outside the Mediterranean, gourmets around the world have sought out Mediterranean olives, high quality extra-virgin olive oil, the finest capers, and spice mixes for their own cooking. Growing international demand for Mediterranean products has sparked innovation and improvement in all aspects of agricultural production and marketing.

There is still a nagging fear, however, that farming may become increasingly less important to the Mediterranean economy, especially if farms remain small and are unable to compete with American agribusinesses. Some industries have risen to the American challenge. For example, the wine industries of Spain, southern France, Italy, Lebanon, and Israel have mechanized or at least found a way to combine human labor with mechanization. They have turned out high quality wines that hold their own against California competitors, and they have used the Internet to market their products around the world. Some industries have been less successful. The productions of nuts—almonds, pistachios, hazelnuts, and walnuts—is still managed on small farms with human labor. These farms are unable to compete with large nut farms from California, which use machines to replace human labor and, in the process, turn out a cheaper product. For Mediterranean nut farmers, mechanization is impractical (the land can be very rocky and uneven) as well as expensive. Although an increasing number of residents in the region have moved from the countryside to the city, many still have ties to rural areas and return there to work. In large cities such as Athens, Istanbul, Rome, and Cairo, the outer districts and suburbs resemble villages and the countryside is not too far away. Citizens in these cities can alternate work in the city with work in agriculture, such as picking grapes or olives, on a seasonal basis. It is unlikely, then, that machines will every fully replace human labor as they have in other parts of the world.

ATTITUDES TOWARD FOOD

Popular attitudes toward food are shaped by many factors. As this chapter has argued, these attitudes are constantly changing because of the history of populations sharing foods and information about food with each other. Of the many factors that influence food choices and ideas about preparing food, one's way of life or livelihood has been important. Of course, one's livelihood dictates how much one can afford to spend on food and in the Mediterranean region, so many residents have been poor for centuries, whether they were peasants, shepherds, or fishermen. For centuries, Mediterranean diet and cuisine were shaped by the principles of peasant cooking, or cooking with little. Peasant cooking relies on grains and limited produce as the main source of nutrition; although farmers produced foods like meat, eggs, dairy products, and more expensive produce, they sold these foods for market instead of eating them. Similarly, fishermen sold almost the entire catch, keeping only fish that were too small or fish parts for personal consumption. Peasant cooking also relied on easy-to-make dishes that stretched the basic ingredients a long way to satisfy hungry family members. Thus there are a lot of stews and soups in which a variety of inexpensive ingredients can be combined to create a satisfying and tasty meal (see chapter 4). Pies, tarts, and omelets were also popular forms of peasant cooking because a wedge or piece could be sliced off and the rest kept for later. And flatbreads topped with a few simple seasonings could be cut up, tucked in one's pocket, and taken out to the fields for lunch or a snack. Peasant cooking relied on few ingredients and few utensils.

Although it relies on an economy of tools and ingredients, peasant cooking is not as easy as it appears to be. Centuries of cooking with few ingredients created a formalistic approach to cooking whereby the exact measure of ingredients and cooking technique matter a great deal to the Mediterranean palate. A Moroccan diner eating a tajine or stew will notice the combination of spices; a pinch too much of a certain spice is cause for embarrassment or apologies from the cook. And for centuries, cooks in the region have tried to make the same foods interesting in many different ways. These efforts to bring variety to the table can be most clearly seen in the Italian art of pasta making. Pasta, which is a paste of flour, water, salt, and sometimes eggs, is available in Italy in hundreds of shapes. Many pasta names reflect the shape of the dried paste: *cavatappi* (corkscrew) for example, resemble corkscrews while *tubetti* are little hollowed-out tubes. The different shapes provide more options and choice for cooks and diners alike. There is also a wide variety of sauces to go with the pasta. Many of these sauces are simple and inexpensive to make, from a pesto (olive oil, basil, pine nuts, and garlic) to an *aglio e olio* (garlic and olive oil) sauce. Although there are lots of different pasta shapes and lots of different sauces, only specific pasta shapes go with certain types of sauces; some pasta shapes and textures are meant to hold small chunks of food in a sauce, whereas smoother sauces cling better to roughly textured pasta. There are definite dos and don'ts for combining sauce with pasta, so it is not as easy as it looks. Pasta shells, for example, are not meant to be served with a smooth sauce, but with a chunkier sauce or with finely chopped ingredients. Some might argue, however, that pasta is pasta, no matter what the shape, and any choice within these limits is an illusion of choice. It is nonetheless important to understand how the art of pasta making and preparation has developed and what this reveals about the nature of peasant cooking or cooking with little. Over the last two or three centuries, Italians have created a sophisticated culinary system out of very little: flour, water, salt, and a few ingredients for sauce. Another example would be the many kinds of zucchini pie in Greek cuisine. They are all zucchini pies, but each one is made slightly different from the other. One may have cheese grated on top, the zucchini used in the pie might be cooked in milk before being baked off in the pie, or a particular spice might be used.

For centuries, Mediterranean cooks have had to cook within certain limits, and although their cuisine reflects the nature of these constraints, their attitude toward food also reflects a tradition of sobriety and thrift. In meal preparation, nothing is wasted; even leftovers are recycled and served in the next meal. And the classic Mediterranean diet relies on a few simple ingredients—bread, vegetables, fruit, fish, olive oil—to create a variety of interesting meals. Although a great deal of ingenuity and creativity go into making entire meals out of only a few ingredients, Mediterranean cooking is not simply about throwing together a few things to see what comes out. There are established rules for making the more traditional dishes, and these rules matter to cooks and diners alike. For example, the citizens of Naples have long maintained that they originated pizza, a flatbread with toppings baked in an oven. As pizza became more popular throughout the world, Neapolitans became nervous. What would happen to their style of pizza in the midst of pizzas topped with ham and pineapple, pizzas topped with sausage and potatoes, or pizzas topped with sushi? Concerned pizza-makers formed the *Associazione Verace Pizza Napoletana* in 1984 to protect Neapolitan-style pizza. The VPN successfully got Neapolitan pizza recognized as *denominazione di origine controllata*, which meant it was certified as authentic. To qualify for authentic status, pizzas had to be made and cooked in a certain way, from specific ingredients. Pizza makers who comply with all the rules receive membership in the association and can advertise this fact to their customers.

Another important set of rules about making and eating food comes from the major religions of the Mediterranean region: Christianity, Islam, and Judaism. In particular, Muslims and Jews still maintain dietary laws that prohibit them from consuming some foods and that dictate how foods are to be prepared for human consumption. All three religions encourage the consumption of specific foods and dishes on special occasions, holidays, and rituals (see chapter 6), whether as a means of bringing the community together or reminding participants of their faith. Given that the Mediterranean Sea is the meeting place for three of the world's major religions, it is not surprising that many food choices are acts of faith as well as acts of consumption.

More recently, demographic changes have played an important role in remaking food habits, as younger generations from the region rely on more prepared and "fast" foods and their attitudes toward these foods is markedly different from those of the older generations. Younger people are more likely to think about convenience and food trends when choosing what to eat. Older consumers are less sure about these American-style trends in eating (McDonald's restaurants, microwaveable frozen food), and some people have protested the opening of a McDonald's restaurant. Others have formed organizations to revere and protect native foods and more traditional food habits. The widening generation gap in eating habits has led to much discussion about diet and health in the Mediterranean region, as doctors and nutritionists examine the consequences of a new Mediterranean diet that contains more meat, fat, salt, and sugar.

In part, food habits and dietary choices are changing because of the region's economy, which in many places is now based firmly on tourism. Tourists from around the world flock to the Mediterranean to go to the beach or to see the many cultural attractions. The islands in the Mediterranean Sea become inundated with tourists, who, among other things, want to enjoy the comforts of home, including food. The Balearic Islands, for example, receive more than 6 million tourists a year, with almost half of the tourists coming from the British Isles. The tourism industry has become the major source of employment on most of the islands, which used to be major exporters of figs, apricots, almonds, and potatoes. As a consequence, the Islands are dotted with British restaurants and pubs. A typical breakfast on the island of Majorca used to be a simple meal of fruit, bread, and coffee. Now, restaurants and cafés offer a British breakfast of eggs, bacon, sausage, beans, tomato, toast, marmalade, and tea. Even one of the most unspoiled of the Mediterranean Islands, Corsica (France), with a population of about a quarter million people, receives well over a million tourists a year. Tourism brings in a great deal of money, but it also affects the environment, as native populations shift economic priorities toward building and accommodating guests, sometimes at the expense of local agricultural production. This shift affects attitudes toward food, as islands and other regions have to import more food because they are growing less. And although there are only a few studies of the impact of tourism on native food habits, preliminary findings suggest that native consumers will buy and eat the foods imported for British tourists, foods like soda, chips, beer, and candy bars.

Tourism, like immigration, colonization, and trade, is the latest historical process or event that brings diverse populations together in the Mediterranean. Mediterranean cooks are a cosmopolitan lot, willing to embrace new foods and new ways of preparing foods. They have had this attitude for centuries, but today, many new foods and ideas about food are coming from outside the Mediterranean region altogether. This has caused some concern among chefs, small farmers, doctors, and others because they fear these external influences will cause the Mediterranean ways of cooking and eating to become less important and even obsolete. The question on the mind of many people in the region is how well Mediterranean cuisine will survive in an era of globalization. In some respects, the globalization of tastes had led to greater interest in local food culture. American fast food restaurants and British pubs have prompted many people in the region to rediscover their Mediterranean culinary roots. There has been a revival of interest in peasant cooking, for example, and restaurants and small hotels now cater to regional culinary traditions. Local and national governments have taken action. On the local level, food fairs and celebrations (see chapter 6) allow tourists and natives to mingle and learn about local food culture. Nationally, small farmers and food artisans receive more protection, either in the form of subsidies or by having certain foods labeled as distinctive or authentic. Local, regional, and national authorities have acted to protect the environment and control the impact of tourism.

It remains to be seen whether people in the Mediterranean will alter their attitudes toward food significantly in the age of globalization, fast food, and agribusiness. Debates and conversations about this matter take on a tone of urgency, in part because of the assumption that for centuries, Mediterranean cuisine has remain unchanged, as permanent a fixture of the region as the sunny beaches and rocky hillsides. This book argues that this assumption is both accurate and misleading. Some foods and dishes have been around for centuries, and Mediterranean cooks and diners have dedicated themselves to making a set of ingredients into a variety of tasty meals and snacks. Yet these same cooks and diners have been open to change, from new ingredients, to the new preparation techniques, to thinking in new ways about the same old ingredients. This curious blend of tradition and innovation characterizes food culture in the Mediterranean, making it a set of practices and attitudes that combines diversity and simplicity, hard work and spontaneity, religious dedication and playful enjoyment. Perhaps the most important aspect of food culture in the Mediterranean is the sheer dedication to, and enjoyment of, food throughout countries as diverse as Egypt, Spain, Israel, Turkey, and Greece. People in the region spend a lot of time thinking about, buying, preparing, and eating food. Mediterranean cuisine has become internationally appreciated, not simply because it tastes good (although that is certainly the case), but also because it embodies the environment, culture, and history of many populations around the Mediterranean Sea.

NOTES

1. Eugenia Salza Prina Ricotti, *Meals and Recipes from Ancient Greece* (Los Angeles: J. Paul Getty Museum, 2005), pp. 1–2.

2. Oswald Rivera, *The Pharaoh's Feast: From Pit-Boiled Roots to Pickled Herring, Cooking Through the Ages with 110 Simple Recipes* (New York: Four Walls Eight Windows, 2003), pp. 18–19.

3. Betty Wasson, *The Mediterranean Cookbook* (Chicago: Harry Regnery, 1973), p. 9.

4. Oswald Rivera, *The Pharaoh's Feast*, p. 61.

5. Sheilah Kaufman, *Sephardic Israeli Cuisine: A Mediterranean Mosaic* (New York: Hippocrene Books, 2002), p. 22.

6. Robert Fox, *The Inner Sea: The Mediterranean and Its People* (New York: Knopf, 1993), p. 8.

7. For a collection of multiethnic recipes from the city, see Daniel Young, *Made in Marseille* (New York: HarperCollins, 2002).

2

Major Foods and Ingredients

Mediterranean cuisine is incredibly diverse: the sweet and sour flavors of Sicilian dishes contrast sharply with the mellow flavors of Turkish specialties and the complex spices that characterize North African cooking are not found in Greek or Cypriot cuisine. In this sense, Mediterranean food culture is as diverse as the societies of the Mediterranean itself. Yet there are several key ingredients or foods that unite the food culture of the region. Today, the phrase "Mediterranean diet" calls to mind foods like olive oil, fish, pasta, bread, as well as fresh fruits and vegetables. Since ancient times, the Mediterranean diet was based on cereals, legumes, fish, and produce. Historians frequently describe how the great civilizations of the past—Phoenician, Carthaginian, Greek, Roman, Arab—have exerted unifying influence on philosophy, technology, and architecture in the Mediterranean region. Without a doubt, these civilizations also influenced food culture as well, and thus there are more similarities than differences in the kinds of ingredients used by cooks throughout the Mediterranean.

GRAINS

Wheat is the most important grain throughout the region, although barley, millet, and rice are also grown in the Mediterranean. Historically, grains like emmer (a bread grain of ancient Egypt) and barley were the most important grains in the region, but wheat now reigns supreme.

Emmer. © J. Susan Cole Stone.

Wheat is grown in Spain, Greece, Italy, Turkey, Tunisia, and Syria. Wheat first appeared as a crop among farmers more than 10,000 years ago and has been the major food for the Mediterranean peoples since ancient times. Hard or durum wheat is the preferred type of wheat, which makes a high-quality, high-protein flour called semolina flour. According to ethnobotanists, durum wheat goes back to the Neolithic era and was probably imported to the Mediterranean from the Middle East. Softer grains of wheat are grown in the Mediterranean and used for foods like bread and pasta, although much of these grains are grown for export.

Bread

It is hard to overestimate the importance of bread throughout the Mediterranean region. It is consumed daily and yet in some rural societies throughout the region, it is treated with a kind of reverence and gratitude that may seem unusual or extreme to Americans and other Western consumers. There are historical reasons for this reverence. Over the centuries, bread was regarded as the most important food, so much so that authorities (churches, governments, rulers) learned to carefully monitor and control the availability and price of flour and bread. If either flour or bread became too expensive or was excessively taxed, citizens would protest and even loot bakeries and flour mills. In some regions of the Mediterranean, notably North Africa and the Middle East, the price of bread is still a political issue and high bread prices in countries like Egypt, where much of the population lives at or near the poverty line, threatens the very existence of the population. Bread prices are less of an issue in countries where the economy is stable and standards of living are high. Today, most bread is purchased in a store or bakery, although in more traditional places it is still made at home or in communal ovens. On holidays or for special occasions, bakers make elaborate breads, often braided or sculpted, that serve as reminders of bread's special place in the Mediterranean diet. Bread is cooked in all kinds of ways, whether in a conventional or wood-fired oven, on the hearth, or on a griddle.

Flatbreads

Flatbreads are just that—flat breads that are made with or without some form of leavening. They are usually baked but are also made on the griddle or other hot surface, and some flatbreads are fried or deep-fried in oil. The list of flatbreads consumed throughout the Mediterranean is endless: pita, *lavosh*, *pide*, pizza, focaccia, to name but a few, and every region within the Mediterranean seems to have its particular kind of flatbread. These breads can be used for dipping, as the pita is used in the traditional meze (appetizers), or they are topped with ingredients and then baked to make a meal, like the Italian pizza. Breads like pita or focaccia are the basis for sandwiches, as they can be stuffed with lots of ingredients and then consumed for a meal or snack. Related to the flatbread is phyllo dough, very thin layers of batter that are never consumed by themselves but always combined with other ingredients. Phyllo dough is layered with spinach to make the Greek spanakopita, or filled with meat or vegetables to make Syrian *boureki* or Turkish *borek*. In addition to savory dishes, desserts can be made with phyllo dough. Perhaps the most famous dish is baklava, dough layered with honey and nuts, that is eaten in Greece, Turkey, and Israel.

Baklava

Pastry

1 pound butter, melted

1 pound phyllo dough

1/2 pound walnuts

1/2 pound almonds

1/3 cup sugar

1 egg

2 teaspoons cinnamon

1 teaspoon allspice

Syrup

1 cup honey

1 1/2 cup sugar

1 cinnamon stick

1 teaspoon of grated lemon rind

Combine syrup ingredients in a saucepan and bring to a boil. Simmer for 15–20 minutes. Strain and set aside. Preheat oven to 350°F. Mix sugar, egg, cinnamon and allspice in a large bowl. In a food processor, coarsely grind the walnuts and almonds together. Add to sugar, egg, and cinnamon mixture. Brush a 13 × 9 × 2 pan with melted butter. Lay a sheet of phyllo dough, brush with butter, then lay another sheet of phyllo dough, and repeat until there are a dozen layers of phyllo dough. Spread a thin layer of nut mixture of top of the layers, cover nut mixture with another layer of phyllo dough, brush with butter and cover with another layer of nuts. Repeat until the nut mixture is used up. Cover with remaining phyllo dough sheets, brushing each sheet with melted butter. Cut the top of the baklava into triangles. Bake 1 hour until browned. Remove from oven and pour prepared syrup over baklava. Cool thoroughly before serving.

Leavened Bread

Leavened bread is made with some sort of rising agent, usually yeast, and baked in an oven. Throughout the Mediterranean, bread is often made with durum wheat flour. Sometimes the flour is coarsely ground and the resulting bread is thick and chewy, as with so-called peasant breads or semolina bread made in southern Italy. More refined flour makes whiter, fluffier bread that was and still is sold for a higher price than "peasant" bread. Historically, consumers were defined economically and socially by which kind of bread they could afford. Bread dough can also be flavored with different ingredients such as olives, rosemary and other herbs, or spices like anise, which is an ingredient in a type of bread consumed in Morocco. Leavened bread is eaten by itself or to accompany a dish like salad, soup, or stew (the bread crust can be used for sopping up broth or dressing). Throughout the western Mediterranean region, toasted bread topped with various ingredients makes a satisfying appetizer or snack; Italian crostini and bruschetta have become popular worldwide. Stale bread is also an important ingredient in Mediterranean cooking, as it is made into salads or soups; grated into sauces, meatballs, or dumplings; and even used in deserts like Spanish *torrijas*, the Sicilian *budino*, and Turkish pudding.

Pasta

Wheat flour is made into a paste with water, salt, and sometimes egg, rolled out into a shape, cut, and sometimes dried. The resulting noodles or pasta as we now know it are boiled, drained, and served with a sauce or tossed with other ingredients. Pasta dishes are best known in Italy, but they are also consumed throughout Turkey, southern France, and Greece. In these regions, pasta is served boiled, or it is sometimes baked in a casserole. In Spain, pasta is cooked in its own broth or sauce and the noodles are called *fideos* or *fideus*. Historians argue about the origins of pasta, specifically whether it was first made in Asia or the Middle East, but it seems likely that Mediterranean cultures learned about pasta from Middle Eastern traders. For centuries, pasta was made at home until the nineteenth century, when industrial production made quick work of a time-consuming task. Because pasta is made with finely milled flour, it was a relatively expensive food and eaten only on Sundays (by Christians) or on special occasions, until mass production methods and a higher standard of living put pasta within the reach of everyone's food budget. Some people still make pasta at home for special occasions, but most consumers purchase dried pasta in stores and supermarkets. Because pasta can be combined with so many other ingredients, it is an extremely versatile dish; and because pasta is inexpensive to buy and make, it remains one of the most popular dishes in the Mediterranean region and has become one of the most popular dishes throughout the world.

Couscous and Bulgur

Couscous is more popular in North Africa and in the eastern Mediterranean and is usually in a dish where it is mixed in with other ingredients to make an entire meal. It can also be served as an accompaniment to other dishes in a meal. Couscous is commonly, and mistakenly, referred to as a grain, but it is actually a technique of making the food. A semolina flour mixture made from durum wheat is placed in the bottom of the dish, dampened with water and stirred by hand to produce small "grains" or nuggets of flour. Alternately, couscous can be made by wetting the palm of the hand and dipping the hand into a bowl of semolina; the hands are then rubbed together gently so that small grains form. Once the grains are formed they are allowed to dry. Couscous is steamed over a broth and, like pasta, couscous is now mass produced and available in shops and supermarkets in the Mediterranean, although it is not precooked as it is in the United States. Bulgur is a cereal food made from wheat, most often durum wheat. The wheat is parboiled, dried, and then the husk is removed; the grain is then cracked. Frequently, bulgur is referred to as cracked wheat, but it differs from cracked wheat in that it is parboiled and the wheat bran is removed. Bulgur is widely used in Turkish cuisine, where fine bulgur is used to make kibbeh (ground bulgur and meat), and coarse bulgur is used to make tabbouleh (a bulgur, tomato, parsley and mint salad). Bulgur is also used to make pilaf or *pilav*, in which the grain is mixed with onions, tomatoes, and peppers, sautéed in butter, and then boiled in meat stock. Turkish people drink *boza*, which is made from bulgur and rice that are left to ferment before being served with cinnamon or roasted chickpeas. For those not brought up on it, *boza* is an acquired taste.

Rice

Rice came to the Mediterranean from the Middle East, and today it is cultivated intensively in Italy, Spain, France, and Turkey. In many regions of the Mediterranean such as Syria, Morocco, Greece, and Turkey, rice is used as an ingredient in dishes or to stuff vegetables or meat. In the eastern regions of the Mediterranean, such as Turkey, rice dishes called *pilavs* are prepared with saffron, nuts, and/or legumes and accompany other dishes in the meal. In Italy, rice is used as the centerpiece of a dish called risotto, in which short-grained rice is cooked in a seasoned broth, giving the rice a creamy (some say mushy) consistency. Rice croquettes are popular throughout Italy and especially in Sicily, where they are filled with different sauces and deep fried. On the Mediterranean coast of Spain, rice is the main ingredient for the famous Catalonian dish paella, which consists of rice, chicken, sausages, shellfish, fish, artichokes, tomatoes, peppers, peas, garlic, and seasonings including saffron, which gives the dish a distinctive yellowish color. Paella can also be made with more exotic ingredients such as rabbit or snail.

VEGETABLES

In addition to cereals, which characterize the Mediterranean diet, fresh vegetables play an important role in both everyday fare and fancy dishes. Because meat and fish can be expensive and because they spoil quickly, vegetables have played a major role in Mediterranean cuisine as a meat substitute. They are frequently considered more of a main dish than a side dish. Considerable amounts of creativity and inventiveness have gone into vegetable recipes, whether cooks have combined vegetables with unusual seasonings or ingredients, or whether they have tried to give vegetables the appearance, texture, and taste of meat. Many of the vegetables that now characterize Mediterranean cuisine were imported from elsewhere: for example, tomatoes and peppers came from the New World, whereas eggplant came from Southeast Asia. It seems that cooks embraced even imported vegetables and applied the same care and creativity to them that they applied to their native produce.

Olives

In many people's minds, no food characterizes Mediterranean food more than the olive. Certainly, olives have a long history in the region. Their cultivation goes back to ancient Egyptian and Minoan cultures, and the ancient Greeks and Romans used olives and olive oil in their cuisine. Olive trees live a particularly long time, some for hundreds of years, and they seem to thrive in the rocky soil of the Mediterranean. The fruit of the olive tree is picked at various stages of ripeness, depending on what the olive will be used for: unripe green olives, mature black olives, and the green-brown or rose-green stages in between ripe and unripe. Curing or preserving is necessary and the most traditional means of curing olives is to dry them in the sun and rub them with a bit of oil to preserve them. When the olive shrivels in the sun, the flavor becomes more concentrated. Olives can also be cured in salt brine or brine flavored with vinegar, citrus juice, olive oil, or a combination of ingredients like oil and vinegar. The olive is split and soaked in cold water first to take out the bitterness; this process allows the bitter oleoeuropein to leech out of the olive. Given the variety of preparation and the variety of olive trees, it is not surprising that olives come in all different shapes and sizes: Nicoise olives from North Africa (not Nice, France) are small, sweet, and black; Italian *Bella di Cerignola* olives are large, green, and tart; Greek kalamata olives are smallish, oval, and purple from being steeped in a red-wine vinegar. Most olives are sold in jars or are available in bulk in markets and stores or sold by street vendors in paper cones. In addition to producing olives for consumers at home, Mediterranean olive farmers also produce a significant number of olives for export around the world. Some of these olives, like the "California-style" olives (these are green olives that are turned black by being soaked in a lye solution), are industrially produced and canned.

A Palestinian woman sorts olives by hand in the West Bank village of Awrta. While some aspects of olive production are mechanized, some farms still rely on human labor. AP Photo/Nasser Ishtayeh.

Olive Oil

Olive oil is another key ingredient for Mediterranean cuisine that has become known the world over and is now produced for domestic consumption, as well as for export. Consumers outside the Mediterranean usually think of olive oil as an Italian product, but it is made in Spain, Greece, Tunisia, Lebanon, and Turkey, as well as in Italy. Before the global boom in demand for olive oil, many governments throughout the Mediterranean carefully controlled olive oil production, so much so that little oil was available for domestic consumers, who had to make do with margarine or vegetable oil. Now, olive oil production for a world market has done much to liberalize the growth of olive trees and oil production, so much so that in many countries, the government has loosened regulations, and so olive oil is available to consumers everywhere in the region. To make a liter of olive oil, about 11 pounds (5 kilograms) of olives are needed. The olives are crushed, and pressed, and then the oil is separated from the olive pulp and pits and stored in tanks or jars. Sometimes the oil is filtered before being stored. Extra-virgin olive oil is a more expensive grade of oil whereby the oil is pressed within 48 hours of harvest, and the oil is obtained in one pressing at room temperature. To qualify for the label of extra-virgin, olive oil must have 1 percent or less of free oleic fatty acid (a measure of oxidation in the oil), and the oil must pass a taste test and not have any defects of taste or aroma. Virgin and light olive oil are refined oils that have a lighter taste and aroma than extra-virgin oil, but they are not light oils in the sense that they have fewer calories than other types of olive oil. Pure olive oil is heavily processed, sometimes with multiple pressings, and the resulting oil has no taste or aroma (sometimes extra-virgin oil is added to give it some taste). Historically, olive oil has been used for medicine, cleaning skin, and for oil lamps in addition to using it for cooking and seasoning food. Jewish populations in the Mediterranean began cooking with olive oil because it contains no animal ingredients (pareve) and therefore can be used to make dishes in compliance with kosher dietary laws.

Peppers and Tomatoes

Peppers and tomatoes are considered classic Mediterranean foods, but both were imported from the New World during the era of the Columbian exchange. Mediterranean populations were already familiar with black pepper when Christopher Columbus brought back a red fruit he called a pepper. Red peppers became extremely popular because they could be grown easily in the Mediterranean climate and were a less expensive alternative to black pepper that could provide the right amount of spicy taste for less money. Peppers are used in all kinds of dishes, but they are perhaps best known for their use in sauces or condiments. In Tunisia, peppers are ground up in a fiery sauce or paste called *harissa*, which is added to many foods and dishes to give it extra punch. In southern France, a red pepper sauce called rouille is used to season dishes and add flavor to fish soups and stews. The popularity of peppers is evidenced by its use in even the most exotic dishes, from a Syrian dish called *muhammara*, a dip made from red peppers, walnuts, and pomegranate, to pepper ices and ice creams in southern Italy. Unlike the pepper, which quickly became popular in the region, the tomato took a longer time to become established after it was introduced to Spaniards by Hernando Cortès after he discovered it in the New World in 1519. Originally, tomatoes were brought back and grown as ornamental curiosities. Most Europeans thought tomatoes were poisonous, most likely because the varieties of tomatoes available were quite sour. Once Mediterranean farmers began cultivating tomatoes, they produced sweet fruit, probably because the soil is rich and ashy in many locations where tomato cultivation occurred. Nonetheless, it took about two centuries for tomatoes to be commonly used, at least according to evidence in printed cookbooks. Now, tomatoes are practically indispensable to Mediterranean cuisine. Dishes that have become universally popular—pizza, gazpacho, pasta sauce—have tomatoes as their primary or characteristic ingredient. Like peppers, tomatoes can be dried and kept for a period of time before being used in dishes. The resulting tomato taste is more concentrated and therefore used more sparingly in recipes. In Sicily, tomato purée is salted and dried out until it becomes like a paste or even like molding clay (it is called 'u 'strattu in Sicilian dialect), it is then kept in jars and used to provide a powerful tomato taste in dishes.

Harissa

12 dried chili peppers
4 cloves garlic, peeled
1/2 cup olive oil
1 teaspoon salt
2 teaspoons cumin
1/2 teaspoon ground coriander
1/2 teaspoon ground caraway seed

Remove seeds from peppers, cut into slices, and soak in warm water for 30–45 minutes. Drain excess liquid and squeeze peppers dry. Put peppers and other ingredients in a blender or food processor and blend until smooth. This can be kept in the refrigerator in a sealed container for two weeks. Use as a paste to add heat to dishes or water down to make a sauce.

Eggplant

Originally from Southeast Asia, the eggplant was brought to the Mediterranean via the Middle East. Eggplant is considered a "poor man's meat" because it can be prepared in many ways so as to resemble meat. One of the reasons eggplant is so versatile is that it has no strong taste, but it tends to absorb the taste of other things. Therefore eggplant is usually prepared in a dish with other ingredients or seasonings. For example, eggplant can be sliced and baked in a casserole-type dish like Greek moussaka or Italian eggplant parmesan, or it can be diced up and mixed with other vegetables like the southern French ratatouille or the southern Italian pasta dish called *pasta alla norma* (pasta in a sauce made from tomatoes, eggplant, olive oil, basil, and hard ricotta cheese). In the eastern Mediterranean region, eggplants are stuffed or filled or mashed up with tahini (sesame sauce) for a dip. A famous eggplant dish in Turkey is called *imam bayildi*, or "the cleric fainted," in which the cooked eggplant, onion, and tomato were so tender that they melted in a cleric's mouth; hence the cleric faints or loses consciousness because of the delicious taste, or possibly because he ate too much of it. In the Catalan region of Spain, eggplants are even fried and eaten as a kind of dessert accompanied by sugar or honey.

Fried Eggplant with Honey

2/3 cup flour

1 cup water

1/4 teaspoon baking soda

Pinch salt

Olive oil for frying

3–4 small eggplants, peeled, sliced, and cut into strips

Honey

Mix the flour, water, baking soda, and salt together. Dip eggplant slices into the batter and fry in olive oil (oil should be 3/4 to 1 inch deep and heated to at least 350°F). Fry until golden brown, then turn and fry on the other side. Drain on paper towels and drizzle with honey.

Greens

All kinds of greens are eaten throughout the Mediterranean: lettuces of all types, arugula, radicchio, spinach, and some herbs. Greens can be mixed together in a salad. A popular version is the French mixed green salad, a combination of arugula, radicchio, frisée, and mâche, dressed with a bit of olive oil and a squirt of lemon juice. In France and Italy, green salads are usually eaten at the end of a meal because they are simple and refreshing. There is great variation throughout the Mediterranean when it comes to making salads. In the eastern Mediterranean, for example, many salads consist of a variety of foods, not just greens: yogurt, cucumbers, tomatoes, legumes, or chopped vegetables. Of course, diners in the eastern Mediterranean will eat green salads as well. Sometimes greens are braised and seasoned and served as a vegetable accompaniment to the main dish. Spinach and radicchio are favorite side dishes. Greens can also be used in soups and stews, or as part of a main dish or appetizer. In Greece and Turkey, spinach, sometimes accompanied by cheese, is layered between phyllo dough or encased in phyllo dough, to create triangles of filled pastry, eaten as appetizers or as a quick snack. Because the Mediterranean climate is so mild, fresh local greens are available year-round.

Artichokes

Artichokes are a prickly, round vegetable that are popular in Italian, North African, and Turkish cuisine. They can be eaten by themselves steamed (and served with a garlic and oil dip), fried, or pickled. They are also cooked with other vegetables, or they can be hollowed out and stuffed with meat, breadcrumbs, or vegetables. Hearts of artichoke, the tender leaves in the center, are considered particularly tasty and are used in dishes, preserved in oil or brine, or breaded and fried. Artichokes are also chopped and eaten raw as a salad.

Onions

One of the oldest vegetables in the world (cultivated in prehistoric times), onions were used by ancient Egyptians, Greeks, and Romans. Along with garlic and chickpeas, onions were a staple of ancient diets. Today, onions are used as both an ingredient and a seasoning in Mediterranean cooking throughout the region. As a seasoning, onions are sautéed in olive oil to flavor the oil before other ingredients are added to the dish. As an ingredient, onions are eaten raw in salads or cooked with meat, vegetables, rice, or eggs.

Potatoes

White potatoes were originally grown in South America and were brought to Spain in 1539 by returning conquistadores. They then followed the same route of popularity as the tomato, first becoming popular with Italian peasants and then moving toward the eastern Mediterranean and south to North Africa. They are hardy and easy to grow, even in the rocky Mediterranean soil. Although not as popular in the Mediterranean as they are in central and eastern Europe, as well as the British Isles, potatoes are prepared in many ways and are used in a variety of dishes. They are invaluable as a way to thicken stews and soups, and they are frequently roasted with a little bit of olive oil, salt, and fresh rosemary and served as an accompaniment to grilled meat. In the eastern Mediterranean, potato pancakes are a savory appetizer, accompaniment, or main dish.

Carrots

Carrots are a particularly versatile vegetable in Mediterranean cooking. They grow nearly everywhere in the region, and they do not require rich soil or lots of water. They are frequently mixed with meats, legumes, and other vegetables in dishes that call for a sweet taste. Because of their sweet taste, they are particularly suited for the complex flavors in North African dishes and the sweet-sour cuisine of Sicily. In Morocco, carrots are sautéed with sugar, spices, currants, and fresh herbs to create a tangy salad.

Okra

Okra is a actually a fruit, but is considered by most cooks as a vegetable. At least it is used in many savory vegetable side dishes and in soups and stews, particularly in North African cooking. A member of the mallow family, okra was first used by the Egyptians as a way to thicken food. A related food that ancient Egyptians used was *melokiyah*, also a member of the mallow family. It is a spinach-like plant that gives off a strong and unmistakable odor when cooked. *Melokiyah* is still used in making soups in Egypt and in Tunisia. It is dried and stored in powdered form, to be added to soups and stews.

Cardoons

An edible thistle, the cardoon looks like celery. It is native to the Mediterranean region and was cultivated and eaten in ancient Rome. Today, it is popular in France, Spain, and Italy. Cardoons are eaten raw in a sauce of olive oil, anchovies, and garlic; or they can be cooked and eaten, usually braised. When they are cooked, cardoons taste something like a cross between celery and artichokes.

Broccoli and Cabbage

Broccoli originated in the Mediterranean region and grew wild there. Originally, people ate the stems but not the flowering heads (what consumers like to eat now). Italians claim broccoli as their own and the name comes from the Italian *brocco* or "sprout." Broccoli can be steamed, braised, stewed, and boiled. A relative of broccoli, known as broccoli rabe, is also popular. Rabe has dark green leaves and its stalks look like broccoli, but it tastes more bitter or pungent than broccoli. Wild cabbage also grew in the coastal areas of the Mediterranean. In ancient times it had a longer stem, which was the part that was eaten. Ancient Romans cultivated cabbage to have a larger, rounder head. Cabbage used to be popular among peasants because it could keep for a long time, especially in cooler weather. Although ancient Greeks and Romans liked cabbage for its medicinal qualities, cabbage was never highly regarded by other

Mediterranean populations, probably because it smells when it is cooked and it is difficult to digest. Cabbage is used in stews and soups, as well as some layered cooked dishes, and it is sometimes consumed raw in salads.

Asparagus

Asparagus was cultivated by the ancient Greeks and was prized by the ancient Romans, both for its taste and its medicinal properties (it was thought to improve kidney function). The vegetable can be either green or white. White asparagus, popular in Spain and France, is produced by heaping soil on the growing stalks to inhibit chlorophyll production, hence the white appearance or color. Asparagus is grown extensively in France and Italy, where it is served as an accompaniment to the main course, steamed and dressed with a simple sauce. It is also used in pasta and rice (paella, risotto) dishes, and can be eaten cold in salads or appetizers.

Legumes

Legumes, like lentils, chickpeas, and fava beans, are as important to the Mediterranean diet as olives and wheat. Originally, these vegetables grew wild throughout the Mediterranean until they were domesticated. Because they are inexpensive, filling, and nutritious, legumes are often referred to as "food of the poor," or "poor man's meat." Although many consumers can now afford meat and other foods, legumes have remained extremely popular; they are eaten by every religious faith in the region and by every ethnic and economic group. Frequently, legumes are served alone or they are seasoned. Legumes prepared in different ways are a popular ingredient for dips and sandwiches: hummus is a dip made with chickpeas, lemon, garlic, and tahini. Mashed, fried chickpeas are called falafel, a specialty found throughout the Levant. *Ful medames* is another popular dish made with fava beans, garlic, tahini, and eggs, meat, or tomato sauce. Mediterranean cooks also use legumes in soups and stews to make them heartier and more flavorful; legumes are thought to go quite well in dishes with salted, fatty meats. Legumes can be dried out and thus keep for a long time. Because dried legumes take a long time to cook, people in North Africa use a special pot, with a wide bottom and a narrow neck, for cooking. The pot's shape allows steam to condense on the sides and slide back down to the bottom, tenderizing the dried legumes more quickly than would boiling in a standard pot. This kind of pot, the tajine, is also the name of a famous Moroccan stew, where legumes are combined with meat, vegetables, and seasonings. A more modern method of cooking is to use a high-pressure cooker. Legumes like chickpeas can be ground up and made into a kind of flour. Chickpea flour is used to make crepes, called *socca*, in southern France, or fried "bread" patties, called *panelle*, in Sicily.

Chicken Tajine

5–6 boneless skinless chicken breasts, chopped

3 tablespoons flour

2 medium onions, chopped

3 garlic cloves, peeled and minced

2 tablespoons olive oil

3 tablespoons tomato paste

3 tablespoons honey

1 cup chicken or vegetable broth

1 teaspoon ground coriander

1 teaspoon ground cinnamon

1 teaspoon ground cumin

1 teaspoon ground turmeric

8 ounces dried apricots

2 cans chopped tomatoes (or use three to four fresh tomatoes)

2 cans chickpeas, drained and rinsed

Sauté onion and garlic in olive oil until soft and translucent. Remove from heat. Add broth and gradually stir in flour. Add tomato paste and honey and stir until mixed together. Add spices and mix. Add apricots, chopped tomatoes, and chickpeas. Mix well and put in a crock pot. Cook in crock pot 2–3 hours, depending on the size of the chicken chunks. Serve with fresh chopped cilantro or coriander on top and serve with couscous.

FRUITS

Fruits occupy an important place in the Mediterranean diet. Like fresh vegetables, fruits are usually less expensive than many other foods, and some fruits (citrus, for example) grow well in the sunny, dry climate. Foreign travelers from the eighteenth century to the present observed an abundance of fruit, in some areas oranges and lemons were left to rot because people could not eat all of them. Fresh fruit is popular as a last course in a meal, served along with nuts, cheese, or a bit of bread. It is also eaten raw as a snack and even unripe fruit can be eaten with a little bit of salt. Fruit is also used in cooked dishes, either as an ingredient in a meat or vegetable dish.

Citrus

Citrus fruits such as lemons, oranges, and citron (which looks like an overgrown lemon) grow in abundance in most parts of the Mediterranean. It is not unusual to see orange or lemon trees in people's yards or in public parks or growing wild by the side of the road. The juice of oranges and lemons is used for cold drinks, including lemonade, and citrus fruits are sweetened with honey or sugar and used in desserts like cakes or puddings. Citrus fruit and juice are also used in salads and soups. Oranges are mixed with chopped onion, fennel, or artichokes in a sweet-sour salad in southern Italy and North Africa. In Greece and Cyprus, lemon flavors a soup called *avgolemono*. Citrus juice is also a staple ingredient for salad dressings, sauces, and as an accompaniment for fish. And in North Africa, lemons are salted and preserved for use in many dishes.

Avgolemono

7 cups chicken stock

3/4 cup rice or orzo

4 eggs

1/4 cup fresh lemon juice

Salt and pepper

Bring stock to a boil. Add rice or orzo and simmer covered for about 20 minutes or until rice is cooked. Lightly beat the eggs in a medium bowl. Add two cups of the hot broth to the eggs and stir constantly. Pour mixture in the bowl into the soup pot. Cook for a few minutes until soup thickens. Remove from heat and stir in lemon juice. Add salt and pepper to taste.

Melons

All kinds of melons are cultivated and eaten throughout the Mediterranean: cantaloupe, muskmelon, and other varieties are eaten for breakfast, for dessert, and even as a first course, combined with cheese or cured meat (as in the famous Italian dish, melon with sliced prosciutto, an Italian ham). Watermelon, which probably originated somewhere in Africa, is also a popular fruit. It is eaten plain, or it can be used in salads to provide a sweet balance to spicy or sour ingredients. Watermelon ices and drinks are good thirst quenchers in the summertime. Sicilians make a type of pudding from watermelon juice, also popular in the summer.

Dates

One of the oldest plants in the world, the date palm, found throughout North Africa and in the eastern Mediterranean, bears fruit that is eaten fresh or dried. For Muslims in the region, dates have a special significance, given that the prophet Muhammed liked them and broke his Ramadan fast with a date. Dried dates are sweet and are frequently consumed as a candy-like snack or for dessert (especially when they are stuffed with nuts). Some prefer dates stuffed with cheese or meat for a sweet/savory snack, whereas other cooks add dates to lamb or chicken to give the dish a sweet taste.

Figs

Figs have been cultivated for thousands of years. Originally from Southwest Asia, figs became a popular fruit in the Mediterranean basin in ancient times. Ancient Romans fed figs to gladiators, to give them quick energy. Packed with sugar, figs are small, pear-shaped, and have many seeds inside. They are grown commercially, for domestic use and for export, and many households have a fig tree in the garden for personal use. Figs are eaten fresh in season, accompanied by sweet white cheese, or a glass of sweet wine. They can also be used as an ingredient in stews (some Moroccan tajines use figs), or meat and vegetable dishes, especially in North Africa. They can be preserved in many ways; they are stewed and made into sweet fig preserves or jam, a popular breakfast treat. Figs can also be dried and eaten later. For centuries, dried figs were a staple food among Mediterranean peasants and were known as poorman's food.

Pomegranates

Cultivated throughout the eastern Mediterranean, pomegranates are a juicy fruit that contain a lot of seeds. Pomegranate juice varies in acidity between sweet, sweet-sour, and sour. Sweet juice and sweet-sour juice are used to make beverages, syrups, jellies, ices, and other desserts. Sour pomegranate juice is used more like vinegar or lemon juice in marinades, salad dressings, and other recipes.

Nuts

Nuts of all kinds are popular in the Mediterranean: hazelnuts, pine nuts, pistachios, walnuts, and almonds are perhaps the most widely consumed.

Preparing tajines in Casablanca, Morocco. AP Photo/Abdeljalil Bounhar.

Nuts are eaten in all kinds of ways: fresh off the tree, toasted, fried, baked, ground, or prepared in both savory and sweet dishes. Nuts and seeds are ground up and made into pastes or "butters"; the most popular is tahini, a sesame-seed paste that is an important ingredient in many of the meze-style dishes in Greece, Turkey, and throughout the Levant. Italian pesto or French *pistou* is a versatile paste made from basil, garlic, and ground pine nuts. Nuts are even used to make drinks. Almond milk is a popular drink in the eastern Mediterranean and is made by grinding almonds and sugar into a paste, adding milk, more sugar, and orange-flower water. The mixture is then passed through a sieve or strainer and then drunk at room temperature.

MEAT

Although there were pockets of great wealth in the Mediterranean region, the majority of the population remained at subsistence level for centuries. Farmers, shepherds, fishermen, and other agricultural laborers preferred to sell more expensive foods such as eggs, dairy products, and meat, rather than consume them. Urban artisans and later factory workers often could not afford to buy meat with their meager earnings. Today, standards of living have improved and intensive production methods have put meat, poultry, and fish within the economic reach of most citizens in the region. Still, old traditions die hard and consumers tend to use what is on hand (sheep, pigs, fish) and use everything in or on the animal. Pigs and tuna are perhaps the best examples of how thrifty Mediterranean cooks can be when it comes to using everything at hand. The two most popular ways meat of all types is prepared are grilling (in *shawarma*, gyros, or kebabs) and stewing (the Moroccan tajine is perhaps the best known example of a meat stew).

Lamb

Lamb is the most popular meat in the Mediterranean region and is grilled, braised, stewed, and baked. One of the most popular ways of serving lamb is something called *shawarma* in Lebanon, Syria, and Israel; gyros in Greece; and doner kebab in Turkey. Lamb meat is sliced into wide pieces, marinated, and then threaded on a long skewer in between slices of fat. The skewer then rotates over a vertical grill for two or three hours until the meat is cooked through. As the meat is cooking, the outer layers can be sliced off and eaten as a meal or stuffed into flatbread for a sandwich. Grilled lamb is also popular as kebab, in which small marinated pieces of meat are put on skewers and grilled. In Lebanon and Syria, a dish called kibbeh is made from a paste of ground lamb, bulgur wheat, onions, and seasonings. And in Turkey, little meatballs called *kofte* are made from ground lamb mixed with onion and seasonings. For Muslim and Jewish populations, lamb sausage is an alternative to pork sausage.

Shawarma in pita. © J. Susan Cole Stone.

Fish

Fish is one of the hallmark foods of Mediterranean cuisine, especially in Greece, Spain, Turkey, and Italy. Mediterranean people eat all kinds of fish: bonito, blue fish, turbot, mackerel, monkfish, and swordfish. These fish are broiled, grilled, baked, stewed, and used in soups. The most popular fish are tuna and cod. Tuna fishing goes back to ancient times and the fish is commonly referred to as "the pig of the sea" because one can eat every part of it, although the best cuts are from the underbelly. Tuna fishing was a mainstay of Mediterranean economies for centuries. Barrels of salted tuna were exported and in the twentieth century; tuna was preserved in oil and canned for export. Recently, tuna has become scarce and the Mediterranean Sea is running out of tuna because of the shift from traditional methods to long-line fishing and factory ships, both of which can harvest much more and usually do so for export. Salted fish like herring, sardines, anchovies, and cod were traditionally consumed by the poor, frequently in amounts so small that the fish acted more like a seasoning for a dish, rather than constituting the main course. Salted cod, known as *bacallà* in Spanish or *baccalà* in Italian, is known for its dense texture and more intense flavor. Once eaten by the poor as cod balls or chopped up in stews, salted cod is now something of a rarity and is usually reserved for special occasions like holidays.

Seafood

Seafood of all types is popular near the shores of the sea: oysters, clams, lobsters, prawns, mussels, squid, and octopus. Seafood can be steamed and served plain or with seasonings. Alternately, it can be made into a more exotic food such as *midye dolmasi,* Turkish stuffed mussels made with rice, raisins, pine nuts, and seasonings. Seafood is used in making Spanish paella and also goes into making any number of fish stews and soups served throughout the region. Snails, known as *cargols* or *caracoles* in Spain, escargot in southern France, or *lumache* in Italy, need to be cleaned or purged (usually by being fed herbs or grain) before being cooked, but they are used in stews and soups. In Morocco a seasoned snail soup called *babouch* is sold as street food.

Poultry

Poultry, especially chicken, is popular throughout the Mediterranean. Like lamb, it is eaten grilled, in kebabs or in *shawarma.* It is also stewed in Moroccan tajines. Turkey, duck, pigeon, and quail are also consumed in the region.

A fisherman sorts fish off the coast of Spain. The European Union has implemented fishing limits to keep Mediterranean waters alive, but fishermen complain these policies are destroying their livelihoods. AP Photo/Jasper Juinen.

Pork

Pork is prepared and consumed by Christian populations in the region, in the form of sausage, ham, bacon, and preserved meats. As with tuna, every bit of the pig is used: livers are fried up and eaten; pig's feet can be boiled, stewed, or fried; and bits of meat from the pig's head can go into sausage. Italian ham, called prosciutto, is an international gourmet specialty, as is the Spanish *sobrassada*, a paté-like sausage that can be spread on bread.

Camel

Camel is favored in North Africa, especially in Egypt, where special markets sell the choicest parts of the animal. The flavor of camel is close to that of beef. The meat is bright red and the fat is translucent. Camels are usually slaughtered for meat between the ages of two and four; otherwise the meat becomes too tough and therefore requires a longer cooking time. A mixture of grated onion, salt, pepper, and cumin is rubbed into the meat to tenderize it and give it flavor. Tougher cuts of meat are boiled, then mixed with rice to make meatballs, or sometimes camel fat is added to tomato juice for a flavorful drink.

DAIRY

Mediterranean consumers are fond of dairy products: Greek yogurt is famous all over the world, as are Italian and French cheeses. Unlike North America, where dairy culture consists mainly of cow's milk products, Mediterranean dairy products tend to come from sheep and goats, animals that were, and to some extent still are, fundamental to a more nomadic lifestyle. Although shepherding is giving way to more industrialized forms of food and clothing production, dairy products made from sheep and goats still remind us of their special place in the rocky geography of the Mediterranean region.

Milk

Cow, sheep, and goat milk is popular either as a beverage or used in recipes. Milk puddings are known throughout Lebanon, Syria, and Turkey; the puddings are seasoned with flavors like orange-flower water and topped with pistachios, raisins, or dates. Throughout the eastern Mediterranean, a clotted cream called *qashta* is thick enough to be cut with a knife; it is used as a topping or filling for pastries and other deserts.

Cheese

Cheese is made from goat, sheep, or cow's milk; and in parts of southern Italy, water buffalo are raised to produce the best soft mozzarella cheese melted on to pizza or used in various appetizers. Although all kinds of cheeses are made, the hard, salty cheeses keep the longest and therefore have been the most traditional cheeses from the region. Greek feta cheese is now known around the world as an important ingredient in Mediterranean cooking, as is mozzarella from Italy and to a lesser extent, *halloumi* cheese from Cyprus, a sheep's milk cheese eaten as fried slices for breakfast, used in salads, or stuffed inside pasta.

Yogurt

Yogurt consists of fermented milk, which is sometimes sweetened. There has been a long-simmering dispute among yogurt's fans as to whether Arabs and Turks invented the food, but all kinds of yogurt are consumed throughout the Mediterranean region. Yogurt is made from cow's milk and goat milk. It can be eaten or used as a condiment plain, or it can be blended with water or juices to make a drink. It is also seasoned with spices for dips in a traditional meze; a popular Greek dip is *tzatziki*, yogurt mixed with garlic and cucumber. In Greek, Turkish, Lebanese, and Syrian cuisine, yogurt is added to meat or vegetable dishes, or it is combined with honey and fruit for a dessert. In Turkey yogurt is made into a savory soup called *yayla corbasi*. In supermarkets across the region, sweetened flavored yogurt is now sold as a breakfast or snack food.

Yogurt Soup

6 cups broth, chicken or vegetable

1/2 cup uncooked rice

2 cups plain yogurt

1 egg

2 tablespoons flour

Salt

Bring broth to a boil in a large soup pot. Add rice and reduce heat. Simmer for 20–30 minutes until rice is done. While rice is cooking, make a sauce by mixing together yogurt, eggs, and flour in a saucepan on low heat. Cook until the mixture starts to bubble. Remove from heat and add to cooked rice soup. Stir constantly for another few minutes until blended through. Add salt to taste and serve. Drizzle soup with olive oil or melted butter, chopped parsley or mint.

DRINKS

Wine

Wine or fermented grape juice was consumed by ancient Greeks, who considered beer or milk drinking to be signs of barbarism. Wine was adopted by Christians and thought to be essential for mass, given that the consecration of red wine transformed it into the blood of Christ during the rite of Holy Communion. Thus wine consumption took root wherever Christianity was popular in the Mediterranean region, as its use was endorsed by the Church. Wine was also one of the most important items for trade in the sea. The environment of the Mediterranean region, specifically the hot dry summer climate, means that the kinds of wines that are produced are very heavy; thus some parts of the Mediterranean (Turkey, Tunisia, Morocco, Israel) were not known for producing very good wine, whereas other regions were thought to make good wine (Spain, France, Italy, Lebanon). Technology allowing for greater control over the fermentation process has evened out the results somewhat, and now wines from all over the Mediterranean are considered quite good. Although alcohol is forbidden for Muslims, wine is made in countries with significant Muslim populations and exported; wine and other alcoholic beverages are sometimes consumed in private, for example, in homes or in social clubs or nightclubs. In countries with large Muslim populations, alcohol consumption is a political issue, especially when governments are urged to take stricter measures against the production and sale of alcoholic beverages like wine. And in countries with large Christian and Jewish populations, alcohol consumption is also a problem and threatens to become a political issue. Although these regions have held a liberal attitude toward alcohol consumption, the

Grapes throughout the Mediterranean are tended and harvested by hand. Here, a woman picks grapes in southwestern France. AP Photo/Bob Edme.

recent rise in teenage drinking and alcohol-related driving deaths has spurred considerable debate over whether governments need to more strictly control alcohol consumption.

Water and Mineral Water

Before the craze for bottled water went global, populations in the western Mediterranean had been drinking special mineral waters in bottles since the late nineteenth century in order to cure all kinds of ailments, aid digestion, or, in some locales, as a replacement for an unsanitary public water source. There was a dramatic increase in bottled water consumption after World War II in the region, as incomes steadily rose, and with more expendable income, consumers chose bottled water over tap water. Today, bottled water is available in natural or in a slightly carbonated form and throughout the Mediterranean; it is offered for sale in cafés, bars, and restaurants. In restaurants, patrons are unlikely to get a glass of tap water served with the meal; instead they must order a bottle of plain or carbonated mineral water.

Coffee

Coffee is a favorite beverage throughout the region and is served in a variety of ways, from the strong cups of espresso in Italy to the weaker, but very thick, Turkish coffee that is served with the coffee grounds still in the beverage. In bars and cafés where coffee is served strong, it is usually served in a small cup or glass, accompanied by a glass of water. In addition to being a morning beverage, coffee is consumed after a meal and is thought to aid digestion. It is also a social drink and has been for centuries, as evidenced by the proliferation of cafés and coffee bars throughout the region. In Syria and Lebanon, coffee is served with seasonings such as cinnamon, cloves, cardamom, or rose water. Whether weak or strong, coffee is sweetened with sugar but is seldom served with milk or cream.

Tea

Tea is brewed English-style in some cafés and at home, but it is more commonly consumed as a kind of infusion, meaning tea leaves are combined with other ingredients—herbs such as mint or chamomile, or spices like cardamom or cloves. In the eastern Mediterranean, mint tea is very popular and in Turkey, tea is more popular than coffee and constitutes the nation's "pick-me-up" beverage.

Soft Drinks

Popular soft drinks include lemonade, drinks made with fruit syrups, yogurt drinks, and fruit juices. Soft drinks are available at every café and bar, and some are also available in bottled form at markets and supermarkets. Carbonated beverages like Coca-Cola have been in the region since the American Coca-Cola company set up bottling operations after World War II, but only after popular resistance. Because Coca-Cola and other American beverages spark economic and nationalist protest, there have been sporadic attempts by various Mediterranean nations to compete with Coke. Most recently, Muslims in France launched Mecca Cola, Turkish people can drink Cola Turka, and inhabitants of the French island of Corsica drink Corsica Cola. Although these beverages are popular on a regional or local level, they have yet to threaten Coca-Cola's dominance in the international carbonated beverage market.

SEASONINGS

The dominant seasonings in Mediterranean cooking are salt, herbs, and spices. Although many herbs and spices are used in the preparation of food—too many to count—Mediterranean dishes are not considered spicy, at least not in the sense that they are spicy-hot. Rather, herbs and spices are considered essential for making the flavor of a dish more complex or intense. The use of spices, many of which originated in Asia, dates back centuries, given the Mediterranean's history as a center for trade. Meanwhile, many of the herbs used in cooking are native to the area and thus a great premium is placed on fresh herbs. And last, perhaps an unusual and ancient characteristic of Mediterranean seasonings is the use of other foods like fish or fish products to enhance the flavor of a dish.

Salt

Commonly referred to as the inner sea, the Mediterranean is a nearly enclosed body of water. Because little fresh water enters the water, the sea is very salty; the dry climate contributes to this situation by creating a constant state of evaporation and therefore high concentrations of salt in the water. Not surprisingly, Mediterraneans have collected salt by drying out sea water and "harvesting" salt. Salt collection goes back to ancient times and because salt was so important, not just as a seasoning but for preserving all kinds of food, it was frequently taxed and controlled by authorities. Because so much Mediterranean food is preserved in salt, cooks are careful to wash the excess salt off most foods before cooking or using them. There is an unusual method of cooking meat, fish, and vegetables that involves encasing food entirely in salt and then baking it. A hard crust forms around the food, keeping the food juicy but not making it too salty. Despite the industrial production of salt, salt is still collected out of evaporated sea water and "sea salt" is favored by many for its pure taste and for its magnesium content. French sea salt, especially *fleur de sel* (flower of salt), is prized by gourmets around the world because of its taste and because it is harvested entirely by hand and therefore scarce.

Garlic

Garlic is a small white bulb that grows underground and can be found all over the Mediterranean region. It is added to dips, sauces, meat dishes, fish, vegetables, couscous, rice dishes, and pasta. It can also be roasted and eaten as a kind of spread, or consumed raw in salads. In parts of the western Mediterranean, garlic and olive oil are blended to make a simple multipurpose sauce. In Catalonia, this sauce is known as *allioli*, or Catalan catsup, and in southern France, it is called aioli. In northern Italy, a peasant dish called *bagna cauda* features a garlic, oil, and anchovy "fondue" for raw or cooked vegetables.

Cinnamon

Cinnamon is an ancient spice, imported to the Mediterranean from Sri Lanka and India, via Egypt. Its use is described in the Bible for scenting clothes and bedclothes. For centuries, cinnamon was used as a spice and as a medicine. Even today, scientific studies claim cinnamon has antioxidant properties and may help with the common cold. In cooking, the spice is used in ground form or the cinnamon stick, or bark, is added whole to the dish and then taken away before serving. Cinnamon is used to flavor sweet dishes and coffee, but it is also used to flavor meat, tomato sauce, and fish dishes.

Saffron

Saffron is a highly prized and expensive spice that has a light flavor and gives dishes a vibrant yellow or reddish-yellow appearance (Spanish paella, for example, has saffron in it). Saffron consists of the dried stamens of the Saffron Crocus; about 150 crocus flowers yield 1 gram (less than one ounce) of dried saffron threads. The crocus originated in Asia and was first cultivated in Greece. Today the Saffron Crocus is cultivated in Catalonia, Spain and Tuscany, Italy, although the majority of the world's saffron is imported from Yemen. Saffron is an expensive spice because the flowers must be hand-picked—a very labor-intensive process. The spice is so prized that there is a thriving market of counterfeit saffron made from crocuses and other substances.

Oregano

Oregano is an herb that is native to the Mediterranean region; it requires little care and thrives in rocky soil. Used fresh or dry, oregano is found in Greek and Italian cooking. Its slightly bitter taste goes well with pickled or preserved foods, as well as in hot and spicy dishes. Oregano is perhaps best known for its use in Italian tomato sauce, Greek salads, and pizza, although it is also used in many vegetable dishes and as a seasoning for grilled meat.

Spice and Herb Blends

Personal mixes of herbs and/or spices are common in the eastern Mediterranean region and in North Africa. Individuals or families make their own blend and store them at home to add to dishes. Spice and herb blends are also commercially prepared and available for purchase in stores and markets. Spice blends are especially popular in North African countries, where individuals and families take pride in their own particular blend of spices to season all kinds of dishes. An increasing number of consumers, however, buy their spice blends from commercial vendors. Perhaps the most famous herb blend from the Mediterranean region is the southern French *Herbes de Provence*, a blend of dried basil, bay leaf, thyme, and sometimes lavender; it has been manufactured and exported since the 1970s for interested cooks around the world. Spice and herb blends can be added directly to the dish, or they can be used in a form that the French call the bouquet garni, a mix of herbs that is tied up in a porous cloth, added to the dish, then removed before serving.

Capers

Capers are the flower buds of the *Capparis spinosa* shrub, a small flowering bush that is native to the Mediterranean region. The plant grows best in rocky soil near the sea, and the immature flower buds are harvested by hand, dried, and packed in salt or cured in vinegar or brine. Capers are cultivated and exported from France, Spain, Italy, Algeria, Greece, and Cyprus. The most sought-after capers are grown on the small Italian island of Pantelleria because they are large and have an intense flavor. Capers have a pungent, peppery taste and they are added to a variety of dishes in Spanish, Italian, Greek, and French cuisine.

Fish Products

The use of small fish and fish products goes back to the ancient food known as garum, or fish sauce, produced in ancient Greece and Rome. The innards of fish such as anchovies, mackerel, or tuna were crushed and cured in brine and left to liquefy. The actual taste of garum was supposedly light, but the production process created such a foul smell that it was carefully regulated by authorities so as not to offend people. The modern version of garum is perhaps the anchovy, a small fish that is usually preserved in oil or brine. When used in recipes, anchovies are sometimes ground up, or the liquid they produce is used to dress pasta or salads. And in southern France, a delicacy known as *pissala* is a paste made from tiny fish (now illegal to harvest, so anchovies or other fish must be substituted), was layered with salt and left to ferment. The paste gave the French version of pizza, *pissaladière*, a characteristic fishy taste. Throughout the Mediterranean, cooks season their food with fish roe (eggs). The roe of tuna or gray mullet are removed, salted, pressed, and dried. It is then coated in wax to preserve it and sold in bricks, or the brick is grated and bottled. The roe is called *bottarga* in Italian, *boutarekh* in Egyptian Arabic, *putargo* in Turkish, *poutargue* in French, and *avgotáracho* in Greek. *Bottarga* can be eaten by itself as an appetizer, but it is frequently used in many dishes as a salty seasoning.

3

Cooking

Many cookbooks about Mediterranean cuisine emphasize how relaxed and casual the process of cooking food is. Cookbooks feature glossy photographs of sunny beaches and olive groves, and the introductory text usually highlights the simplicity and freshness of ingredients and dishes. Although these books try to distinguish what is unique or interesting about Mediterranean cuisine, readers might get the impression that people in the Mediterranean go out to their gardens, pick a few ingredients, and throw them in a pot to create a delicious meal. This may be the case on occasion, but it is perhaps more accurate to think of Mediterranean cooking as a complex process of measuring ingredients in exact proportion to achieve a particular kind of taste. Although it is easy to throw together a salad or a sandwich, it is much more time-consuming and complicated to put together a Moroccan tajine or a French bouillabaisse. Cooking across the Mediterranean involves a lot of preparation in the form of shopping for or storing certain foods to be used later, and the actual preparation of the dish, or multiple dishes, can be complex indeed.

Cooking is not only a potentially complicated task, it is a necessary and ongoing process. People throughout the region are known for their hospitality, and cooking is perhaps the most common way to express it. Families, including extended family, might dine together three times a day; guests and neighbors might come over for dinner; special meals mark significant life events and holidays. It is not surprising, then, that people spend a great deal of time thinking about, and preparing, food for family and friends.

For many people, cooking is more than a skill to learn in order to stay alive or eat well. It can be a means of expressing love for one's family or a way to demonstrate one's fitness for marriage and a family. And for people who cook professionally, whether in hotels, restaurants, or street market stalls, cooking is a way to earn a living. Cooking is also a way that people relate to other people in the Mediterranean. People throughout the region not only define themselves and their relationships through cooking, but they see cooking as an important and distinctive feature of their societies. People in the Mediterranean are quick to offer a snack or home-cooked meal to friends or even strangers. The process of cooking matters; individuals may buy something like pizza or a sandwich for a quick snack, but they are not content to pop a frozen meal in the microwave or to throw together a sandwich for a meal, at least not on a regular basis. Cooking, like hospitality, not only defines the Mediterranean diet, but who people in the Mediterranean are and how they relate to each other.

Of course, social and economic influences continually reshape food habits, and some people in the Mediterranean are changing their perspectives on cooking. Among the younger generations (university students, young families), microwave ovens and frozen foods are considered useful and convenient. Because of changing family structures in the Mediterranean (larger multigenerational families have given way to smaller nuclear families), there are fewer older family members nearby who pass down information about how to cook or who share favorite recipes from the past with their children and grandchildren. New work patterns and expectations make it difficult for factory workers and office workers alike to come home for a multicourse lunch. Shifting relations between men and women have recast expectations of who will do the cooking and how much cooking will go on in the household. And a growing number of chefs are trying to breathe new life into old favorite dishes by making them lighter and more healthful. These changes have occurred at an uneven pace throughout the region, and it is difficult to say whether these changes have significantly affected the role and significance of cooking in everyday life. What does seem clear is that the role of cooking in people's lives is currently being redefined.

This chapter first looks at who does the cooking in the household, restaurant, or market stall. Both men and women share the task, although it generally falls within women's responsibilities to do most of the cooking at home. Men do cook, either in public or private, but defining cooking as a male task depends on the type of dish being prepared, as well as the place it is prepared; it also depends on the dominant attitudes toward cooking as a form of housework. Next, this chapter explains the rather unique places and spaces for cooking in the Mediterranean. Kitchens can be anywhere: inside an apartment building or house, outside in a courtyard or on the street, and even in the middle of the desert! Although the Mediterranean kitchen is sometimes small and sparsely appointed, it is a place of constant activity, given the workload Mediterranean cooks and chefs must bear if they are always cooking for friends, family, and guests. Learning to cook in such a kitchen, then, means learning to organize space and time. Learning to cook also means understanding how to work with a few basic ingredients to produce many different types of dishes. Because so many Mediterranean dishes are based on the principle of "cooking with little," cooking involves a lot of thinking about the proper mixture of ingredients and a lot of preparation to store, preserve, and make the most of the ingredients on hand. Last, this chapter charts the recent social, cultural, and economic changes that have shaped contemporary food habits in the region. The most noticeable, and most controversial, change in food habits is a greater reliance on food that is already prepared (frozen foods, fast food, convenience foods). Some consumers worry that these recent changes are unhealthy. They also worry that young and future generations will not regard cooking with the same respect and understanding as have older Mediterranean cooks.

It is too early to measure the full impact of recent changes in Mediterranean food habits, but it seems clear that cooking is still an important activity. Whether it is done at home, on the street, or in the middle of the desert, cooking powerfully shapes attitudes toward food and defines relations among people across the region. Although it is sometimes difficult or time-consuming work, cooking is also entertaining, fulfilling, and meaningful.

WHO COOKS?

Determining who does the cooking in various parts of the Mediterranean depends on what kind of meal is being prepared, as well as where it is being served. In other words, there is no general rule regarding who cooks what, given the diversity of cultural practices and traditions throughout the region. In Western countries, feminist scholars have found that there is a "culinary hierarchy" that assigns more visible status and social value to public and professional cooking, usually, but not exclusively, performed by men. Private cooking in the home merits less status and frequently falls under the category of "housework," to be performed, usually but not exclusively, by women.[1] This culinary hierarchy is slowly giving way to a more equitable division of labor within the kitchen, but in western Mediterranean countries, it still holds true that many four-star chefs are men and in many households, women do more housework, including cooking, than do men. The culinary hierarchy is not a hard-and-fast rule, then, but its presence indicates that different cultural values are assigned to different types of cooking.

Western assumptions about the gendered nature of cooking as an aspect of housework do not hold up to the diverse cultural practices throughout the Mediterranean, particularly in the eastern and southern regions. As chapter 5, "Eating Out," describes, much of the street food (snacks and meals that are prepared, sold, and consumed on the streets, popular in the North African and Middle Eastern regions of the Mediterranean) consumed in the Mediterranean is prepared and sold by men. One might assume, then, that for some reason, women are discouraged from cooking food that will be sold in the public sphere. And one might assume that the top professional chefs in hotels and restaurants in these regions are men. Yet in Morocco, women are esteemed as the best chefs in restaurants, so much so that locals will check to see if a woman is cooking in the kitchen before eating at a restaurant!

It is difficult to generalize about the gendered nature of cooking, as it seems to be divided between men and women depending on the type of food being prepared and where the food is being served. Women throughout the Mediterranean tend to do the cooking in the private sphere of the home, especially on holidays and special occasions that call for elaborate preparations and special ingredients. It is difficult to say that this type of work is somehow not valued because a woman performs the task; cooking for one's family or guests is regarded both as a significant obligation and achievement. Women consider cooking to be an important duty, but it is more than a duty or obligation; cooking can be considered an art and it is a point of pride to be able to prepare a tasty dish for extended family or for company. Women also understand the importance of more specialized tasks such as bread-making. Since ancient times, women have been involved in milling flour and preparing and cooking bread, a time-consuming and sometimes difficult task. A certain amount of social status was assigned to this task, however, given that bread was the chief staple of the Mediterranean diet. And, for Christians and Muslims, bread contains God's blessings and is of symbolic and cultural significance as well. Today, commercial bakeries and bread-making factories have largely replaced women's work in this area; anthropologists studying the industrialization of bread-making in the Mediterranean have noted that women experienced a loss of status when their jobs were taken over by machines and factory workers. Anthropologists believe that the duty of bread-making raised women's status in society. When these tasks were taken away from them, women felt a loss and experienced nostalgia; cooking at home was not the same anymore.[2] Thus good cooking is more than just following recipes; it is a socially valued process to shop, prepare, and present meals for families that do not eat prepared foods or eat out much. This workload is compounded in some cases by having to work within a limited budget or within the confines of a small kitchen with few appliances.

In the United States and other parts of the world, prepared food is relatively inexpensive, convenient, and available. Consumers may prefer to buy frozen meals or fast food meals rather than cook for themselves, particularly if they regard cooking as a chore. Similarly, working families and single people might opt out of cooking at home because of the time and preparation needed to prepare attractive meals. Mediterranean consumers view cooking from a slightly different perspective; they do not regard it as a chore or an inconvenience but as something that fills an important social and nutritional need. For example, Greek university students studying in the United Kingdom prefer to cook in their dormitories rather than eat sandwiches or fast food. They see cooking as an important way to nourish themselves, provide better tasting food, and continue family traditions they experienced at home in Greece. And in some North African countries, people hesitate to dine out in restaurants, preferring a home-cooked meal in someone's house to a fancy meal out. Cooking has a different status, then, as an activity that is both necessary and desired. Women who cook at home and men who cook outside the home have an important obligation to prepare satisfying, healthy, and tasty dishes.

COOKING IN THE KITCHEN AND OUTDOORS

The warmth of the Mediterranean climate necessitated a house structure that was more open, and most houses in rural and urban areas were built around a central outdoor courtyard. Since ancient times, food was usually prepared in the courtyard, whether women roasted or grilled foods there or finished important tasks like pickling and preserving. In more populous areas, houses had indoor kitchens, but cooking was still done over an open hearth. In ancient Egypt, the kitchen was well ventilated, with a covered clay oven for baking; inside the oven were shelves for placing containers at different levels. In ancient Rome, meals were cooked in a cauldron or pot set over a fire, or they were cooked in vessels set on a

gridiron. Because of the open fire, indoor kitchen areas were well ventilated, either through a hole in the ceiling or a vent in the wall. In more
densely populated areas, houses lacked cooking facilities and ancient Romans would go to outdoor communal kitchens to prepare their meals.

Today, in rural regions of the Mediterranean (especially in North Africa), some houses do not have an "official" kitchen. Instead, people cook
in an inner courtyard of the house, either over an open fire (for roasting
or grilling) or in a barrel-shaped oven (known as a *tandir*, tandoor, or
tanuur), well suited for baking bread. In Turkey, flat loaves of dough are
stuck to the wall of the tandoor; they then drop off when they are crusty
and baked through. In urban and suburban regions of the Mediterranean,
the inner courtyard may exist in a house, but most of the cooking is now
done in a kitchen. Porous boundaries still remain between the indoors
and the outdoors, however. For example, where people still tend small
gardens for herbs and vegetables, the indoor kitchen is usually connected
to the outdoor garden. Another type of kitchen found in Sardinia is called
a *cucina rustica*, which is not a kitchen per se but an area in the back of the
house, partially covered, which opens to an outdoor courtyard. The *cucina
rustica* has a fireplace and a large table; this area used to be a space for preparing food. Cooks would do everything from butchering a pig to making
pasta in this spacious area. Today, many Sardinians have converted these
spaces into large dining rooms, work areas, or family rooms by enclosing
the outdoor portion, remodeling and refurbishing the more rustic aspects
of the space.[3]

The average Mediterranean kitchen seems small and sparsely appointed,
at least compared with the average American kitchen. In Catalonia, essential items are few: a *cassola* or clay casserole, a paella pan, a mortar and
pestle. In North Africa and throughout the eastern Mediterranean, cooks
make do with a few good knives, pans, steamers, a pressure cooker or tajine, mixing bowls, and serving platters. In North Africa, many women
cook in small kitchens where little space is wasted. The kitchen may lead
to an outdoor courtyard and usually there is one table or counter for prep
work, a charcoal brazier, a gas or electric stove, a refrigerator and a freezer.
In eastern Mediterranean countries such as Turkey, most food is cooked
over an open fire (grilling and roasting) or on the stove top; there is little
need for the oven, except to make baked desserts. Most bread is purchased
in stores or in bakeries.

There are few high-tech appliances like blenders, microwaves, and mix-
masters in the average Mediterranean kitchen. This is more a matter of
preference than necessity. Although many high-tech tools and appliances
are available in stores and the standard of living in many parts of the

Mediterranean is high enough for consumers to afford them, most cooks prefer to grind food with a mortar and pestle, not a food processor, or they will have a microwave oven but use it less often than would an American cook. Mediterranean cooks have always been able to turn out highly sophisticated meals using little equipment. Growing up in Egypt during World War II with her wealthy Egyptian grandmother, food memoirist Collette Rosant remembered the sparse yet efficient kitchen that the servant used. Even though the kitchen was stocked with all the latest technology (a refrigerator, a gas oven), the cook used very little to assemble rich, extravagant meals:

I spent a lot of time with Ahmet in the kitchen despite my grandmother's admonition that this was not the place for *une jeune fille de bonne famille*. The kitchen was very large, with two windows overlooking the back garden. There was a wide, deep stone sink with a copper faucet, and a large counter with bowls of limes and lemons and jars of spices. On the floor near the window were "primus" kerosene burners on which most of the cooking was done. A large refrigerator dominated the corner of the kitchen, and on the opposite corner was a large gas oven for baking. Near the counter were a couple of high stools where I would often sit watching Ahmet prepare lunch or dinner, or just put up pickles for the family.[4]

Cookbook author Fiona Dunlop traveled the countries of North Africa to collect recipes and cooking tips. She noted in many cases that most of the women (and a few of the men) she met worked in extremely small quarters with only a few appliances and utensils. Even the wealthier families she met had smallish kitchens in their apartments or houses, especially in urban areas where space comes at a premium. A small kitchen can be difficult when a cook is trying to make a large meal for company; access to an outdoor cooking space like a courtyard makes the process flow more smoothly. A small kitchen can also be a problem for Jewish cooks trying to follow kosher dietary rules, which call for separating meat and dairy in the preparation of meals. In practical terms, this translates into keeping different cooking utensils and plates in limited space and making sure the sink is emptied out between the washing of dishes and utensils. Small kosher kitchens require the cook's attention and organizational skills so that the family does not eat something forbidden or so that the meal is not rendered unsuitable for consumption by carelessness.

There are, of course, elaborate kitchens in the homes of the wealthy or in luxury restaurants and hotels. The most elaborate kitchens in history were located in the eastern Mediterranean during the time of the Ottoman Empire. Turkish cuisine in the palaces of the Sultans became more elaborate and ritualized. Whereas the early sultans ate simply and often in the company of ministers of state, it became customary for the sultan to eat more elaborate dishes, in isolation, after the conquest of Istanbul in 1453, an event that marked the transformation of the Ottomans into a world power. The staff of the palace kitchen ballooned, from a modest 200 persons at the end of the sixteenth century to more than 1,370 persons by the mid-seventeenth century. Within this enormous staff, an elaborate hierarchy of responsibility developed. Supervisors oversaw the creation of all sorts of dishes, and all work was broken down according to the type of food prepared, as well as the person who was going to eat it. The sultan and his immediate family had their own cooking staff of 12 who worked in a separate kitchen from the rest of the staff, who fed between 5,000 and 10,000 people in the palace every day. Not surprisingly, the grocery lists were huge: in 1661, one list showed that 36,000 bushels of rice, 3,000 pounds of noodles, 500,000 bushels of chickpeas, and 12,000 pounds of salt were used in the palace. In 1723, the annual meat supply for the palace numbered 30,000 head of beef, 60,000 of mutton, 20,000 of veal, 200,000 of fowl, and 100,000 pigeons.[5] The preparation of each type of food or dish (soups, pilafs, vegetables, fish, bread, pastries, candies, jams, syrups, drinks) was treated as a separate and meaningful art. As one Turkish food expert noted, "so thoroughgoing was the specialization practiced in the palace kitchens that by the mid-eighteenth century the preparation of each of six varieties of halvah (a sweet made from sesame paste) had been entrusted to a separate master chef, assisted by a hundred apprentices."[6]

Not every kitchen was as elaborate as those of the Ottoman sultans. Most peasants made do with a cauldron on an open hearth, and in some regions, kitchen facilities were not available. In parts of rural Tunisia, a Tunisian tajine (a baked stew; see chapter 4) is still made outside. The cook puts an earthenware dish filled with the tajine over lighted olive wood. The pan is then covered with a flat plank and hot coals are piled on top. The nomadic Tuaregs of Libya and southern Algeria used to bake *tgilla*, or "ash bread" in a shallow hole in the sand. Once a staple of the Tuareg, *tgilla* is now made mostly on long trips or for special occasions. Whether the kitchen is in the desert, on a hill by the sea, or in a crowded city, it is usually considered the most important place in the home. People across the Mediterranean region love a home-cooked meal; in many places, restaurants are reserved for tourists because one can always make something tastier at home. Emigrants, students, and travelers who leave the region will pine away for home-cooked meals or the foods they can buy only in their native country. One study of Greek university students studying in the United Kingdom found that they frequently not only took ingredients (olive oil, feta cheese) with them back to school, but they took entire cooked meals in their checked baggage or on board planes return- ing to the United Kingdom! One student even brought back 16 kilograms (about 35 pounds) of meat to London:

I go to Greece almost every month because I want to see my boyfriend. Every time I carry back food. Last time I brought 16 kg of meat. Not only mine; my friend asked me to bring some for her too. I shape the meat in small portions in cellophane, freeze it and bring it over frozen. I also brought cheeses . . . I put everything in the suitcase among my things.[7]

Greek students were generally reluctant to try meats or cheeses not pre- pared in Greece, so attached were they to the flavors of home. Although Mediterranean kitchens may look small and simple to the unknowing eye, they are nonetheless significant places to both cooks and eaters. First and foremost, kitchens are places where one learns and then practices particu- lar methods of meal preparation, but they are also places where women and some men express their concern for the health and well-being of their family and friends.

LEARNING TO COOK

Recipes and cooking methods are usually transmitted orally. There is not the same mass market for glossy cookbooks and "how-to" books in the Mediterranean as there is in the United States, although there has been a great deal of international interest in the Mediterranean diet (see chapter 7) and the dishes that make up Mediterranean cuisine. One Tu- nisian woman, now considered a good cook, described how she learned at an early age about cooking because the ability to cook was tied closely to the prospect of finding a good husband:

I first learned to cook from my mother . . . and since then I've collected ideas chatting with women friends—we share tips and recipes. I was 15 when my mother first said, "I'll die one day soon so you've go to learn cooking—NOW!" She'd stand over me and hit me if I got it wrong, saying "You won't find a hus- band like that!" . . . I'm now trying to convince my 15-year-old daughter to learn—though she's doing her best to avoid it![8]

Young women and an increasing number of young men usually train under their mothers' watchful eye. A young cook-in-training might start by making a simple soup or stew and then progress to making part, then all, of an entire meal. A generation or two in the past, women married early (in North Africa, sometimes as young as 14 or 15 years) and many now recall having to learn how to cook on their own, without a lot of input or supervision from their mothers. Across the region, women are marrying at later ages and many go to university, attend graduate school, or work before marrying. Learning to cook, however, is still important so that young women and men can learn to feed themselves.

Some experienced cooks in the Mediterranean write off the ability to cook by explaining that the process of cooking is simple or straightforward. One Moroccan woman summed up her approach to cooking by stating that "[t]here's no secret, you just have to get on with it! I never throw anything away and keep all the leftovers to make a gratin or pie using an easy pastry. You just need to know the basics."[9] Knowing the basics, however, means really understanding how to use everything available, as well as knowing that one must waste nothing. For centuries, the culture of poverty throughout the Mediterranean has dictated culinary style and form. Mediterranean culinary style relies on the need to improvise and the ability to make something out of very little. Mediterranean cuisine is characterized by the simplicity of ingredients and the ingenuity of the chefs who make the dishes. In Italy, for example, pasta is garnished with little more than olive oil, garlic, and hot pepper or a sauce of olive oil, anchovies, and leftover breadcrumbs. In both cases, a few ingredients bring sharp and interesting flavors to the pasta. Or in Turkey and other parts of the eastern Mediterranean, vegetables are stuffed with a mixture of ground meat, rice, and seasonings to make a dish called dolma. The stuffing is a clever way to stretch the supply of meat to feed more for less.

Dolma or Stuffed Zucchini

6 medium or large zucchini

1/2 pound ground beef

1 medium onion, chopped

4 cloves garlic, peeled and minced

1/2 cup white rice, cooked

1 tablespoon tomato paste

2 tablespoons vegetable oil

1/4 teaspoon salt

2 medium tomatoes, seeded and coarsely chopped

Olive oil

Preheat oven to 350°F. Cut zucchini in half and scoop out the inside, leaving at least a half-inch thick shell. In a large bowl combined meat, onion, garlic, rice, and tomato paste, oil, and salt. Add 1/3 cup water and mix well. Let mixture sit for a few minutes to allow the flavors to blend. Stuff the zucchini with the meat mixture and place in a 13 × 9 × 2 pan or similar baking pan. Sprinkle chopped tomatoes on top of the meat mixture and drizzle with olive oil. Add a cup-and-a-half of water to the baking pan and cover tightly with foil or, if using a casserole dish, the fitted lid. Cook in the oven for 35–45 minutes, checking the water level to make sure there is enough to steam the zucchini. Remove from oven and let rest for 10–15 minutes. Serve with plain yogurt.

"There is no better sauce than hunger" a Sicilian proverb states, but this does not mean that poor people will eat whatever is in front of them, although this certainly may be the case in many circumstances.[10] Rather, it means that poor people, whether peasants or city dwellers, will use only a few ingredients to create everyday dishes, but those ingredients matter. Knowing how to cook, then, means knowing what a pinch of salt or the addition of a certain herb will bring to a dish. It also means knowing how to chop or dice vegetables in a certain way to bring out their full flavor. Learning to cook in this way entails understanding the exact and proper balance among only a few ingredients. "Cooking with little" has been a peasant method for preparing food that has been around for centuries, although it is reinforced now and again according to contemporary circumstances. During World War II and in the postwar recovery period, women in Italy, southern France, and in Greece had to make do with very little. Even the most humble ingredients—cornmeal, legumes, vegetables, innards, or sweetmeats—were scarce; and it was not unusual to see dishes like meatballs made out of breadcrumbs or rice, or imitation green beans made from spinach stalks. Today, rising poverty in countries like Egypt necessitates the same skills that "cooking with little" has required over the centuries. Under such conditions, cooking is a creative achievement that is frequently overlooked or undervalued by historians of food and cooking, who tend to focus on the more elaborate culinary achievements of individuals or societies.

Elsewhere in the Mediterranean, the standard of living is higher than in Egypt, and many consumers can afford to buy and cook whatever pleases them, including a variety of more expensive cuts of meat, types of cheese, and exotic produce. Still, old habits die hard and many traditional dishes are still made and savored by the working and middle classes, as well as the wealthy. Cooks and diners have rediscovered peasant cooking because it tastes good, it represents more authentic regional cooking style, or it is something unusual to try. There is also a growing interest in peasant cooking because it is seen as a simpler form of cooking, relying as it does on only a few ingredients and not a lot complicated cooking equipment. Consumers living in a world saturated with goods and services might yearn for the simple and sustainable life. The rise of the Slow Food movement (founded in 1989), discussed later in this chapter, has brought new meaning and life to cooking with little, now seen by some as a political choice rather than an economic necessity.

THE WORK OF COOKING

Mediterranean cuisine has the reputation of being simple. Glossy cookbooks and articles in magazines tend to represent Mediterranean cuisine as a collection of dishes that can be easily and quickly assembled out of a few fresh ingredients. Readers of these books and articles might assume that all Mediterranean dishes are easy to make. This assumption is somewhat incorrect, given that for some dishes and specialties, preparation and cooking can be very time-intensive and complicated processes. Some dishes take a long time to cook, like the Moroccan tajine. Other dishes involve extensive preparation. For example, in Catalonia, Spain, a mixture called *picada* is added to a dish at the very end to provide additional flavor. To make a *picada* (the word means pounded), the cook uses and mortar and pestle to grind together a mixture of garlic, parsley, nuts, toasted fried bread, and various spices. Although this may not sound difficult, preparation of a *picada* adds additional steps to what might be an extensive preparation list.

The French fish stew known as bouillabaisse looks simple enough: fish, potatoes, and seasonings in a broth. Bouillabaisse is one of many fish stews made in the Mediterranean; each region has a slightly different version. In Greece, fishermen make a soup called *kakavia,* named after the pot in which the soup is prepared, called a *kakavi.* The soup is made from whatever fish cannot be sold on the market; the fish, along with olive oil, lemon juice, onions, and potatoes, are cooked at a high heat until the soup becomes a thick stew. In Sardinia, fishermen make a stew called, *zeminu* out of fish, calamari, crab, clams, mussels, or whatever is on hand, along with tomatoes, wine, herbs, olive oil, and sometimes hot pepper. *Zeminu* is usually eaten with *pane carasau,* a thin toasted flatbread, which is also known as Sardinian "music bread," so named because it resembles sheets of music. French bouillabaisse originated with fishermen throwing their unusable fish and fish parts into a cauldron with sea water and stale bread, boiling it all together to make a thick stew.[11] Today, bouillabaisse is a sophisticated concoction, made from select fish, potatoes, and saffron. Making the "simple" stew involves a two-step process in which a rich fish stock is made from a combination of fresh fish, and then the stock is used to poach more fish, vegetables, and potatoes. Rare and expensive saffron, along with other seasonings, is added to the stock and each restaurant has its own unique blend. French fishermen are more likely to throw together a simple fish stew, boil it once, and then eat it. Bouillabaisse, on the other hand, involves a sophisticated process of balancing delicate flavors. Its preparation is both expensive and time-consuming. In the case of Mediterranean cooking, one must not equate simplicity with ease. Cooking can be a lot of hard work.

Kakavia

2 medium onions, chopped

1/2 cup olive oil

4 tomatoes, seeded and coarsely chopped

1 stalk celery, chopped

3 tablespoons fresh chopped parsley

1 bay leaf

1 sprig of fresh thyme

6–7 cups water

4 pounds of assorted fish (bass, cod, halibut, trout, pollack, whiting), sliced or cut into chunks

1 pound of shrimp, peeled

French bread, sliced and toasted

In a large soup pot, sauté onions in oil until soft. Add tomatoes, celery, herbs, and water. Bring to a boil and simmer one hour. Add salt and pepper to taste. Pour mixture through a sieve to strain. Return to soup pot and bring to a boil. Salt and then rinse the fish, lower into soup and add water if needed to cover the fish. Simmer five minutes then add shrimp. Taste and adjust seasoning. In soup plates, put a thick slice of toasted bread and carefully ladle soup on to bread.

Mediterranean food culture values both hospitality and home cooking. The burden, then, falls on the cook (usually the oldest woman in the household) to work throughout much of the day. Mornings are time for cooking and serving breakfast, which is less work in Italy, where most Italians opt for a quick coffee and pastry on the way to work or school; but more work in Syria and Lebanon, where families might enjoy a breakfast consisting of several dishes, all made at home. In areas where families still bake their own bread, mornings are a time for making the day's or week's supply of bread. Making and baking bread dough can be labor-intensive, especially if one has to work the dough, let it rest, then work it again before ensuring the oven is at the right temperature for baking. These tasks are frequently shared by the community in areas where bread is still home-made. Throughout her travels in rural Turkey, one author observed that in many places, flatbread is still made by hand:

[V]ery young girls join in the garrulous group of women who frequently gather together for the task. Each takes a small piece of dough and rolls it out to paper thinness, using a long, wooden pole. There may be as many as ten women working together- but usually only one in charge of the upturned dome of metal over burning wood on which the bread is cooked. The rolled-out dough is deftly draped over the wooden pole and passed over the chief cook, who puts it swiftly on to the hot, greased surface, flipping it over as soon as it starts to bubble and brown. Within a minute, the sheet of bread is cooked and transferred to a growing pile in the corner.[12]

Making bread from scratch is becoming a thing of the past . . . but not everywhere. In Morocco, for example, an estimated 80 percent of households still bake their own bread. Women make the dough at home then take it to the communal bake house. Waiting for the bread to bake provides ample time to catch up on local news or gossip. Once the bread comes out, each woman "stamps" the bread with her fingers while the dough is still warm, marking off her family's bread.[13]

An Egyptian woman with a tray of bread at a public oven in Giza. AP Photo/ Amr Nabil.

Morning is also a time for shopping, especially if one wants to get the freshest foods available at outdoor markets. Depending on the meal plan for the rest of the day, shopping for the right ingredients could take up much of the morning. If the cook prefers to go to the open market instead of a supermarket or grocery store, shopping involves stopping at multiple stalls and negotiating the best price for the highest quality foods. In markets where live animals are sold, shoppers might be asked to select a chicken or pigeon for slaughter. Shoppers might stop and chat with, or sample the wares of, a particular vendor and if they run into family or friends, they might have to stop for coffee or tea. For women (and some men) who stay at home to take care of their children or grandchildren, shopping in the open air market is a daily ritual. Working women and men are more likely to opt for the greater convenience of grocery stores and supermarkets.

Outdoor markets specialize in certain foods and are open only at certain times of day. The Campo de'Fiori market in Rome, Italy, has a variety of fresh produce and fresh fish. AP Photo/Angelo Scipioni.

Shoppers can find anything at an outdoor market in Damascus, Syria, even pickled vegetables. AP Photo/Bassem Tellawi.

If women are cooking for the family lunch, then late morning is the time to start preparations for the meal. If the meal is simple—salad, a main course of meat or fish with rice or couscous and vegetables, and fruit for dessert—then there are vegetables to be washed and chopped, meat to be marinated or seasoned, rice to be cooked perfectly, additional vegetables to be cleaned, chopped and cooked, as well as a table to be set. This may not sound like hard work, but it takes coordination and organization to ensure that the lunch is served quickly for family members who may not have a lot of time to eat. In the early afternoon, the family cook might be preoccupied with food to be preserved for later: meat to be salted, vegetables to be pickled, lemons to be salted and stored, and biscuits or cookies to be made and stored away for later. In Tunisia, cooks make and store *harissa,* a fiery paste made from hot and sweet peppers, olive oil, salt, garlic, and up to 20 different spices (some spices, like coriander and cumin, are more common while other spices, like cinnamon or rosewater,

of fast food, prepared foods, and other convenience foods. Having someone else do the cooking is becoming an increasingly popular and profitable
trend throughout the Mediterranean. Among younger consumers (30 and
under), fast food, especially American-style fast food like McDonald's or
Pizza Hut, is popular. When American fast food franchises first arrived in
the Mediterranean (many of them during the 1980s, which was a decade
of global expansion for several American fast food companies), they were
viewed with disdain by older consumers, although teenagers and young
adults liked to hang out in McDonald's restaurants because it was a space
of their own and sometimes, their parents disapproved of their eating fast
food. Now the teenagers who ate at McDonald's to rebel against their parents take their children there for a quick lunch or dinner. Within a generation, then, fast food restaurants like McDonald's or Pizza Hut went from
exotic to everyday. Although American fast food outlets have spread like
wildfire across the region, not every consumer is happy. Angry protesters
have demonstrated in front of McDonald's restaurants and sometimes acts
of vandalism are committed. In many cases, protesters and vandals are
making a statement against the Americanization of the Mediterranean
diet, or in cases where protesters object to U.S. foreign policy (such as
the recent wars in Iraq), they target McDonald's because it symbolizes the
United States. Consumers who object to American fast food may refuse
to eat there, or some entrepreneurs have established fast food restaurants
of their own which compete with McDonald's. In Egypt, the fast food
chain *Mo'men* (the word means believer) serves chicken and beef burgers
and seafood sandwiches that are halal (permissible according to Muslim
dietary rules). Part of the restaurant chain's mission is to support the Egyptian economy, although a few restaurants also exist outside of Egypt.

Of course, the recent trend of buying prepared food or fast food is not
an entirely new phenomenon. Mediterranean consumers have been enjoying "fast food" for a few centuries, given the region's fondness for street
foods like pizza, doner kebab, and gyros (see chapter 5). Mediterranean
consumers who object to the most recent trends argue that fast food is less
healthy than traditional street food because it is not as fresh. Consumers
also object to the fact that most profits from restaurants like McDonald's
and KFC line the pockets of Americans, not Italians or Turks. Concerns over what is truly "Mediterranean" versus what is "American" have
fueled objections and even protest. These same concerns, however, have
prompted many people in the Mediterranean to go back to their culinary
roots and discover the traditional ways of preparing and cooking foods.
Ironically, modern technology has helped many consumers and cooks rediscover the culinary past. The Internet provides a continuous forum for

people to exchange recipes and tips for cooking, as well as information about holiday traditions or directions to local farms that sell produce, cheese, olive oil, or honey. And a growing number of television cooking programs introduce viewers to the culinary traditions of their country and their region. In Morocco, the television cook Choumicha shows viewers how to make interesting dishes from all the regions of the country. Choumicha puts a distinctly modern spin on the recipes, however, by making them lighter and healthier for viewers and their families. On Lebanese television, the most popular cooking show is hosted by Ramzi N. Choueiri, who likes to demonstrate forgotten recipes while answering viewers' questions about cooking problems, issues, or disasters.

Other well-known chefs in the Mediterranean work outside of the Internet and television to change local eating habits. One of the most famous chefs in Egypt, Abdel Hamid Badawy, set the standard for lighter and more innovative dishes by cooking on his own. His recipes were then imitated in other hotels, restaurants, and even in market stalls by street food vendors. Badawy's innovations, such as combining fish and lentils in the same dish, challenge ideas about cooking that have been in existence for centuries in Egypt. He complains that "[t]he whole world is changing, and only we Egyptians adamantly stick to our inflexible traditions without giving much thought to how we might be able to develop our culture," but he never hesitates to suggest improvements or innovations whenever he samples a local dish.[14] Although France and Italy have been renowned for their cooks and chefs, the rest of the Mediterranean only recently gained international recognition in the restaurant and tourism industries. For example, top chefs from the Muslim world now compete with chefs around the world, gaining greater recognition for North African or Middle Eastern cuisine. Gourmet cooking in the top restaurants and hotels in the Muslim Mediterranean presents its own problems for chefs. Hotels catering to an international clientele require an international repertoire of cuisine for customers, but how do Muslim chefs create certain Western dishes without alcohol? Chefs have substituted everything from fruit juices to balsamic vinegar for wine. Another challenge is running a large kitchen during Ramadan, when devout Muslims fast from sunrise to sunset. Stefan Hogan, who is not Muslim, is a chef at the Corinthia Bab Africa Hotel in Tripoli, Libya, where he supervises a largely Muslim staff. During Ramadan, his staff is unable to taste what they have created, leaving the non-Muslims to do the necessary tasting. "For a whole month, I have to taste everything myself . . . every couple of minutes one of my guys holds a spoon under my nose and says, 'try this for me, boss.' It's a complete muddle: meat, rice pudding, soup."[15] These challenges and problems are relatively minor, however, and the restaurant, hotel, and hospitality industries in the Muslim Mediterranean are clearly thriving.

Despite a thriving food industry throughout the Mediterranean region, many chefs and consumers are worried that traditional Mediterranean cuisine is losing ground to American-style fast food and processed foods. In parts of the Mediterranean, there has been a collective response to the increase in American-style foods in the form of an organization called Slow Food. Slow Food originated in the Mediterranean; it was first launched in 1989 in response to the opening of a McDonald's restaurant in the Piazza di Spagna in Rome in 1986.

Slow Food seeks to mobilize consumers against fast food and the impact of globalization on local eating habits. To do so, they have launched numerous initiatives, including the creation of local eating societies called *convivia*, which bring people together to enjoy a range of local food specialties. Slow Food urges its members to slow down and enjoy the range of tastes and foods available to them locally. The organization alerts members and the general public through its Web site about how to prepare home-cooked meals or where to buy locally produced foods. Thus, Slow Food plays an important role in supporting local farmers and encouraging the artisanal, not industrial, production of foods like cheese, sausage, and wine. The movement is political in its opposition to corporations like McDonald's and the industrialization of agricultural production. Members object to the standardization of taste and seek to defend and preserve a way of life that is disappearing, a way of life that is readily measured by food habits. In addition, the *convivia*, as well as the Slow Food Web site, encourages members and others to cook slowly. This means thinking about the ingredients to buy, returning to traditional methods of preparation and cooking, and sharing the finished meal with friends, relatives, and guests.

In addition to Slow Food, several individuals have become outspoken critics of American fast food and globalization generally. A French farmer named José Bové, for example, attracted international attention when he and other members of his community disassembled a McDonald's restaurant as a protest in 1999. Bové has since become a leading spokesperson against big business and globalization as they affect the ways in which people farm and consume agricultural produce. Individuals like Bové and organizations like Slow Food emphasize the way food habits are tied to a whole way of life. When they protest the opening of a fast food restaurant like McDonald's, they are protesting much more than the hamburgers, fries, and sodas inside. They also object to the industrialized forms of agricultural production, the organization of retail outlets through franchise systems, and intensive and targeted marketing to existing and potential consumers.

Many consumers worry that "American-style" eating habits will become increasingly more popular across the region, and consequently Mediterranean habits and customs will become less popular and eventually die out. It is easy to understand their concern: American-style eating habits frequently translate into increased obesity rates and nutrition-related problems or illnesses. And when American companies are interested in keeping the profits, Mediterranean consumers see few benefits or conveniences attached to fast food. Yet it seems difficult to imagine how Mediterranean habits and customs will ever completely die out, given that cooking food is a practice so firmly embedded in cultures throughout the region. As the next chapter explains, there is much diversity and complexity in Mediterranean cooking style. For example, similar dishes are served throughout the region; yet in each country, the differences in ingredients, preparation technique, or cooking time, matter. They matter because cooks and chefs are intensely proud of their skills and desire to transmit the knowledge of these skills to future generations.

NOTES

1. A summary of this scholarship can be found in Vicki A Swinbank, "The Sexual Politics of Cooking: A Feminist Analysis of Culinary Hierarchy in Western Culture," *Journal of Historical Sociology*, 15 (2002): 464–494.

2. See Carole Counihan, "Bread as World: Food Habits and Social Relations in Modernizing Sardinia," in Carole Counihan and Penny Van Esterik, eds., *Food and Culture. A Reader* (New York: Routledge, 1997), pp. 283–295; and Willy Jansen, "French Bread and Algerian Wine: Conflicting Identities in French Algeria," in Peter Scholliers, ed., *Food, Drink and Identity. Cooking, Eating and Drinking in Europe Since the Middle Ages* (Oxford: Berg, 2001), pp. 195–218.

3. Efisio Farris, *Sweet Myrtle and Bitter Honey* (New York: Rizzoli, 2007), p. 101.

4. Colette Rosant, *Memories of a Lost Egypt. A Memoir with Recipes* (New York: Clarkson Potter, 1999), p. 62.

5. Nur Ilkin and Sheilah Kaufman, *A Taste of Turkish Cuisine* (New York: Hippocrene Books, Inc., 2002), pp. 6–7.

6. Ayla Esen Algar, *The Complete Book of Turkish Cooking* (London: Kegan Paul, 1985), p. 5.

7. Student interviewed in Elia Petridou, "The Taste of Home," in Daniel Miller, ed., *Home Possessions. Material Culture behind Closed Doors* (Oxford: Berg, 2001), p. 91.

8. Dalila Amdouni, quoted in Fiona Dunlop, *The North African Kitchen* (Northampton, MA: Interlink, 2008), p. 97.

9. Latifa Alaoui, quoted in Fiona Dunlop, *The North African Kitchen*, p. 40.

10. Clarissa Hyman, *Cucina Siciliana* (Northampton, MA: Interlink, 2002), p. 9.

11. Daniel Young, *Made in Marseille* (New York: HarperCollins, 2002), p. 122–26.

12. Sarah Woodward, *The Ottoman Kitchen* (Northampton MA: Interlink, 2002), p. 110.

13. Florian Harms and Lutz Jäkel, *The Flavours of Arabia* (London: Thames and Hudson, 2007), p. 22.

14. Harms and Jäkel, *The Flavours of Arabia*, p. 130.

15. Harms and Jäkel, *The Flavours of Arabia*, p. 101.

4

Typical Meals

To try to find and describe a typical meal, or even several typical meals, that characterize dining in the Mediterranean would be an impossible task. Although most experts think there is something clearly identifiable as a Mediterranean cuisine, they are usually referring to the basic ingredients or components of the Mediterranean diet, and not to the many ways in which these ingredients are put together in dishes and in meals. Mediterranean food expert and cookbook author Paula Wolfert has thought about Mediterranean dishes in terms of key flavors and tastes; for her, the major ingredients define what Mediterranean cooking is about: "In the diversity of ingredients lies the unity. These ingredients constitute the bounty of the Mediterranean, the stuff of which its cuisines are built."[1] Her cookbooks, then, organize Mediterranean dishes according to their most important ingredients—olive oil, peppers, fish, lamb, eggplant, garlic, and legumes. Her approach to understanding Mediterranean cuisine is one of many, and it makes sense when one thinks about how Mediterranean food is characterized or defined by a set of tastes. When one begins to put these essential ingredients into varying combinations and cook them in certain ways, however, a wide variety of tastes emerges. For example, garlic creates different tastes when it is fried in olive oil, ground with cured olives and seasonings, mixed with eggs and lemon, or stuffed into a chicken. Here lies the paradox, perhaps, of Mediterranean cuisine. When compared with the repertoires of industrialized, modernized cuisines, where artificial ingredients and manufactured tastes create so many different flavors and tastes (although some would argue that all processed food tastes the same), Mediterranean cuisine is based on relatively few ingredients. Yet out of these few ingredients a complex and diverse set of dishes has emerged. There is no typical Mediterranean meal, but the kinds of meals and the way they are consumed reveal a great deal about diverse eating practices and attitudes towards food across the region.

This chapter first looks at the order of meals in terms of how the meal is presented to diners. Understanding how food is presented—in what order, which dishes are served with what—reflects popular attitudes about, and the rules regarding, food. Next, meal order is described in terms of how meals are served throughout the day and what kinds of dishes characterize the standard meals of breakfast, lunch, dinner, and snack. There is considerable variation as to what constitutes "breakfast" or which foods are snacks and which are meals. Typical menus for the countries of the Mediterranean describe more than just who eats what when; they express the full complexity of meal structures and the variety of foods offered for meals. Menus also reveal the relative weight assigned to meals throughout the day. The chapter then breaks down meals by examining the many dishes that make up a meal: appetizers or first courses, main dishes, side dishes, and desserts or final courses. Although this list is not exhaustive, it describes some of the most typical dishes consumed throughout the region. Of course, there is considerable variation in the way even similar dishes are prepared. Each country may have its own version of a fish stew, a type of pizza, and a vegetable relish; but the addition of a particular herb or spice, or a particular cooking technique, can make a substantial difference in the way the dish ultimately tastes. Such variation proves that there is no one typical meal in the Mediterranean; it also demonstrates the creativity and resourcefulness of Mediterranean cooks, who have developed sophisticated cooking traditions based on years of scarcity. Thus a typical Mediterranean meal is much more than a group of dishes; it provides an interpretation of the region's culinary past and offers a fresh perspective on contemporary eating habits and ideas about food.

MEAL ORDER

The order of a meal says a lot about a society's attitudes toward food. It can express personal or social preferences about what tastes good together, it can highlight the significance of a special occasion or holiday, and it even influences how diners relate to each other. Anthropologists have studied the structure of meals to understand how societies differ from each other in thinking about, and through, food. In the region of the Mediterranean, it seems clear that there are multiple eating styles; meals are defined in different ways across geographical boundaries. One major difference in meal order lies between the eastern and western Mediterranean. In the eastern Mediterranean, courses are less formally structured. Salad, for example, illustrates a more informal attitude toward the structure of a meal in the eastern regions; diners are not particularly concerned with having salad as a distinct course. Rather, it is served at the beginning of the meal and remains on the table throughout the rest of the meal. In restaurants, salad is consumed while diners think about what to eat for the main course. In Turkey and Greece, a salad is brought out and the ingredients are chopped up and dressed in yogurt or oil and vinegar. In Lebanon or Syria, a plate of vegetables and a sharp knife are brought to diners, who make their own salad while thinking about what to eat later. In someone's home, salad will remain on the table throughout the meal, in case a diner wants to nibble on it later. Then, diners will eat salad along with meat and other vegetables. Meal order is a less formal affair in the eastern Mediterranean; tastes mingle as diners enjoy different types of food all at once.

Compare this attitude toward salad with attitudes in the western Mediterranean, namely in Italy, France, and Spain. In these countries, salad is enjoyed as a stand-alone course. It frequently comes *after* the main course of meat or fish, as it is supposed to cleanse or refresh the palate. Salad is dressed sparingly, often with salt, olive oil, and a bit of vinegar or lemon juice, so that diners enjoy the full taste of the vegetables comprising the salad. Often, only one type of vegetable or green will be served, so it is not unusual to enjoy an arugula salad or a tomato salad without heavy dressings or additional ingredients. The salad course in western Mediterranean countries typifies a more formal meal structure, in which great care is taken to present the meal in distinct stages, with each food coming out one at a time, to be enjoyed as a separate taste by diners. It is worth noting, for example, that in Italy there is a specific language attached to meal courses. Diners enjoy an antipasto before the meal, followed by a *primo*, or first course, usually soup, pasta, or risotto. This is followed by the *secondo*, or main course, usually meat or fish, accompanied by a *contorno*, cooked vegetables and/or potatoes served as an accompaniment to the meat. After the main course, a salad is served, followed by coffee, fruit, or a sweet dessert. In restaurants, diners might order their meal one course at a time, so that there is a longish pause between courses, as the chefs or cooks prepare the next item. This more structured order of the meal allows diners more time to consider, and appreciate, each dish as a distinctive taste or flavor. Such a formal attitude may seem extreme to Americans; for example, in Italian McDonald's restaurants where there are antipasto bars, diners will enter, select and pay for an antipasto, and then when finished with that course, wait in line again to order and pay for a hamburger and French fries.

This example seems extreme to Americans because they are used to having meals served all at once, or courses that come in quick succession during a meal. The eastern Mediterranean meal structure is less formal as well; a typical meal might be a meat or grain dish, accompanied by salad and yogurt. Also on the table are bread, olives, pickles, or raw vegetables. Food is kept on the table and diners serve themselves, family-style, throughout the meal. A more formal meal for company might be appetizers (meze), followed by two main dishes (a stew, stuffed vegetables, meat such as lamb or chicken) and salad; the appetizers remain on the table throughout. Dessert might be coffee, fruit, or pastry, and only then are the main dishes cleared away (although in the presence of company, coffee and dessert might be served in a separate room, like the living room). Nothing typifies this informal and communal style of eating than the popularity of meze in the eastern Mediterranean. Meze, also known as *mezze* or *mazza*, are little dishes of food served either before a meal or as a meal. No one knows the origins of the word meze for certain, but some believe

Turkish meze. AP Photo/Murad Sezer.

that in Byzantium, it was customary to serve five or six little dishes of food as starters. These would be vegetables, or legumes, and were intended to be enjoyed while diners waited for the main dish. Meze then became appetizers or dishes meant to whet the appetite for the main course. Other food experts believe the practice of eating meze dates back to ancient Persia, where diners consumed different fruits to counterbalance the taste of bitter wine. Meze became foods to be consumed with wine or other alcohol. Whatever the origins of the word and the practice of eating meze, the tradition of sharing meze is popular in Egypt, Greece, Israel, Lebanon, Syria, and Turkey. Several dishes are prepared and eaten communally; diners usually scoop up the relishes, salads, and dips with flatbread, or they might also have finger foods.

Meze are usually served before a meal as appetizers, but diners can also make an entire meal out of meze plates. In some restaurants in Lebanon, for example, an elaborate variety of meze are presented, with some establishments offering as many as 50 different dishes at the same time. Ideally, a combination of meze should strike a balance of flavor, temperature, and texture. A smooth pureed dip will contrast sharply with crisp, raw vegetables or a chewy bulgur salad. A room temperature salad will contrast with a very cold one; nutty tastes will balance spicy or sweet tastes. A meze dinner will have standard favorites, as well as more substantial foods to appeal to every diner:

A typical meze dinner:

- Toasted almonds and roasted pistachios
- Assorted olives
- Raw vegetables (crudités)
- Hummus (chickpea and tahini dip)
- Baba ghanouj (eggplant and tahini dip)
- Cheese
- Pepper dip
- Tabouleh (bulgur, vegetable, and parsley salad)
- Fattush (bread salad)
- Ful (fava bean salad)
- Stuffed grape leaves or other vegetables
- Falafel (fried chickpea balls)
- Kibbeh (ground raw meat)
- Spinach or other savory pie
- Meat turnovers

The entire meal is accompanied by flatbread like pita, and diners serve themselves, making sure to leave enough for others. Those who prepare an elaborate assortment of meze or a meze dinner place great emphasis on the abundance of dishes, ingredients, and tastes for their fellow diners. Although each dish is prepared and served separately from the other dishes, the flavors of meat, vegetables, and grains all mix together, sometimes in the same bite. The formal order of the meal matters less than the emphasis on abundance and hospitality.

This basic difference between the eastern and western regions of the Mediterranean is not set in stone. Certainly there is variation, and continued immigration throughout the region has meant that North Africans have brought their less formal traditions with them to France or Italy, or Europeans settling in Israel have maintained their more formal approach to meal order. The basic difference between east and west, along with the myriad variation on these meal orders, indicates that meal order is just one indicator of the diversity of attitudes toward food in the Mediterranean region.

Tabbouleh

2/3 cup bulgur wheat

1/2 cup fresh mint leaves, chopped

2 cups flat-leaf parsley, chopped

1 cucumber, peeled, seeded and chopped

1/4 teaspoon cayenne pepper

1/4 teaspoon allspice

1/4 teaspoon cinnamon

1/4 teaspoon nutmeg

4 tablespoons olive oil

2 tablespoons fresh lemon juice

2 large tomatoes, seeded and chopped

Place bulgur in cold water and soak. Combine herbs, spices, cucumber, oil, and lemon juice in large bowl. Drain bulgur well and add to bowl. Mix well. Cover bowl and refrigerate overnight. Mix in chopped tomatoes right before serving.

Fattush

Stale bread (preferably pita)

1 cucumber, seeded and chopped

1/2 onion, chopped

1/4 cup of fresh chopped parsley

2 large tomatoes, seeded and chopped

Dressing

1/2 cup olive oil

2 tablespoons of lemon juice or vinegar

1 clove garlic, minced

Salt and pepper

Break the stale bread into small pieces. Make a dressing with lemon juice or vinegar to taste. Mix dressing, stale bread, vegetables and parsley together to blend the flavors. Let sit for a few minutes before serving.

Spinach Pies

1/4 cup olive oil

1/2 onion, chopped

2–3 pounds of spinach, washed and drained thoroughly

4–5 tablespoons of chopped parsley

1 tablespoon of chopped dill

1/2 pound of crumbled feta cheese

3 eggs, lightly beaten

12 sheets of phyllo pastry dough, plus melted butter

Heat oil in pan and sauté onions until soft. In a separate pot, cook spinach in a few spoonfuls of water, drain thoroughly. Preheat oven to 350°F. Add spinach to onions and mix in herbs; add salt and pepper to taste. Cook on low heat for 5–10 minutes. Cool. Stir in feta cheese and eggs. Brush some melted butter on the bottom of a 13×9×2 pan, then lay down six phyllo dough sheets, brushing each layer with melted butter. Gently spread spinach mixture over dough, then cover with remaining six phyllo dough sheets, brushing each layer with melted butter. Score the top few phyllo dough sheets with a knife, or prick the dough with a fork. Bake until golden brown, about 45 minutes. Cut into triangles or diamonds.

TYPICAL MENUS

Menus or meal plans throughout the Mediterranean might have some of the same dishes or ingredients, but the combinations of foods, as well as the times diners eat them, varies a great deal across the region. Because many people eat so much fresh local produce, menu plans differ depending on the fruits and vegetables available at that time. Although an increasing number of supermarkets in the region offer certain types of produce year round (via imports), most consumers prefer to buy the choicest seasonal goods from local growers. Another factor affecting menu planning is the rhythm of the day for the individual or family. A single working individual might have a radically different menu plan compared to a family where the wife/mother stays at home to care for the children. Families where individuals work and go to school are less likely to eat a home-cooked lunch and perhaps are more likely to eat a rushed breakfast on the way out the door. Also, there are regional differences based on custom and traditional attitudes toward certain foods and meals. On much of the European side of the Mediterranean, breakfast is not that important; young and old alike make do with a hot drink and a roll or pastry. Even manual laborers do not eat that much for breakfast, preferring instead to eat a heavier lunch and dinner. In other countries, breakfast is considered a more important meal and is more substantial and perhaps more elaborately prepared. Of course, menu plans vary according to individual preference, occupation, and ability to prepare and cook food, but there are some common trends worth noting.

First, breakfast is a meal that is wide open to interpretation across the region and occurs at different times. People dashing off to work or school may eat something first thing in the morning, but those who stay at home might eat breakfast at mid-morning, as late as 9 or 10 in the morning. As previously mentioned, European consumers frequently make do with little more than a roll and a cup of coffee. Many adults stop by a café on their way to work to down a croissant and an espresso or perhaps a cappuccino. Grocery stores offer American-style breakfast cereal or European-style muesli, but these are not very popular options. Instead, Italian children might eat packaged biscuits, toasts, or breakfast "cookies" along with milk and yogurt. In Catalonia, Spain, early breakfast or *desayuno* consists of rolls and coffee or hot chocolate, or bread and tomato. Later in the morning, at around 11:00 A.M., consumers might eat a more substantial breakfast of eggs and sausage or a few appetizers to hold them over until a later lunch, at around 2:00 or 3:00 P.M. In places where breakfast is more substantial, there is considerable variation in thinking about breakfast as either a sweet or savory meal. In the eastern Mediterranean, for example, a traditional sweet breakfast consists of yogurt with honey and/or fruit preserves made from figs, oranges, and lemon. A savory breakfast, on the other hand, consists of sweet black olives, feta cheese, sliced tomatoes, and cucumber. Both sweet and savory breakfasts are served with bread, either plain flatbread served in Lebanon or Syria, or white bread sprinkled with sesame seeds in Greece and Turkey. Black tea or coffee usually accompanies either type of breakfast. In Israel, breakfast is hearty and combines whole grains (bread and porridge) with dairy foods (yogurt and cheese) and fruit. In the early years of Israel's existence, hotel breakfast buffets became world famous, because they offered so much: eggs, herring, bread, vegetables, fruits, milk, cheese, yogurt, and hot cereals.[2] Workers on a kibbutz also ate heartily: milk, fruit, fresh-baked bread, eggs, and vegetables. Today, Israelis are more likely to get their breakfast from a grocery store or supermarket, although Sabbath breakfast is still special, with Turkish Jews consuming *burekas*, filled turnovers; Central European Jews eating coffee cake; and Middle Eastern Jews preparing *kataif*, pancakes filled with nuts or cream and served with syrup. Pancakes are a popular food in Israel and are consumed for breakfast and other meals. Special pancakes are made for certain holidays or special occasions. For example, pancakes with cottage cheese are served on the holiday Shavuot, which celebrates Moses receiving the Ten Commandments.

If breakfast is light, lunch is more substantial. And in many countries, if lunch is the main meal of the day, it occurs later in the day, sometimes as late as one or two o'clock in the afternoon. On the other hand, if lunch is a hurried affair in between university classes or meetings for work, it can occur much earlier, as early as 11 in the morning. As chapter 5 explains, families throughout the Mediterranean used to gather at home for a lunch that consisted of several courses. For peasants and urban workers alike, lunch was the main meal of the day and therefore was an important time for the family to gather together. This habit is slowly giving way to new habits, as people eat their lunch outside the home, either at work, in school, or in restaurants and cafés. If people do go home for lunch, they usually eat something hot. Lunch at home might be a bowl of soup or pasta, followed by a small portion of meat or fish with some vegetables. A salad or fresh fruit completes the meal. Lunch at a nice restaurant might also consist of multiple courses or dishes. Students and workers who do not have enough time for a long lunch will grab something at a café or street vendor's cart: pizza, a bowl of soup, kebab, or a sandwich.

Generally speaking, most people in the Mediterranean strike a balance between lunch and dinner. That is, if lunch is a big meal, dinner will be light and vice versa. Dinner is usually eaten in the home (either one's own home or someone else's) in much of North Africa and parts of the eastern Mediterranean; diners in the European countries and in parts of the Levant will either eat dinner at home or out in a restaurant. There are multiple dishes served for dinner, except in cases where an individual or family consumes only a sandwich, an omelet, or a bowl of soup. The main meal is usually followed by fruit or a sweet dessert. Although Mediterranean pastries, candies, cookies, and other treats are known for being particularly sweet and rich, they are not always consumed as desserts. Adults prefer to eat fresh fruit for dessert; they might enjoy some candy or baklava with a cup of coffee for a snack. Children, on the other hand, will eat sweets at any time of day or night. In the Levant and in North Africa, dinner occurs in the hours after work, whereas in the European countries of the Mediterranean, diners eat dinner much later, sometimes as late as 9 or 10 o'clock in the evening.

Given the fact that street food is so popular in the Mediterranean, it is not surprising that snacking is common practice throughout the region. Sweets are a good example of a popular snack. The country of Turkey is famous for pastries and candies, including baklava (squares of phyllo dough layered with honey and nuts) and a chewy candy called Turkish delight, or *rahat lokum*, which means giving rest to the throat. Turkish delight was reportedly the favorite treat of the ladies of the harem in the Ottoman Empire. Today, many varieties of Turkish delight, flavored with nuts and flower water, are sold in street markets, bakeries, and grocery stores. Inhabitants of the island of Sicily are famous for their fondness for sweet snacks; they can put away pastries, cookies, candies, and ice cream at any hour

Sweets are a popular snack for both adults and children throughout the Mediterranean. Here, shoppers buy sweets in downtown Damascus during the holy month of Ramadan. AP Photo/Bassem Tellawi.

A customer of Turkey's best-known confectioner, Haci Bekir, waits as a salesman wraps her purchase of Turkish delight, a traditional candy. AP Photo/Burhan Ozbilici.

of the day. In the summer, some cafés offer a pastry filled with ice cream or *granita* (a flavored crushed ice) for breakfast. Any special occasion or holiday in Sicily is sure to have plenty of sweet snacks for Sicilians to purchase and eat while celebrating. Savory snacks are also popular: nuts, fritters and turnovers, sandwiches, and potato chips. In places where dinner is not served until later in the evening (after 8 P.M.), an afternoon snack is a necessity; young and old alike pack cafés or buy an ice cream cone to eat on the way home. For adults, a coffee or tea can be an important pick-me-up in the mid-morning or afternoon. Because of its unique position as a trading point between east and west, the Mediterranean has a long history of coffee houses, cafés, and coffee bars. The first coffee houses in the region appeared in Turkey in the sixteenth century. Turkish coffee is internationally famous for its taste and elaborate preparation: water and sugar are brought to a boil in a small copper pot with a long handle, coffee is stirred in and the mixture is brought to a boil four times and then poured, hot and fizzing, into small cups. Today, Turkish citizens are more likely to drink more tea than coffee. Midnight snacks are also popular for those who stay up late; Italians who enjoy parties, movies, or the theater return home and make "midnight spaghetti" for themselves and friends. A favorite is something called *aglio e olio*, pasta tossed with garlic, olive oil, and a little hot pepper.

Midnight Spaghetti

1 pound spaghetti

1/2 cup olive oil

4 cloves garlic

1/4 teaspoon hot pepper flakes

2 tablespoons fresh chopped parsley

Salt and pepper

Grated parmesan cheese

Boil spaghetti in salted water until al dente. Meanwhile, fry the garlic in the olive oil, either by frying garlic slices in the oil then removing them, or by gently frying minced garlic. Be careful not to burn the garlic. Add hot pepper flakes and parsley and cook for a minute. Toss oil mixture with spaghetti and serve with generous amounts of grated cheese.

Typical Menus in Italy

Breakfast

Brioche or croissant

Coffee

Lunch

Pasta alla Norma (pasta with eggplant sauce)

Chicken cutlet

Tomato Salad

Cheese

Fruit

Coffee

Dinner

Vegetable soup with bread

Meatballs (*polpette*) with roasted potatoes and green beans

Green salad

Fruit and cookies

Coffee

Typical Menus in Greece

Breakfast
Roll
Fresh fruit with yogurt
Coffee

Lunch
Mezedes: tzatziki (yogurt and cucumber dip) with pita bread, fried meatballs,
    octopus, cheese, sausage, fava beans
Fruit

Dinner
Salad of cheese, olives, and tomatoes
Beef stew with onions (*stifado*)
Baklava
Coffee

Typical Menus in Turkey

Breakfast
Turkish bread with preserves, honey and butter
Boiled Egg
Olives
Tomatoes and Cucumbers
Cheese
Tea

Lunch
Lahmacun (Turkish pizza)
Mixed salad
Fruit
Tea

Dinner
Melon and white cheese
Lamb stew with vegetables
Pilav
Tea

Typical Menus in Syria

Breakfast
White Cheese
Olives
Pita
Tea

Lunch
Artichokes with fava beans
Chicken and rice
Salad
Fruit
Tea or Coffee

Dinner
Cheese dip with toasted sesame seeds
Lamb and vegetable stew
Rice with vermicelli
Salad with greens, tomatoes, and cucumbers
Fruit, cookies
Coffee

Typical Menus in Lebanon

Breakfast
Baked eggs in yogurt
Bread
Fruit
Tea or coffee

Lunch
Chicken kebabs
Bread
Salad
Lentils and Rice

Dinner
Cheese turnovers
Fish baked in spicy sauce

Saffron Rice
Salad with lemon dressing
Orange Cake
Coffee

Typical Menus in Egypt

Breakfast
Vermicelli with sugar and milk
Cheese
Bread
Tea with milk

Lunch
Stewed spinach and chickpeas
Rice with Tomatoes
Green salad
Fruit

Dinner
Lentils with rice and pasta
Eggs
Salad
Pudding

POPULAR DISHES

Most meals are made up of several dishes or courses. Although there are diverse practices throughout the Mediterranean in terms of how food is consumed and when it is consumed, the most popular dishes in the region share similar ingredients, given the region's geography and topography. Thus the people of the Mediterranean eat many of the same ingredients (discussed in chapter 2) even though they prepare and consume those ingredients in different ways. Many cookbook authors and experts on Mediterranean cuisine group the diverse dishes served in the region according to the main ingredients that characterize each dish. It is fairly common to find a Mediterranean cookbook that has sections on olive oil, garlic, and peppers as opposed to sections on appetizers, main courses, and side dishes. This common type of organization suggests that local ingredients unify

Mediterranean cuisine. Not surprisingly, the major dishes that people prepare and eat are similar in terms of their major ingredients. They can also vary a great deal in terms of other ingredients or special preparation techniques. The following sections illustrate many of the most popular dishes in the Mediterranean. These dishes are presented roughly according to the order in which they appear at a meal. And although not every dish can be described and discussed, the most characteristic or representative dishes will provide a clear sense of what diverse populations make and eat throughout the region.

Appetizers

Appetizers go by many names throughout the region—tapas, meze, antipasti, hors d'oeurves—each type is designed to be a little bite of food, to whet the appetite for more, to accompany a drink before dinner, or to provide something to eat until the main course is served. Meze, referred to earlier in this chapter, are served throughout the eastern Mediterranean and the Middle East. Because meze are intended to be scooped up with bread, so many of them are spreadable: relishes, dips, or salads. The most well-known meze dish is hummus, a dip made from cooked chickpeas, sesame paste, or tahini, and seasonings like garlic, lemon juice, salt, and pepper. A similar dip is baba ghanouj, which substitutes roasted eggplant for cooked chickpeas. To contrast the sharp taste of tahini and garlic-based dips, usually a milder dip is offered as well. In Greece, a popular dip is *tzatziki*, made with yogurt, cucumbers, and seasonings. Or a dip made from roasted peppers and pomegranates provides a sweet contrast to the sharp tang of hummus or baba ghanouj. Throughout the eastern Mediterranean, yogurt is mixed with cucumbers, peppers, eggplant, and legumes to make different dips. Salads are also popular as meze. Ingredients are finely chopped so that diners can pick up mouthfuls with a piece of flatbread. Marinated, seasoned green beans, salads made with fava beans or lentils, and tabbouleh, a cracked bulgur, tomato, and parsley salad (in Syria, a salad called *ksir* is made with bulgur, tomatoes, peppers, and herbs) are all popular items for the meze plate.

Most of the relishes and dips for the meze plate are made from vegetables and legumes, but meat and seafood are popular additions to meze. In Greece, marinated seafood, such as mussels or squid, are popular appetizers. In Lebanon, *kibbeh nayé* is a rare treat. *Kibbeh nayé* consists of raw lamb, which is ground with bulgur and spices, then dressed with olive oil and seasonings. Making *kibbeh nayé* is time-consuming; the lamb has to be ground several times to give the meat an elastic texture. Consequently, it is usually prepared as a special holiday food, but it can be served as a meze dish on occasion. Kibbeh also refers to a crisply cooked lamb and nut mixture. Finger foods are also popular meze: cheese, served plain or fried; grape leaves stuffed with a mixture of rice, pine nuts, raisins, and herbs; and little turnovers or savory pastries made with layers of dough, called phyllo dough (in Greece, spanakopita or *tiropites*, in Turkey, *börek*). Savory pastries are usually filled with cheese, spinach, lamb, or chicken.

The Italian version of the appetizer is called antipasto, or that which comes before the meal. Anything made with bread is a popular antipasto: crostini, which are small toasted slices of bread spread with dip or relish; bruschetta, or grilled bread topped with chopped ingredients or melted cheese; and various flatbreads, baked with ingredients such as olive oil, grated cheese, or herbs sprinkled on top. Italians dining at a restaurant that offers pizza will sometimes eat an individual-size pizza as a first course or antipasto. They will then eat a main course of meat or fish, or perhaps finish the meal with just a salad. Otherwise, Italians enjoy marinated seafood and vegetables, chopped salads, or cured meat, either sausage or cured ham (prosciutto) slices with melon. Italian restaurants will have an antipasto table, laden with a variety of different appetizers, but in the home, cooks usually prepare only one appetizer for the family. On the French coast of the Mediterranean, appetizers are considerably less elaborate than meze. Hors d'oeurves might consist of tapenade, a spread made from ground olives, anchovies, capers, garlic, olive oil, and lemon, or *anchoïade*, an anchovy and garlic paste that can be used as dip for raw vegetables or spread on toast or bread. French diners also enjoy finger foods such as *panisse* or *socca*, chickpea pancakes, served before a meal or as a street snack. In Catalonia, Spain, diners enjoy tapas (see chapter 5), either at restaurants or bars, or in the home.

Stews and Soups

Stews and soups are the quintessential Mediterranean food because they best exemplify the tradition of peasant cooking in the region. Whether farming the land or fishing the sea, peasants frequently had to make do with very little when it came to cooking meals. Soups and stews can be assembled out of whatever the cook has on hand, and slow simmering blends even a few tastes into something unique and appealing. Stews and soups stretched the peasant food budget by stretching a small piece of meat to feed an entire family. Stews and soups can be prepared and put on the fire to simmer for a long time, making them the ideal meals for those who had to labor in the fields all day or juggle farming tasks with family caretaking. A contemporary comparison to the traditional stew would be meals made in a crock pot. The cook in a busy family puts all the ingredients in the pot and plugs it in; a hot meal is waiting when the family returns from work and school. Although soups and stews started off as humble peasant coping strategies, they have undergone numerous refinements and today, they can be quite sophisticated and expensive, like bouillabaisse, a complicated fish and saffron stew. Although the preparation of stews and soups can be sophisticated and refined, there is still a great deal of individual variation when it comes to making these dishes. A cook or family might have a particular ingredient or preparation technique that makes their dish a unique creation. Throughout the Mediterranean, soups and stews are either the first or main course. Depending on when and how the dish is served, a soup or stew may consist of vegetables, legumes, grains, meat, fish, and even dairy products, either cooked together or added at different times.

Perhaps one of the most famous stews in the Mediterranean is bouillabaisse, a fish stew, made on the French coast, but particularly in the city of Marseille, where restaurants and hotels all offer their own version of the stew. The origins of the stew come from French fishermen, who would boil the fish and fish parts that they couldn't sell, add some potatoes and seasonings, and eat it. This rustic fishermen's stew is still made today, either by fishermen and their families on a Sunday afternoon, or by those vacationing at beach houses or picnicking in beachside cabins. Bouillabaisse, however, is a more refined version of fish stew. First, an intensely flavored fish stock is made from fish, sea water, vegetables such as fennel, tomatoes, and potatoes, and seasonings such as olive oil, parsley, orange peel, basil, thyme, and bay leaves. The stock is put through a food mill so that it is smooth, seasoned with saffron, and then it is used to poach other fish and vegetables. For the stew to be a proper bouillabaisse, *rascasse* or scorpion fish is used. The finished stew is eaten with bread spread with rouille, a spicy, garlicky mayonnaise. Throughout Marseilles, each restaurant, hotel, and individual make bouillabaisse with their own special ingredient: orange peel, fennel, a certain type of pepper, legumes, or salt cod. Versions of bouillabaisse include stews made from chicken, or something called bouillabaisse borgne, or "poor-man's bouillabaisse," a vegetable stew with a poached egg on top.[3] There are variations on the fish stew made throughout the region. In Turkey, a soup called *balik* consists of a fish stock that is simmered, strained, and then used for a soup consisting of the stock, vegetables, eggs, and lemon.

A stew is a collection of foods that has been simmered together so that the flavors blend together in new ways. The Moroccan tajine has become the most famous stew in North Africa and it represents Mediterranean cuisine in the same way as Italian pasta dishes, Greek salads, and the eastern Mediterranean meze foods (hummus and baba ghanouj). The name tajine also refers to the funnel-shaped terracotta dish where meat, fruits, vegetables, and seasonings are slow-cooked. A tajine pot must be made of clay, not metal, porcelain, or glass, and it is usually pointed or rounded at the top. The clay is fired twice to ensure that it can withstand the heat of cooking; a good pot doesn't crack and the food inside doesn't burn. The unique conical shape of the tajine pot allows the food to steam; condensation drips down off the sides of the pot, concentrating and intensifying the flavors of the stew. Steam cooking also tenderizes the ingredients, such that the stew is never stirred, or else the ingredients would become mush. Some stews, called *marqas*, are prepared in pressure cookers, but Moroccans and Moroccan food connoisseurs agree that the cooking method of the tajine makes stew taste better.

Mediterranean cookbook author and food expert Paula Wolfert has observed that the tajine is an ingenious way of making less palatable cuts of meat delicious: "Most tajines involve slow simmering of less expensive meats. The ideal cuts of lamb are the neck, shoulder or shank cooked until it is falling off the bone."[4] To make the meat so tender, fat or oil is used in the cooking liquid. The other ingredients in a tajine can be fruits, vegetables, and seasonings like spices and herbs. The cook needs to find appropriate vegetables that will go with the meat and seasonings for a sauce that will go with both the vegetables and the meat in the stew. There are four basic sauces for tajines: *m'qualli* or a yellow sauce (made with oil, ginger, onion, saffron, salt, and sometimes cilantro), *m'hammer* or red sauce (butter, sweet paprika, garlic, saffron, ginger, and onion), *k'dra,* a light yellow sauce (onions, butter, pepper, salt, and saffron), and *m'charmel* another red sauce (sweet paprika, garlic, cumin, coriander). A great deal of thought needs to go into the preparation of a tajine to achieve the proper combination of vegetables, meat, and sauce. This is because the process of cooking really concentrates the flavor of all the ingredients, and using the wrong spice or vegetable can result in something that does not taste very good. Many of the taste combinations in tajines mix sweet and savory, as ingredients such as dried fruit, sugar, cinnamon, and honey are frequently added to the stew. Popular combinations include lamb, prunes, and almonds; or eel, onions, and raisins. A tajine is eaten as the main course and it is usually accompanied by preserved lemons, which are lemons that are soaked in water then treated with salt. They are kept in water and can be used in cooking or as a condiment for up to a year.

There is also a dish called a tajine in Tunisia, but this stew involves a different, more complicated, cooking process. First, a stew of veal or lamb is made with onions and spices, either a combination of sweet spices such as cinnamon or dried rosebuds or other spices such as coriander and caraway. A starchy food is then added to thicken the stew; ingredients like chickpeas, bread crumbs, and potatoes are the most popular. When the stewed meat is tender, it is flavored further with herbs, vegetables, and even stewed calf's brains. Then eggs and cheese are added and the stew is baked in an oven until the egg is set and it is cooked through. A Tunisian tajine is then turned on to a plate and cut in to squares, so it becomes more like a pie or frittata. A simmered stew in Tunisia is called a ragout or *marquit*.

Most countries in the Mediterranean have a traditional stew. In Greece, a food made *stifado-* or *stifatho*-style refers to the way veal, rabbit, or beef is stewed with small white onions (and sometimes eggplant) over a long period. *Stifado* is usually cooked very slowly the day before serving, then reheated slowly before the meal, thus allowing the ingredients to blend together over a long time. And in southern France, *daube* is a traditional beef stew. Beef and vegetables are marinated in wine overnight. The stew is then cooked for several hours until the meat is very tender. Daube is served over pasta, polenta, or baked potatoes. Popular Italian stews include *pasta e ceci*, a Tuscan pasta and chick pea stew that also includes meat and seasonings such as rosemary or basil, garlic, and onion. A similar dish is *pasta e fagioli*, a stew made with pasta and beans. Stews and soups are served as a first course in Italy, although they can also be consumed as a main course.

Soups are just as important to Mediterranean cuisine as are stews. Soups can be made of unusual flavor combinations, such as cold garlic soup with almonds and raisins (Spain), soup made with zucchini flowers (Italy), and yogurt soup (Turkey). Most soups, however, are made of combinations of vegetables, meat, and spices are simmered long enough for the flavors to blend thoroughly. Soups like Moroccan *harira* are substantial and intended to be a main course or, during Ramadan, *harira* is eaten during fasting because it is so satisfying. Making *harira* is complicated. Chickpeas are soaked overnight and the soup is made by sautéing meat (usually beef) and onions with spices. More ingredients, like tomatoes, rice, chickpeas, and lentils, are added along with water and additional spices at 15-minute intervals. A good *harira* should be smooth and the lentils, chickpeas, and rice should be well cooked without being burned. Because of its time-consuming and layered preparation, *harira* has become a sort of test of one's cooking skill; if it is well made, the cook is considered accomplished. *Leb-lebi*, a chickpea soup from Tunisia, is also time-consuming to make. Chickpeas are simmered overnight with calf's feet or marrow bones, and the soup is served over stale bread cubes with lemon juice, olive oil, and *harissa* (a fiery pepper paste) on top. A proper bowl of *leb-lebi* should make your nose run because of the spicy intensity of the *harissa*.

Leb-Lebi

2 cups dried chickpeas. Soak overnight with a pinch of baking soda and rinse thoroughly. Or use 2 cans of rinsed and drained chickpeas.

3 cups broth: vegetable, beef, or chicken

4 cloves garlic, minced

1 tablespoon ground cumin

4 tablespoons olive oil

6–8 eggs

Stale French bread cut into cubes

Olive oil

Lemon wedges

Harissa (see recipe in chapter 2)

Put chickpeas, broth, garlic, cumin, olive oil, and extra water to cover chickpeas in a large soup pot. Add salt and pepper and boil until peas are fully cooked, at least one hour. Soft boil eggs, one per person. Put stale bread in bottom of soup bowl, cover with chickpea stew and set peeled, soft boiled egg on top of soup; cut the egg so that the yolk runs. Drizzle with olive oil and squeeze a lemon wedge on soup. Combine *harissa* with water to make a sauce and drizzle on top of soup.

Grain Dishes

The Mediterranean diet (see chapter 7) is based on plenty of whole grains: pasta, rice, bread, and bulgur. Certainly, people around the world associate Mediterranean cuisine with pasta dishes, lots of fresh bread, and rice dishes like paella and *pilav*. Pasta or noodles are served throughout the region, either boiled and tossed with ingredients or a particular kind of sauce, or baked in layers with other ingredients. Pasta is extremely versatile: just about any ingredient—fish, seafood, meat, vegetables—can be combined with noodles to make a satisfying first course or main dish. Italians in particular have turned pasta production into a highly developed art form; there are hundreds of different shapes of pasta and usually the name of the pasta shape tells you what it might look like. For example, *orecchiette* means little ears, or caplike shapes that resemble tiny round ears. The kind of sauce or ingredients used in the dish depends on the shape of the pasta. Pasta with grooves (*rigate*) are suited for holding smooth sauces; hollowed-out shapes, like *orecchiette*, are suited for capturing small chunks of food like peas or bits of potato. Pasta with a plain tomato sauce is perhaps still the most popular first course for lunch or dinner, despite the infinite variety of pasta dishes produced in Italy. Special occasions call for baked pasta, usually in the form of lasagna, pasta sheets baked off with meat or other ingredients in a tomato or béchamel sauce. Southern Italians might prepare a *timballo*, cooked pasta layered with meat, sauce, and a variety of other ingredients, everything from vegetables to livers to cinnamon. Similar to the *timballo* is the Greek pastitsio, a layered dish of baked pasta, meat, tomato or white sauce, and cheese. And on the island of Malta, a special dish is *timpano*, a deep-dish casserole of pasta, chopped meat, and hard-boiled eggs within a pastry crust. The Maltese also have an ingenious way to prepare leftover spaghetti. Known as *froga*, the dish consists of leftover spaghetti mixed with eggs and ham, seasoned with cumin and pan-fried until crispy. *Froga* is eaten as a snack or appetizer.

Froga

1 pound cooked cold spaghetti

1 cup ricotta cheese

2 eggs, lightly beaten

1/4 cup grated parmesan or Romano cheese

2 cups tomato sauce

Combine all ingredients in a large mixing bowl. Mix thoroughly. Season with salt and pepper. Heat olive oil or cooking oil in a heavy skillet. Add a small portion (1/4) of spaghetti mixture to skillet and lower heat. Gently turn over spaghetti fritter and cook on both sides until golden and crunchy. Drain on paper towels and serve.

Most pasta, macaroni, and noodles in the Mediterranean are made from semolina flour. In some regions, people like their pasta to have a slightly (or very) sour taste. In Greece, people make and eat *tahana*, which is a pasta made from sour milk and in Tunisia, noodles called *hlalems* are made from lightly fermented semolina flour dough. These noodles have a sour or nutty flavor and are usually served plain. Another pasta-like dish is couscous, tiny nuggets of semolina flour and water that are steamed, not boiled, and served as an accompaniment to meat, fish, or vegetables. Like pasta, couscous is a versatile ingredient for main dishes and even desserts. It can be prepared with hearty vegetables like eggplant, or cooked with meat or fish to make a main course. As an accompaniment, it can be flavored with herbs, seasonings, or a sweet-pungent flavor combination like onions and raisins. Couscous is also prepared with honey or sugar and eaten as a kind of dessert. Although couscous is most popular in North Africa, it is also eaten in Greece, Turkey, and in Sicily, where a dish called *cucusu* is made from much larger nuggets of semolina paste. Because couscous is an accompaniment to the main course, it is often served plain. In Tunisia, cooks steam couscous in a covered pot, whereas Moroccan and Algerian cooks do not. Tunisian couscous is tender and moist; the Moroccan and Algerian versions are lighter and fluffier.[5]

Paella, Spain's best known dish, is seasoned rice with shellfish, meat, and sausages. Paella was first made in Valencia, a city on the Mediterranean, about 200 years ago. Originally a Lenten dish, with rice, local vegetables, salt cod, and snails, paella became more elaborate as cooks added chicken, sausages, and shellfish, and local restaurants added special seasonings or expensive ingredients like lobster. The dish is named after the iron skillet in which the rice is cooked. The skillet is round, about 15 inches across, with two handles and slanted, shallow sides. Traditional paella is made outdoors over a wood fire, although it can also be made on the stovetop and finished in the oven. Paella is still served in restaurants in Catalonia, or it is made at home for special occasions. It is eaten as a first course even though it has so many ingredients as to be a meal in itself. Farther east in the Mediterranean, *pilav* is a dish made famous in Turkey (in the United States, it is known as rice pilaf). A *pilav* is a seasoned rice that accompanies meat. Some elaborate *pilavs* contain lamb, chicken, and even quail and are served as the main course of the meal. Other ingredients, such as currants, pine nuts, tomatoes, eggplant, and chickpeas, can be added for additional

Paella. © J. Susan Cole Stone.

flavor, but the key to a good *pilav* is cooking time and technique. Cooks need to be careful about the amount of time and the temperature at which the rice is cooked, depending, of course, on the type of rice being served for the *pilav*. The rice must be perfectly cooked, not too watery or overdone. Some *pilavs* use bulgur as their main ingredient, but rice is more popular. Proper cooking also characterizes Italian risotto. Ingredients are cooked with arborio rice (a special short-grain rice) so that the grains of rice absorb their flavor. A good risotto has a creamy, not watery, texture.

Stuffed and Layered Foods

Stuffed foods—stuffed vegetables, layered dishes, meatballs—are also good examples of peasant cooking, or cooking with little. The stuffing used is usually stale bread, rice, or bulgur, foods that are less expensive and therefore stretch more expensive ingredients, like meat, further. A classic example is the meatball. In Italy, *polpette* are made from ground meat, bread crumbs and seasonings. They are served as the main course along with vegetables; only Italian Americans serve meatballs with their spaghetti. Turkish meatballs, or *köfte*, are made from seasoned meat or the meat is stretched further with rice, stale bread, eggplant, or other vegetables. Greek *keftedes* are made with beef or veal, lots of spices and herbs, and stale bread. A seasoned meat mixture is also used to stuff vegetables (dolmas) in Turkey, Greece, and other parts of the eastern Mediterranean. Vegetables that can be stuffed include squash, eggplant, tomatoes, peppers, and grape leaves, which are pickled first. Sicilians stuff meat, in a special dish called *farsumagru*, a recipe that dates back to the thirteenth-century Angevin occupation (the dish takes its name from the French word *farce* or stuffing). Originally, *farsumagru* was a thin piece of meat rolled around a breadcrumb filling. Through the centuries, the dish became more and more complicated, including such ingredients as eggs, peas, cheese, ham, ground beef, currants, and pine nuts. Today, the dish is reserved for special occasions.[6] Sicilians are much more likely to eat a dish called *involtini*, skewered meat rolls with a filling, for ordinary meals.

The Mediterranean is also home to many layered dishes, where ingredients are assembled then baked. Baking allows the tastes of the many ingredients to blend together and create new tastes. Lasagna, *timballo*, and *timpana*, previously mentioned in this chapter, are all examples of layered foods made with pasta. Another famous layered dish is Greek moussaka, lamb with layers of eggplant, potato, and béchamel sauce. Spanish, French, and Italian tarts are also layered foods; cooked vegetables (peppers, potatoes, tomatoes, eggplant) or meat are layered on a pastry crust and an egg custard is poured over everything. Pastry crusts are stuffed with vegetables, meat, and legumes. A favorite savory pie in Morocco is *bisteeya,* a pastry crust stuffed with chicken or pigeon. A mixture of seasonings—nutmeg, saffron, parsley, and cinnamon—deepens the flavor of the poultry used. A mixture of sugar and almonds is also added to the pie, which provides a sweet taste.

Meat and Fish

Historically, populations in the Mediterranean have not consumed much meat. The Mediterranean diet is based on carbohydrates, not proteins. In fact, there were many folk sayings that indicate meat was a rarity on most people's tables. One Italian phrase recalled that if someone eats a chicken, either the person or the chicken is sick. Today, people eat all kinds of meat and there is plenty of meat for sale in grocery stores, outdoor markets, and supermarkets. Beef, not traditionally associated with the pastoral and seafaring ways of the region, has become more available, but many Mediterranean consumers prefer lamb, chicken, goat, pork (for Christians), and even camel. When meat is served, it is usually roasted, which was popular with peasants because it can be done easily and out of doors. From ancient times forward, armies and nomadic peoples would gather food as they went. When they set up camp, they would gather firewood then slaughter a few sheep or goats and grill the meat. Although it is one of the oldest ways of cooking meat, roasting is today a refined cooking technique. During the Ottoman Empire, for example, palace cooks would try out various types of wood to impart different tastes on the meat. Today in Turkey, barbecue is still wildly popular for holidays and special occasions, as well as in restaurants, where the barbecue is brought to the individual table and customers can cook meat and vegetables to their satisfaction.[7]

In many parts of the Mediterranean, roasted meat or barbecue is a highly sophisticated enterprise. Kebabs (shish kebab, doner kebab) of all types are popular street foods, and each street vendor has his or her individual recipe for marinade. Some of the most popular ingredients for marinade include yogurt, olive oil, lemon juice, and a mind-boggling variety of herbs and spices. Although a simple kebab will consist of chunks of meat on a skewer, meat can also be ground up with different seasonings then shaped around a skewer and roasted. Moroccan *kefta* is ground meat mixed with seasonings. The mixture is shaped like a sausage, threaded on to a skewer, broiled, and served over couscous. Rotisserie-cooked meat is also popular, especially in the eastern Mediterranean. Greek souvlaki is lamb or chicken that has been marinated first and then threaded on a long skewer, sometimes between vegetables and bay leaves. The cooked meat is served on pita bread with salad and yogurt. Greeks also make a dish called gyro on the rotisserie. Made of ground lamb mixed with bread crumbs and seasonings, gyro is cooked on a vertical spit and slices are cut off and eaten with bread, tomatoes, parsley, and yogurt. Similar to gyro is *shawarma*, eaten in the eastern Mediterranean, especially the Levant. Meat is marinated and grilled, then served with pita bread, tomatoes, garlic sauce, and French fries.

Given the peasant traditions and uneven economic development in the Mediterranean region, it is not surprising to note that every part of the animal is eaten; nothing is wasted. After the choice parts are roasted and eaten, less desirable parts of the animal are ground up, cooked, seasoned, and stuffed into intestinal casings for sausage. Animal innards are also put into stuffed vegetable dishes to stretch the supply of meat even further. Animal tongues and some of their internal organs (sweetbreads) can be cooked into layered dishes or roasted on skewers. Even the lining of the cow's stomach, tripe, is consumed in stews and soups. Some of the more unusual parts of animals are considered delicacies. Pig's feet are cured and sold for special occasions in Italy. And in Greece, lamb's heads are a delicacy. The head is soaked in water and then split in half. It is usually brushed with a light marinade before roasting, and it is ready to serve when the brains are tender.

Because fish play such an important role in the region's economy and ecosystem, they are prepared in many ways. The most common way to prepare most fish is roasting or broiling. Fish and seafood are also sautéed with a few vegetables and seasonings. And fish eggs are a particular delicacy, either as roe to be used in recipes or cured as *bottarga*, blocks of fish eggs wrapped in thin wax. Fish eggs are tossed with pasta, or used in salads to add a distinctive salty flavor, or they are eaten with bread and a drizzle of olive oil as an appetizer. Some fish dishes are more complicated. Fish

Tripe. © J. Susan Cole Stone.

are used as stuffing for vegetables or conversely, vegetables like zucchini are used to cover fish before cooking. Fish and seafood are frequently used in complex tajines and paellas. And on the French Mediterranean coast, fish is layered with tapenade, tomato confit, and phyllo dough and baked off, to make a kind of fish "pastry." Another exotic fish dish is *lampuki* pie, made from a popular fish in Malta. The *lampuki* fish is deboned and fried, then mixed in a pie with onions, cauliflower, spinach, tomatoes, olives, and raisins. When fish is broiled or sautéed, it is usually seasoned with a bit of olive oil, lemon, and a few herbs; but it can also be marinated in a sweet-sour mixture, which is popular in north Africa and in Sicily.

Side Dishes

Side dishes are usually fresh vegetables or legumes. Historically, legumes were popular foods in the region because they provided nourishing protein, they were versatile, and they kept well in dried form. Lentils and chickpeas are popular additions to stews and soups; they can also be cooked with seasonings and served either hot or cold. Further, they can be ground up and fried into patties or balls for snacks and appetizers. Another legume, the fava bean (also known as the broad bean), is popular throughout the region. Fava plants grow long pods in which there are three to eight beans inside each pod. Like other legumes, fava beans are versatile: they can be steamed, boiled, or fried. But unlike other legumes like lentils or chickpeas, fava beans are not typically used in main course dishes. Instead, the fava bean is the quintessential side dish legume. In Morocco, cooked fava beans are tossed in a spicy dressing made with coriander, cumin, and garlic, or in Algeria, more simply, cooked and tossed with cumin and salt. In Tunisia, a side dish or type of salad is *ftet*, a fava bean, noodle, and dry fish dish, where fava beans are simmered with dried fish and seasonings in a tomato paste, then mixed with noodles. In France, fava bean salad is made with cooked fava beans, herbs like parsley and basil, and some grated cheese. Or a more elaborate salad is made in Spain with Spanish ham (*jamón Serrano*) and mint; also used are eggs and tomatoes. In Italy, fava beans are made into a soup, simmered with fennel and hot peppers, and served over toasted bread and drizzled with olive oil. In Greece, fava beans are cooked with leeks and potatoes.

Vegetables served as side dishes are cooked many ways, whether baked, simmered, braised, or grilled. Vegetable mixes are also popular, providing more variety and again, different tastes, than a single vegetable. One of the most common vegetable side dishes consists of eggplant, peppers, and tomatoes. In Provence, this is known as ratatouille, a dish that is eaten both hot and cold; in fact, it tastes better the day after it is prepared, as the blended flavors become even stronger. Ratatouille is made by sautéing eggplant, peppers, and tomatoes (sometimes zucchini is included in the mix) with garlic, thyme, basil, and parsley. A similar dish is Tunisian *mechouia*, a mixture of roasted peppers and tomatoes seasoned with garlic, capers, and various spices. *Mechouia* is usually garnished with tuna or sliced hard-boiled eggs. In the Middle Eastern part of the Mediterranean, diners eat a dish called *mnazzalleh*, eggplant with tomatoes, chickpeas, and seasonings such as mint, parsley, and sometimes cinnamon. The mixture is left to sit for several hours to allow the flavors to blend together. Another dish that is left alone for the flavors to blend is Sicilian caponata, a combination of eggplant, celery, pepper, tomatoes, and onions seasoned with capers, olives, raisins, and vinegar.

Dessert

The preferred end to most meals in the Mediterranean is fresh fruit, sometimes combined with cheese, biscuits, and coffee or tea. Prepared fruit is also a popular dessert choice. Sometimes fruits are stuffed with sweetened ricotta cheese, or they are poached and served with fruit syrup. Dried or fresh fruit is stewed into a compote and flavored with nuts, honey, or yogurt. Fruit is also used as the main ingredient in flavored ices, puddings, tarts, and ice creams. Another dessert preferred by Mediterranean diners is pudding. Usually made from milk, cream, or yogurt, Mediterranean puddings are made with corn starch or mastic, a North African ingredient that gives the pudding a chewy texture. Frequently, puddings are topped with nuts, toasted seeds, dried fruit, and honey.

Fruit and pudding are simple desserts enjoyed at home. In restaurants or when entertaining company, Mediterranean hosts and hostesses may make something more elaborate, like pastries, cookies, or even a cake. Cookies studded with nuts or dried fruit are often accompanied by coffee or tea. Pastry is made with either a sweet dough made with eggs and butter, or with phyllo dough, delicate rolled-out layers of dough. The rich dessert baklava, a layered honey, ground nut, and phyllo dough pastry, is most often associated with Greece, but it is also enjoyed in Turkey and throughout the Levant. More elaborate pastries are made in southern France and Italy; bakeries offer a wide variety of layered, filled, or frosted pastries; and lunch or dinner guests usually buy a tray of pastries to take to the home of their host or hostess. It is said that no one eats more pastries than Sicilians; this may be debatable, but it is true that

Sicilian pastries and cakes are the most elaborate in the Mediterranean, difficult to make and syrupy sweet. For example, the cake called *cassata* is a sponge cake, layered with a sweetened ricotta cheese mixture and wrapped in marzipan (almond paste); as if this weren't enough, the confection is then frosted!

Dried Fruit Compote

1 cup raisins

1 cup dried apricots

1/4 cup chopped walnuts

1/4 cup chopped almonds

1/2 cup sugar

3 tablespoons honey

Rinse raisins and apricots then place in a bowl and soak with about 1 quart of cold water for 4 hours. Put nuts in a bowl and cover with boiling water. Soak for an hour and drain. Leave fruit in liquid and add sugar and honey, stir until sugar is completely dissolved. Add nuts and serve.

It seems clear, then, that no one dish or meal or menu adequately characterizes all the tastes and techniques of the Mediterranean region. The same ingredient can be prepared in hundreds of different ways and enjoyed at any time of the day or night. Although there are no typical dishes for the region, there are some similarities between countries in terms of meal order, preparation of certain foods, and food combinations. What seems clear is that Mediterranean dishes are based on a fairly elaborate culinary system that embraces or incorporates difference while preserving certain trends (peasant cooking, for example) for future generations. And, as the next chapter demonstrates, people across the Mediterranean region enjoy these dishes both in and out of the home. Just as there are hundreds of typical dishes and meals, there are dozens of ways to enjoy them.

NOTES

1. Paula Wolfert, *Mediterranean Cooking* (New York: Harper Perennial, revised edition 1994), p. xii.

2. On the history of the hotel breakfast buffet see Joan Nathan, *The Foods of Israel Today* (New York: Knopf, 2001), p. 25.

3. Daniel Young, *Made in Marseille* (New York: HarperCollins, 2002), pp. 122–126.

4. Paula Wolfert Web site, http://www.paulawolfert.com.

5. Wolfert, *Mediterranean Cooking,* p. 149.

6. Clarissa Hyman, *Cucina Siciliana* (Northampton, MA: Interlink, 2002), p. 76.

7. Sarah Woodward, *The Ottoman Kitchen* (Northampton, MA: Interlink, 2001), p. 61.

5

Eating Out

"Eating out" means a lot of things to people in the Mediterranean region. People might eat out at an elegant restaurant, but they are just as likely to stop by a café or snack bar for a quick bite. They might sample the seasonal delicacies at a stand in a street market, or they may be invited to dine at a friend's house. Just as there are all different venues for eating out, there are also different reasons to do so: convenience, circumstance, hospitality, and a desire to do something out of the ordinary. In all these cases, eating takes place outside the familiarity of one's home and kitchen; for some Mediterranean diners this is an anxious moment, but for others it is an opportunity to try something new or to see how others cook familiar food. People from all walks of life eat out, from those who do not have proper kitchen facilities and subsist on varied forms of inexpensive fast food, to those who can afford to try the latest trendy restaurant or attend an elaborate dinner party. Making and selling food to others constitute a vital part of the small business economy in this region, and just about anyone can find a bit of start-up money to become an ambulant vendor.

This chapter explores the different places where people eat out: street markets and stands; informal dining establishments such as cafés, bars, and coffee-shops; and more formal places such as restaurants and other peoples' homes. Food bought at market stalls and from ambulant vendors is perhaps the equivalent of American fast food in the sense that it is inexpensive and quick, but this is where the comparison ends. Mediterranean street food is by no means standardized like American fast food. Instead, diners can choose from a variety of dishes: breads, sandwiches, soup, snails, savory and sweet pies, ice cream, candy, and just about every other kind of snack or meal one could imagine, each prepared by an individual cook or baker. And hundreds of years before Starbucks, parts of the Mediterranean had a thriving coffee-shop culture. The popularity of coffee and tea has ebbed and flowed, but a café, bar, or coffee shop can still be found on nearly every street corner. Drinking caffeinated beverages is not only an important aspect of consumption and leisure activities in the Mediterranean, café culture provides a space for various communities, whether defined by gender, age, class, religion, politics, or occupation, to foster important social bonds. The restaurant, from the humble trattoria in Palermo, to the trendy brasserie in Tel Aviv, to the Michelin-starred restaurant in Nice, offers locals and tourists alike a chance to sample neighborhood specialties or food from around the world. In some areas of the Mediterranean, however, restaurants are usually for tourists; locals prefer to dine in their own or in someone else's home before dining out in a restaurant. Although a tremendous variety of food is served in restaurants and in other peoples' homes, these places share some common dining rituals, as well as basic ingredients for meals.

MARKETS AND STREET FOOD

Cooks throughout the Mediterranean are likely to purchase their food at a local outdoor market or at a small specialty shop, rather than at a large supermarket. Historically, small shops and markets were important for consumers in the Mediterranean region, often because shopkeepers extended credit and offered gifts during the holidays to create and sustain a reliable customer base. Food prices were not advertised and shopkeepers would make adjustments according to the market or to adjust to the economic circumstances of the consumer. When large chain stores and supermarkets first appeared in the Mediterranean region after World War I, they were very unpopular. Not only did customers dislike the shopping experience, but shopkeepers in major cities organized and protested this way of doing business. Today, when consumers shop at a small store, they are more likely to buy just a few items, maybe just what they need for dinner. They are also more likely to stop and chat with the storekeeper or the help, if only to find out what meat is at a good price or to see how everyone's family is. They might sample a new type of cheese, and their children might get a sweet from the shopkeeper. Small shops and markets now have to compete with an increasing number of supermarkets where consumers can drive to the store, park their cars, and fill up on groceries for the week. Supermarkets are popular with younger people and tourists who might prefer the faster but less personal service and the standardized, clearly visible prices. Supermarkets are also popular with working families who appreciate the hours they stay open (some small shops still close at lunch time and most outdoor markets are open only in the morning) during the week and on Sundays.

Because the climate in much of the Mediterranean is generally mild, outdoor markets can be found year-round. These markets are places to buy ingredients for meals as well as prepared foods, which range from simple snacks and treats to more elaborate cooked meals. Outdoor markets are set up in towns and villages and in cities. Some are more specialized, selling mostly fish or eggs or fresh produce; others are big sprawling affairs selling all kinds of food and other goods and services as well. Whereas markets in small towns and villages usually open one day a week, from dawn until mid-day, more permanent markets in cities, like the Marché Central in Tunis, stay open five or six days a week. The Marché Central is famous for carrying everything from spices to cheese, from octopus to crusty bread, from rose petals (for making rosewater) to candy. Another famous market is the Djemma el-Fna in Marrakech, Morocco, which covers an area of about 12 acres. Here shoppers can find any kind of food they desire, and there are lots of nonedible goods for sale as well. Entertainment is provided by street performers, who might amuse shoppers or the patrons enjoying mint tea at any of the numerous cafés that surround the market area. After about five in the afternoon, mobile cooking stands are set up by vendors who make and sell all kinds of Moroccan dishes: *harira* (a nourishing and inexpensive soup), couscous, snails, and grilled sausages. The outdoor market, or souk, in the northern Syrian city of Aleppo, covers 10 kilometers (about 6 miles) of winding alleyways; inexperienced shoppers can easily get lost in the maze of food and goods. Classic souks are arranged so that all the stalls of a particular trade (or good) are grouped together in one section. For example, all of the spice vendors are in one area and the nut vendors are in another. This arrangement allows for easy comparison shopping by consumers.

Because outdoor markets have no formal inventory control or consumer survey mechanisms, they tend to offer local produce or food specialties only when they are available. On the coast of Italy or in Sicily, shoppers can buy fresh citrus in season, or pastries and candies during special religious holidays. In Catalonia, the local markets sell everything from locally made sausage to wild mushrooms. A popular seasonal item are *calcots*, a variety of onion that is served roasted with *romesco* sauce (made from peppers, tomatoes, garlic, toasted almonds or hazelnuts, olive oil, vinegar, salt, and pepper). Local specialties and produce are purchased on site and then prepared at home. In the eastern Mediterranean region and throughout North Africa, food is prepared and cooked right in front of the customers, who either sit down at tables or eat standing up. Sometimes, communal utensils are washed off or kept in water for the next customer. Traditionally, street food has been associated with the lower classes, especially with workers, who did not have adequate time or money for a home-cooked lunch. What people refer to now as "fast food" has really been around for centuries. In eighteenth-century Naples, for example, citizens who lived in the slums by the bay of Naples did not have kitchen facilities, so they subsisted on street food: octopus, bread, pizza, stews, and even pasta served street-side. Hungry Neapolitans would pay vendors whatever they could afford, and the vendor would give them the appropriately size portion. Sometimes the customers would argue with the vendor over the size of the portion, or they would ask for some extra seasoning. Other times they would eat the food quietly and quickly, either standing or sitting.

Pizza maker Gennaro Bruno prepares pizzas in a restaurant in Naples, Italy. The Italian government has issued strict guidelines to protect real Neapolitan pizza from impostures. AP Photo/Salvatore Laporta.

Today, workers still buy a nourishing meal or quick snack on the street, but some upper-class consumers might consider it inappropriate to buy and eat something made right there on the street. Although there is something democratic about being able to buy and eat just about anything on the street, there are still class- and status-based prejudices against those who would slurp soup on the street corner or eat a folded-over slice of pizza while sitting on the steps of a building. Certain codes of manners and family traditions have always held some people back from partaking in this kind of consumption. For example, in 1889, the king and queen of Italy, King Umberto and his wife, Queen Margherita of Savoy, were traveling through Naples and desired to taste pizza because they had heard so much about it. Nineteenth-century codes of conduct forbid royalty from engaging in such a plebeian activity as eating food on the street or in a humble pizzeria; instead a pizza maker was summoned to prepare several different types of pizza and deliver them to their hotel. The Queen communicated her thanks through the head of the Royal Household and, presumably, the pizza she enjoyed the most, a tomato, basil, and mozzarella cheese pizza, was named the pizza margherita in her honor. Cookbook author Anissa Helou recalled growing up in Beirut, Lebanon in the 1950s and 1960s, where, along the seaside, street vendors would sell "all kinds of tempting goodies: sesame galettes that looked like handbags, grilled corn, mountains of seeds and nuts spooned into cones made out of old newspapers, luscious sweets and candies, ice cream, and refreshing drinks." Yet Helou was never allowed to satisfy her appetite there on the street because she came from an upper-class family. Every time she would ask for a treat, her uncles would reply: "Girls from good families don't, but you can buy whatever you want and take it back home and eat there."[1] Today, children and young adults seem less concerned about the unspoken codes of conduct when it comes to eating street food or fast food. Their parents and grandparents, however, might still want them to take the food home and eat it privately.

Pizza Margherita

Dough

1/2 cake compressed fresh yeast

2 cups of warm water

1 cup pastry flour

1 tablespoon salt

5–1/2 to 6 cups unbleached, all-purpose flour

In a bowl, stir the yeast into warm water until it dissolves. Add the pastry flour and salt and mix well. Add the all-purpose flour one cup at a time, kneading until the dough is smooth. Shape the dough into a ball and leave it in the bowl; cover with a towel and let rise for four hours. Punch the dough down and divide into pieces; the dough should make five to six pizzas.

Toppings

1 large can of peeled tomatoes, chopped

1 1/2 cups diced mozzarella cheese

Fresh basil

Salt

Olive oil

Pinch dough out into a small circle on a pizza peel or pan. Distribute a small amount of the chopped tomatoes on the dough and swirl around with your fingers. Dot the dough with chunks of mozzarella, then sprinkle some salt over the pizza and add several fresh basil leaves. Swirl about a tablespoon full of extra-virgin olive oil on top of the pizza and put in a very hot oven (500°F) and bake until gold brown, about 5 to 10 minutes.

The distinction drawn between eating food in public and private is perhaps more important in regions of the Mediterranean where street food is, literally, food that is prepared and eaten on the street. For example, throughout Egypt, men set up carts or street-side stands to cook *koshari*, a mixture of pasta, rice, and legumes. Customers get a bowl full and may even use a communal spoon that is kept in a pot of water. Frequently, food is prepared and cooked right in front of the customers, who may make special requests for certain ingredients, but who do not, as a rule, offer suggestions in terms of preparation. Although there has been no exhaustive study of the types of street food prepared in the region, anecdotal evidence suggests that proper street food, sold by ambulant vendors and consumed on the street, is more popular in the eastern and southern regions of the Mediterranean, where all sorts of dishes are prepared, not only simple sandwiches, but also more elaborate dishes like soups, stews, tajines, and even desserts. Throughout the European edges of the Mediterranean, street food refers to the specialties that are usually prepared indoors and then taken away to be eaten on the streets or at home. An example would be the *pizza a taglio* (pizza by the slice) stores where customers can select from a wide variety of prepared pizzas, choosing the type and quantity of pizza. Sometimes the pizza is reheated or the customer can take home some wrapped pizza to eat later. Diehard fans of street food would argue that there is not much "proper" street food on the western or

European side of the Mediterranean. This may be the case today, but it was not necessarily the case in the past, given that Italy, Greece, Spain, and southern France had ambulant vendors and hawkers who sold food on the streets for people to eat.

One of the most popular street foods in the eastern Mediterranean is the kabob or kebab, which is meat or ground meat threaded on a skewer and grilled. During the last 20 years, kebab has become adopted by many around the world as a favorite fast food. Thanks to the recent emigration of peoples from Turkey and the Levant to parts of Europe, kebab stands compete with pizzerias and snack stands selling local specialties in cities like Stockholm, Berlin, and Copenhagen. One kind of kebab is *shawarma*, sold on the streets of Lebanon, Syria, and Israel. *Shawarma* is a very large, fat "kebab" made with either lamb or chicken. The meat is sliced into wide pieces and marinated overnight. It is then threaded on a long skewer in between pieces of fat. The skewer is placed on a vertical grill and left to rotate. As the meat cooks, the layers of fat baste the kebab, keeping it moist. Once cooked, the outer layers are sliced off and served on pita bread with tomatoes, onions, pickles, tahini (sesame paste) or garlic sauce. The Greek version, made with pork, is called souvlaki and the Turkish version, made with beef or lamb, is called doner kebab.

Sandwiches like doner kebab are popular street foods because they are portable. Variations on sandwiches are plentiful throughout the Mediterranean. Italians duck into cafés and bars to purchase and eat panini, sandwiches made out of large slices of white bread. The sandwiches are filled with a variety of ingredients—cheese, eggs, meat, vegetables—then sliced into triangles and kept in stacks under cloth napkins. Customers choose which ones they want and the barista toasts the sandwiches as they wait. In Tunisia, a popular sandwich in the coastal areas is *casse croute*, which means breaking the crust, a sandwich stuffed with varied ingredients made to order, but most commonly made with tuna, potatoes, and salad loaded into a sliced baguette. Tunisians also enjoy a filling sandwich called fricassée, fried bread filled with tuna, potatoes, and olives. The Tunisian fricassée has nothing to do with the French fricassée, a stewed chicken dish. Fans of French street food have their own version of the take-away sandwich, *pan bagnat*, which means soaked bread, originally a specialty of Nice and now sold throughout the Riviera. *Pan bagnat* consists of a sliced baguette that is rubbed with garlic and then filled with ingredients such as tuna, hard-boiled eggs, and vegetables. Perhaps the most famous street food sandwich is falafel: crispy fried chickpea balls layered into pita bread with tahini sauce, lettuce, tomatoes, radishes, pickles, and even potato chips or French fries. Falafel originated in Egypt, where

Falafel—served with pita bread, lettuce, and tahini sauce—is made from ground chickpea flour. AP Photo/Larry Crowe.

it is called *ta'miyah*, and it also took root in Syria and Lebanon, where the chickpea balls are smaller and crisper. Today, falafel has become part of the global fast food market, along with pizza and kebab, available on street corners throughout the world as a quick and filling snack.

Pan Bagnat

Dressing

1 tablespoon red wine vinegar

1/2 teaspoon Dijon mustard

3 tablespoons olive oil

Salt, pepper

Whisk together vinegar, mustard, salt and pepper. Add olive oil gradually, stirring constantly, set aside.

Sandwich

1 large baguette

2 cans tuna, drained

2 onions, sliced into rings

2 hard boiled eggs, sliced

1 pepper sliced into rings

1 cup kalamata or brine-cured olives, chopped

1 tomato, sliced

Slice baguette horizontally and pull out the soft bread center, making a well in both halves of the bread. Place tuna, onion, eggs, pepper, olives, and tomato in the bottom half of the baguette. Drizzle dressing over the filling. Top with other half of baguette and wrap entire loaf tightly with plastic wrap. Let sit one hour at room temperature. Unwrap, slice, and serve.

Related to the sandwich are a variety of filled breads and flavored flatbreads, usually prepared in advance but sometimes made on the street for customers. Ancient Greeks and Romans mixed together flour, water, and olive oil and sprinkled the dough with more oil, honey, herbs, or a sauce. They then baked the dough on a hot stone. Leavened and unleavened breads were prepared throughout the Mediterranean region, as both daily staples and ritual foods. Today, Italians eat focaccia, in southern France consumers eat *fougasse*, and in the eastern Mediterranean one can buy seasoned pita. In Morocco and Tunisia, the herbs and other ingredients (such as anise seeds or sesame seeds) are kneaded into the dough before baking. The most popular version of flavored flatbread is, of course, pizza. Once found exclusively in the city of Naples, Italy, pizza's popularity spread as Neapolitans immigrated to the rest of Europe, as well as North and South America. The original pizza was little more than a flatbread with tomatoes, salt, herbs, and sometimes lard, cheese, or tiny fish larvae. Related to pizza is *lahmacun*, or "Turkish pizza," in which a ground lamb mixture is spread on flatbread and baked. Turkey, along with Greece, specializes in stuffed breads and savory pastries like the Turkish *borek*, filled with cheese, spinach, potatoes, or meat; or the Greek spanikopita, a phyllo-pastry triangle layered with cheese and spinach. Turnovers, flatbreads, and pizzas are sold in bakeries, storefronts, and from sidewalk stands; they are usually eaten throughout the Mediterranean as a snack, although with pizza, special restaurants (pizzerias), where one can sit down and order a pizza with specific toppings, cater to customers for lunch and dinner.

Lahmacun

1 package of pita bread, separated in halves

1 pound ground beef or lamb

2 onions, chopped coarsely

1 cup parsley

2 tomatoes, seeds discarded and chopped

1/2 teaspoon red pepper flakes

2 garlic cloves

1 teaspoon salt

Using a food processor or blender, chop up and mix together all the ingredients except for the meat. Then mix in the ground meat and refrigerate mixture to blend the flavors for about an hour. Preheat oven to 500°F or broil; take some of the meat mixture and spread in a thin layer on a pita bread. Place as many pitas as will fit on a cooking sheet and cook for about five minutes until pita is golden brown and crispy.

Sandwiches and light snacks offered as street food are not unusual; what is worth noting about breads and sandwiches in the Mediterranean is the variety of ways these foods are prepared. A simple food like bread is prepared in hundreds of different ways, altered by the addition of a single ingredient or topped with an array of interesting tastes; however, ingredients are not added indiscriminately or carelessly. Instead, much thought and consideration goes into the preparation of a particular kind of bread; a pinch of salt can make a dramatic difference to the discerning customer. No doubt this is the case because the poor populations throughout the Mediterranean frequently had to make do with few ingredients. Thus simple foods like bread and flatbread became complex forms of cuisine with the addition of only a few ingredients. The pinch of salt matters, then, in distinguishing one form of flatbread from another.

More complicated, even elaborate, dishes are also served on the street. In Tunisia, one street specialty is called *brik*, a pastry pocket filled with minced lamb, beef, or vegetables. An egg is cracked over the ingredients, the pastry folded over and sealed, and the whole thing is deep fried in oil. *Brik* is a very messy food, popular with tourists even though it takes an experienced consumer to eat the pastry pocket without incident. More popular with locals than with tourists, *koshari* is a meal served on the streets in Egypt. Broken-up bits of macaroni, vermicelli, and rice are cooked with chickpeas, lentils, and onions in a seasoned tomato sauce. The mixture simmers in big vats and is served up on the street. It is a favorite with many Egyptians because it is inexpensive and filling. Soup is also a popular street food in the southern and eastern Mediterranean; *harira* can be found throughout North African and Middle Eastern markets, especially during Ramadan. Chickpea and egg soup, or *leb-lebi*, is also popular on the streets of Tunis. Customers crumble white bread into a bowl and then the vendor adds a ladleful of chickpea, lemon juice, and cumin soup into the bowl. Then he stirs in a raw egg. The soup is finished off with *harissa* (red pepper paste) and olive oil. Inexpensive sources of protein—eggs (served at egg counters in street markets), snails, tripe, and chitterlings—are prepared in different ways, sautéed, fried, and simmered in soups and stews.

Koshari

Tomato Sauce

4 tablespoons olive oil

1 small onion, chopped

3 cloves garlic, minced

1 large can of chopped or crushed tomatoes

Salt, pepper

Sauté onions until soft. Add garlic and cook briefly, then add tomatoes. Simmer for 20 minutes or so until thickened. Season with salt and pepper.

Koshari

8 tablespoons of olive oil

2 medium onions, sliced

1/2 cup vermicelli, broken up into pieces

1 cup dried lentils

1 1/3 cup rice

Cook the onions in the olive oil until they are caramelized. Remove from oil and dry on paper towels. Add vermicelli to oil and fry until browned. Remove from heat and set aside. Put lentils in 6 cups of water and bring to a boil, reduce heat, and simmer, covered, for 30 minutes or until lentils are tender. Add rice to the lentils and simmer for 15 minutes, then add vermicelli and oil from the pan. Remove pan from heat and let sit covered for 10–15 minutes or until liquid is absorbed and vermicelli and rice are tender. Stir in caramelized onions and top with tomato sauce.

Sweets and desserts are also popular street foods in all regions of the Mediterranean. Ice cream in one form or another is a popular summer treat that has become a year-round institution. In Italy, gelato, a creamier iced treat made with milk, is sold in hundreds of flavors, including unusual ones like rice, kiwi fruit, jasmine blossom, and even tomato. Customers can duck into a *gelateria* to choose several flavors for a cup or cone to take away, or there are bars and cafés that have a gelato case, usually with a sign boasting that the gelato is made on the premises. Ice cream (*glace*) is also popular in the Côte d'Azur, where vendors sell cones and cups to hungry beachgoers. In the Levant, a popular iced milk treat is *büza*, usually made with fruits and nuts and stuffed into a rectangular cookie "box." Another sweet treat popular throughout the Mediterranean is pudding, usually made with milk and other ingredients, and sold by ambulant vendors as well as in sweet shops and ice cream stands. In Lebanon and Syria, *m'hallabiyeh* is a simple milk pudding served in tiny bowls and piled high with different nuts. Sicilians make pudding out of more unusual ingredients such as watermelon or chestnuts. Very sweet desserts and candy are available everywhere in the Mediterranean, whether in the form of baklava, a sweet honey and nut filled pastry; marzipan (almond paste) candies; or Turkish *lokum* (also known as Turkish delight), a candy made with corn starch, sugar, nuts, and coconut. For many people, candy and pastries are special treats and not everyday fare. Adults prefer to have fresh fruit as the last course of the meal, although they may indulge their children in an afterschool snack of an ice cream or a bag of candy. On religious holidays (see chapter 6), candy is one way to mark the occasion as special. Some of the desserts served on the street can be quite elaborate. In Syria, pancakes are cooked on a griddle; stuffed with cheese, walnuts, or clotted cream; folded over and pinched shut; then deep fried and covered in sugar syrup.

Büza

1 1/4 cups whole milk

3/4 cup sugar

About 2 1/2 cups chopped fruit (strawberries, watermelon, peaches, mangoes, bananas)

1 cup crème fraîche

Pour milk in medium saucepan and bring to a boil without boiling over. Pour into a mixing bowl and stir in sugar until sugar is dissolved. Process chopped fruit in a blender or food processor until smooth. Stir into milk and add crème fraîche. Pour into ice cream maker or put mixture in the freezer, checking it every half-hour and stirring it until it reaches the right consistency.

Street food is more than just a quick snack or meal in the Mediterranean. It plays a vital role in the local community. It provides opportunities for small businesses to start and grow. One does not need much in terms of start-up funds, and some ambulant vendors make do with a bicycle, a tajine pot, a few utensils, and a bag of ingredients. In this era of increasing consolidation and globalization, street food vending offers one way for small businessmen and women to survive and even thrive. Moreover, street food vendors make available all kinds of foods to those who might not have the time or opportunity to cook. This includes single people who do not feel like cooking for themselves, working people who may not have the time to cook, and those who do not possess adequate supplies or facilities for cooking. In providing adequate and varied nourishment for these populations, street vendors offer a vital community service. And by preparing and cooking popular dishes in public, street vendors keep certain food traditions alive, offering an opportunity to customers to witness and partake in a different type of community, one defined by taste and tradition.

CAFÉS, BARS, AND COFFEE SHOPS

Coffee and tea both have a long history in the Mediterranean region. The leisurely consumption of these beverages has long been a part of the consumer culture in urban areas. For example, the first coffee house in the Mediterranean was opened in Istanbul in 1554, during the Ottoman Empire. Coffee houses soon became meeting places for intellectuals to meet, talk, and write. They also became places for leisure; playing games was a popular pastime at coffee houses. Sometimes, discussion became lively or focused on political issues. Authorities were quick to close coffee houses if they thought these places were or would become hotbeds of political unrest. In the mid-seventeenth century, the Sultan Murad V not only closed coffee houses, he also forbade the drinking of coffee. Coffee houses soon spread to Europe, but the premiere coffee shops were located in areas where there was trade or diplomatic relations with the Ottomans: Venice and Vienna, for example, and not the cities along the European Mediterranean coast.

Tea is more popular than coffee in parts of the Mediterranean such as Turkey, Morocco, and Tunisia. Although tea was a prized import from China for centuries, it did not become a drink for the masses in these regions until well into the nineteenth and even twentieth centuries. Tea lovers can buy their favorite drink in cafés, or they can purchase it from a street vendor or a tea cart at work. Tea is also served at the end of a meal in restaurants and in homes. Brewed from loose tea leaves, not teabags, Mediterranean tea is quite strong and is served highly sweetened and with mint in Morocco and Tunisia. In restaurants and in people's homes, tea is poured out from a special pitcher with a long spout, into glass cups, which allow the drinker to appreciate the full color of the tea. No one drinks

A man drinks coffee at an outdoor café in
Athens, Greece. AP Photo/Petros Karadjias.

more tea in the Mediterranean than the Turkish population. Turks take
numerous tea breaks at work throughout the day, and they like to joke
that the nation's economy would come to a halt if the tea supply were cut
off. A popular joke or story tells of a lion escaping from the Ankara Zoo
and taking up residence in the basement of a building (an office building,
Parliament, a government office). The lion proceeded to eat important
people like politicians, businessmen, or reporters, but no one did anything
until the lion ate the tea-vendor of the building. Only then did people
organize to capture the lion and return him to the zoo.

Today's coffee shops (or as they are also called, cafés, bars, and *kafeneion*)
are not usually hotbeds of political dissent. Instead, they tend to be places
where patrons can relax and discuss the news, play cards or other games,
and socialize. Many cafés have indoor and/or outdoor seating, and now
it is common to see televisions that blare out music videos or the latest
installment of a popular reality show. In Greece and in the eastern Mediterranean, some cafés are male domains, where (usually older) men can
retire to smoke, talk politics, and play cards, dominos, or backgammon.

Throughout the Mediterranean, however, cafés catering to younger patrons attract both men and women, who may come to study, flirt, and drink Coke instead of coffee or tea. Starbucks has expanded into some countries in the Mediterranean (Greece, Cyprus, Lebanon, Turkey) and is popular with younger customers, who enjoy the drinks and the ethos of "hanging out," although the U.S. company is currently cutting back on its international expansion (having closed outlets in Israel, for example). Locally owned cafés are neighborhood institutions, places where one comes to get the news, hear the gossip, or reconnect with neighbors and friends. Some patrons do not mind lingering and chatting over their drink, but others prefer to duck in, grab a quick cup of espresso, which they drink standing up, wolf down a sandwich or pastry, and then leave. Cafés also offer a variety of other products: candy, cigarettes, lottery tickets, and postage stamps; and barkeepers are reliable sources of information about neighborhood services and activities. In the age of Starbucks, none of this may seem unusual, but café culture made the Mediterranean area distinctive in the years before and after World War II, in the sense that it supported neighborhoods and more specific communities (artistic, literary). Moreover, cafés offered fast, convenient food, as well as a stimulating beverage in the years when people in the Mediterranean adjusted to new work patterns, changes in family structure, and social habits. Still prominent on practically every street corner, cafés, coffee shops, and bars are anchors of neighborhood communities and constitute an important part of small business practices in the region.

RESTAURANTS AND HOMES

There are many ways to "eat out" in the Mediterranean, including the more formal occasions of visiting restaurants and dining in someone's home. Hospitality is a critical aspect of Mediterranean culture, and thus eating out often means a visit to a friend or relative's home, to enjoy an evening of food and conviviality. Among Muslims, hospitality during a meal has ritualistic dimensions; a host or hostess will serve more food than guests can possibly eat—not to show off, but to show respect for the guests. Dining in a Muslim home takes on spiritual dimension, according to two German observers of Middle Eastern food habits, who describes the hospitality ritual by noting carefully the language used at the beginning and end of the meal:

The head of the house selects the finest piece of meat for his guest and then keeps pushing bowls of food towards him: *inshaallah 'adjabak* ("Hopefully it is to your taste"). When the guest has eaten his fill, he offers thanks, for example, by saying *daime*, an expression used throughout the Levant meaning "(may your reward) be eternal," to which the host may reply, *sahteen*, "double health (be given back to you)," before the visitor rounds off the exchange with "*ala qalbak*, to your heart."[2]

In regions where most socializing takes place in people's homes, restaurants are usually reserved for tourists or for special occasions. In other regions of the Mediterranean—the Côte d'Azur or in Catalonia, for example, restaurants are much more popular. They are important venues for socialization and express the vibrancy of local food habits and rituals.

Perhaps the most popular places for eating out are the outlets where diners can get a quick meal without a lot of fuss or formality, for example, cafeterias, snack bars, and other self-service dining establishments. Turkey, for example, has restaurants called *hazir yemek*, or ready food, which function like self-service cafeterias. Steam tables keep a variety of dishes warm and patrons grab a tray and select the items they like, pay for them, and eat, usually one flight above the cafeteria or in some cases, on an open air terrace. In Italy, the *tavola calda*, or hot-table, offers a similar variety of foods to customers who eat them in the cafeteria or take them home. Other informal dining establishments are popular neighborhood places. In Greece, the taverna and *kafeneia* tend to attract locals, and more upscale restaurants cater to tourists. In Italy, the trattoria is more casual and less expensive than a *ristorante*. And on the Mediterranean coast of France, "mom-and-pop" establishments serve indigenous cuisine at lower prices, whereas higher priced restaurants tend to be starred Michelin restaurants; this means they have to adhere to strict national standards and the food is classic French cuisine. At a starred restaurant, one is more likely to get a meal there that resembles something at a restaurant in Paris.

Over the last 20 years, one of the most noticeable changes in the region is the trend toward eating lunch outside the home and family. In many Mediterranean countries, workers and students used to return home at lunchtime for a home-cooked meal and a rest before heading back to work or school. Shops, schools, and offices would close for one or two hours, much to the frustration of foreign tourists, who expected goods and services to be open nonstop during the business day. In particular, American travelers on a tour of Europe would frequently remark that the Spanish, Italian, and Greek way of life seemed too slow paced, given that everything shut down for two hours in the afternoon.

Lunch was such an important meal that it was usually the most substantial meal of the day. Lunch would consist of several courses, usually a beginning course like soup or pasta, followed by a main course of meat or fish with vegetables, then a fruit course. And depending on the location, salad was served either before, during, or after the main course. Dinner, on the other hand, was frequently lighter than lunch: a bowl of soup and some bread, an omelet and some salad, or maybe just a sandwich and a piece of fruit. There are still places in the Mediterranean, especially in rural areas, where stores and businesses might shut down for lunch; but in cities and suburbs, schools and businesses tend to stay open and workers and students consume their lunches away from home. People may work or attend school far from their homes and going home is not practical or even possible in some cases. And in the age of the Internet, the pace of work and school has quickened; workers and students are expected to get more done in a day. There is no longer time for a one- or two-hour break in the middle of the day

Nevertheless, one still might find on the streets of Barcelona, Naples, or Athens, an auto mechanic, plumber, or shopkeeper who works down the street from his house or flat. He leaves at one for a home-cooked lunch prepared by his wife and returns to work after an hour or so. Usually, he leaves a note on the door of this workplace, or he shuts the outer door and turns off the lights. Now it is far more common to see people leaving their jobs for a quick bite at the snack bar or café, or hustling into a casual restaurant where they can get a fast meal. A quick bite or a fast meal does not necessarily mean bad food, however. Patrons of a humble trattoria in Italy can find a reasonable fixed-price lunch, consisting of a pasta or soup, followed by a meat dish and a vegetable, with fruit for dessert. The trattoria only has a few options to choose from and the servers work to feed the patrons quickly and efficiently. At the very least, patrons in a snack bar can get their sandwich toasted so the cheese melts and the taste of the ingredients blends together in a satisfying way. Large offices and factories have cafeterias or canteens, where workers can buy either a hot or cold lunch at a reasonable price.

It used to be traditional for children in school to go home for lunch, but increasing numbers of children are taking their lunches with them. In many schools there is now a cafeteria that serves prepared meals for kids or at least a canteen where kids can buy sandwiches or other packaged foods to eat. Children eat their lunch at school either because they live far from the school or both parents work. At some schools, it is not unusual for kids whose parents work to stay at school and eat lunch while other kids go home to have lunch. And, as children get older and attend high school, they prefer to take their lunch break outside school and home, usually by hanging out in the school parking lot or at a local snack bar or fast food outlet like McDonald's.

After lunch, the afternoon snack becomes the next occasion for eating out. Schoolchildren might grab a bag of potato chips at a café, or they might have an ice cream cone or some candy. The culture of eating out at dinnertime varies by region, as well as the type of restaurant and the clientele it caters to. In Catalonia, especially in the cosmopolitan city of Barcelona, people love to eat out, especially for dinner. Breakfast may be a rushed coffee and pastry, but lunch out is a more leisurely affair. Restaurants open for lunch attract patrons at about one or two in the afternoon and, if one takes coffee and desert, the meal can take over an hour. After work or school, they will enjoy a snack or *merienda*, maybe coffee and pastries, or wine and tapas at a bar or café. While eating tapas and drinking wine, diners might linger a bit and turn the snack into an early dinner. Tapas are little appetizers, served on small plates to diners in bars and patrons. Tapas are never served at home. The origin of the word, tapa, literally means cover. In nineteenth-century Andalucía, "roadside innkeepers used to cover the glass of wine they served to tired and thirsty horsemen with a slice of ham, cheese, or bread." The food was meant to protect the wine inside the glass from dust or rain. The customer paid for the wine but not for the complementary tapa.[3]

In bars, patrons can choose from a variety of dishes and in restaurants, waiters will bring out a *tapita*, or "little tapa," a small plate with sausage, olives, or some almonds. In fancier restaurants, the *tapita* will be something more elaborate, perhaps a bit of salt cod with potato and garlic, or a flavored anchovy. A variety of tapas can make an entire meal and not surprisingly, many people who frequent bars after work will fill up on tapas then return home later, either to sleep or to make a simple sandwich or omelet for dinner. Those who do go out for dinner will head out late in the evening, around 9 or 10 P.M., for *cena* or dinner. Dinner consists of a multiple course meal and can take several hours. Restaurants are also open very late in Greece and in Cyprus, but dining out is less of a cosmopolitan activity than it is a family affair. The dress code in most restaurants is casual, and it would not be unusual to find extended family dining together, with grandparents, parents, and children all sitting together. Like Catalonian restaurants, Greek restaurants open late by American standards (1–2 P.M. for lunch and 8–9 P.M. for dinner) and stay open as long as the customers linger. Servers avoid rushing customers out of the restaurant, and everyone assumes that patrons have the table for as long as they wish, even if this means the entire evening. It is not unusual, then, for people to stay an hour or even two hours after the last plates are cleared.

One of the most vibrant restaurant cultures in the Mediterranean can be found in Israel, which hosts a booming hospitality industry including hotels, restaurants, and wineries that cater to tourists and citizens alike. This is somewhat of a recent development, as the region was not known for having fine cuisine until the last decade. Israeli chefs, hotel owners, sommeliers, and vintners have made great strides in terms of professional training and quality control. It is not unusual, for example, for top chefs in city hotels to have received training in Paris, New York City, or London. Israeli wines are also gaining international recognition at competitions and in the export trade. Because so many citizens have immigrated to Israel from elsewhere, restaurants in cities and suburbs offer a wide range of ethnic foods: not only Middle Eastern specialties, but Italian, French, Greek, Russian, Ethiopian, Balkan, Thai, Chinese, American, and fusion cuisine. Israel has the most multiethnic restaurant culture of the region, but other countries offer a variety of cuisines as well. This has been the case historically, given the legacy of imperialism, immigration, and tourism. In Tunisia, many restaurants with French names ("Monte Carlo" or "Le Pub") serve local and French dishes. In Cyprus, there are British pubs alongside the traditional tavernas, where one can drink a pint of beer or ale and play darts.

In some parts of the Mediterranean, it is thought the best meals are served in people's homes, not restaurants, which are reserved for tourists and traveling business people. Eating out, then, means eating in someone's home. In Morocco, dining in someone's home is made more formal by a premeal hand washing ceremony and a blessing pronounced before the meal. Many different foods are served in abundance, usually hot and cold salads followed by a tajine, then the heartiest dish like lamb or chicken followed by couscous topped with meats and vegetables. In North Africa and the Middle East, it is important not to eat everything set out for guests. This act demonstrates that the host has set out more than enough food to satisfy everyone's hunger. Everyone eats quickly and usually in silence. After the meal, diners retreat to the living room for sweets, coffee, and conversation. Here, the party can continue through the night, especially during holidays like Ramadan (see chapter 6).

Whether one is dining in a restaurant or at someone's house, the meal usually begins with something before the main course. In the Côte d'Azur, this means hors d'oeuvres, tapas in Spain, antipasti in Italy, and meze in Greece and the eastern Mediterranean. The purpose of this first course is to whet the appetite for the main course or in some cultures, they are intended to go with whatever wine or alcohol is served before the meal. These foods are served in small bite-size chunks and are frequently salty or pickled. Although many Mediterranean cultures share a preliminary course, there is a wide range of practices in terms of how these foods are consumed. In Italy, for example, diners will find an antipasto bar or table at the front of the restaurant; this table is usually loaded with the local specialties as well as some standard "Italian" appetizers such as roasted vegetables, prosciutto, and fresh mozzarella cheese. Individuals can browse and either help themselves or order from their server. Tapas in Spain are brought out to diners on little plates, although the plates are usually shared by everyone at the table. Meze are intended to be shared; diners pass around a communal plate, dipping their flatbread into the offerings. Whatever the medium of the appetizer, the ingredients are usually similar. Eggplant, for example, can be roasted and spread on toast (crostini) in Italy, roasted and mixed with tahini as baba ghanouj in Lebanon, sautéed with tomatoes, peppers, and spices and served as a meze in Morocco, or chopped into a salad with roasted peppers, tomatoes, and spices in Spain.

After the appetizer, there is considerable variation in the presentation of the meal, depending on location and the occasion, as the previous chapter explained (chapter 4). There is little difference, however, between restaurants and homes: if the pattern of the meal is casual, as in the eastern Mediterranean region, then this will be the case for restaurants as well as in people's homes. And in European countries in the Mediterranean, guests in people's homes are treated to the same formal order of dishes that they will encounter in restaurants. There may be some variation to the meal order if one is eating out at a picnic; here all the food is usually served together no matter where the picnic is held. It is worth noting, however, that in Italy, campers will bring cook stoves and pots with them so they can prepare a plate of hot pasta to be eaten as a first course, even in the middle of the woods or on the beach.

Eating out means so many different things: grabbing a quick sandwich from a street vendor, buying a hot lunch in a school cafeteria, spending a lot of money at a fancy restaurant, or feasting at a relative's house on a holiday. The diversity of experiences demonstrates that hospitality is more than custom or ritual in the Mediterranean—it is a way of life. Eating out is also a social expectation and frequently a necessity. The many venues for eating out constitute a foundation of the local economy and the relationships between cook, vendor, and consumer build a sense of community and illustrate how people of the Mediterranean relate to each other. Despite frequent worries and even protests against American fast food chains, it seems unlikely that such a lively and diverse street food culture, especially in North Africa and in the eastern Mediterranean, will ever die out. And restaurant culture, whether humble or luxurious, continues to evolve, creating ever more sophisticated cuisine while still maintaining great respect for tradition. One of the most noticeable characteristics of eating out across the Mediterranean is how much people enjoy being, and eating, together. Even in cafés or outdoor markets, individuals who do not know each other will sit or stand elbow to elbow and eat, either in quiet appreciation of the food before them or in conversation with each other. This is not to say that people in the Mediterranean do not eat a sandwich alone in a car, or a snack in front of the television; they do, although they would prefer not to. Eating is a shared event and, by extension, eating out is more than just about the food; it is about human relations and a sense of community.

NOTES

1. Anissa Helou, *Mediterranean Street Food* (New York: HarperCollins, 2002), p. xv.

2. Florian Harms and Lutz Jakel, *The Flavours of Arabia. Cookery and Food in the Middle East* (London: Thames and Hudson, 2007), p. 9.

3. Marimar Torres, *The Catalan Country Kitchen* (Reading, MA: Aris, 1992), p. 33.

6

Special Occasions

Food plays an important role in defining special occasions in the Mediterranean. Food preparation and consumption bring people together during a celebration for a shared meal that frequently becomes a central activity, if not *the* central activity of the day. Designated foods or dishes are reserved for a particular holiday; thus food reinforces the meaning of the occasion by marking the day as a special or significant one. Food's symbolic qualities can reinforce the values that individuals or communities want to think about on that occasion. Particularly for religious holidays and rituals, symbolic food serves as a medium of communication for the community to express their faith or commemorate the past. For life celebrations such as the birth of a child, weddings, or funerals, food is the medium through which people come together and express their collective feelings, whether they are joy, respect, or sorrow. Because food and its consumption make an event or celebration special, the dish or food item usually consists of something unusual or out of the ordinary. Either the food is an expensive or rare luxury (an entire roast pig or caviar) or it involves more elaborate preparation than everyday fare (a layered and decorated cake). Food both reinforces the unique qualities of the occasion and becomes one of the main reasons for individuals to gather together.

Special occasions vary greatly across regional and cultural divides. Every culture honors certain passages of life, but life celebrations can occur more or less randomly. Weddings can be planned in advance, but events like birth and death are more or less beyond the control of most individuals. Organized or planned holidays occur with greater regularity and can be dedicated to any number of causes for celebration and commemoration. Holidays are special days, marked off not only by the kind of food people eat, but frequently by time off from work and the usual rhythms of life. Celebrants may attend an elaborate feast in someone's home, or they may take a drive into the countryside to have a picnic. Given the cultural diversity of the Mediterranean, secular holidays like national or patriotic holidays differ between nations and even within nations. Even an intentionally universal holiday like International Worker's Day (May 1) is not celebrated as much as it was when it was first proclaimed a holiday in 1889, and when it is celebrated, it is less about paying tribute to workers and more about staging concerts or promoting political causes. People throughout the Mediterranean are connected through the celebration of religious occasions, however, given that the Mediterranean is the meeting place of three of the world's major religions: Christianity, Islam, and Judaism. In all three religions, food plays a significant role in bringing people together, imparting certain lessons or values, and serving as the bridge between the externally visible routines of ritual or everyday practice and the inner life of faith and belief. Each of these religions maintains a vibrant food culture, expressed not only through holidays but also through everyday practices.

In examining the role that food plays in defining and commemorating special occasions, this chapter focuses primarily on religious events: holidays, celebrations, and everyday practices. Specific foods are prepared and eaten on special days and in certain ceremonies or rituals. Moreover, in two of the major faiths, Judaism and Islam, dietary laws or restrictions play an important role in making the everyday practice of preparing and eating food a special event in itself, symbolizing one's community, one's belief, and one's relationship to God. In effect, dietary laws make every day a special occasion. This chapter first describes the special foods and rituals of Judaism, followed by Islam and Christianity, noting which foods and meals define special occasions, as well as how those foods are prepared and used for the event. The rest of the chapter discusses the role of food in nonreligious events or foods that are eaten for special occasions that have nonreligious symbolic significance. Local holidays that celebrate some aspect of community or history, as well as national secular holidays and celebrations of the harvest, use food in ways that are similar to those of religious events: to bring the community together, to symbolize certain values or myths that individuals live by, and to mark the day or event as being out of the ordinary.

In all these cases, food performs a variety of social and cultural work. Most important, shared meals and feasts bring the community together, re-affirming the bonds between family, friends, neighbors, or citizens. Because food can be prepared in a variety of ways (roasted, boiled, baked, molded, or stuffed), it can symbolize certain events, individuals, or qualities the special occasion commemorates. Food's symbolism can be quite obvious: a loaf of bread can be shaped to resemble a Christian saint, or the symbolism can be more abstract: in some cultures, fava beans have come to be associ-ated with death and the dead. In either case, people have actively assigned meanings to food that stretch beyond simple nourishment and sustenance. And when particular foods are eaten for a special occasion, food makes abstract values like community, faith, and veneration more real. An event is marked as special not only by the presence or abundance of food but fre-quently by the absence of food through fasting and abstention from certain foods. Both practices reaffirm community or remind individuals of certain obligations. And last, because food for special occasions is prepared in a certain way, even using special utensils or tools, individuals who prepare and eat the foods tend to remember the holiday through the preparation and consumption of certain dishes or meals. Memories of these foods are preserved in people's minds, passed down through generations, or perhaps even described in a cookbook. Certain foods, their preparation, and con-sumption bring people together not only for the special occasion, but by tying people together in the realm of memory, in terms of thinking with and through food about a shared past, a sense of community in the present, and hope for the future.

FOOD AND RELIGION: SACRED CELEBRATIONS AND EVERYDAY LIFE

Because the Mediterranean is home to three major religions, there is a diversity of religious practices regarding food, both for special occasions and for everyday life. Yet each faith—Judaism, Islam, and Christianity—shares certain attitudes and practices regarding food. In all three religions, for example, the faithful are supposed to offer thanks to God before a meal, usually as a measure of gratitude for providing the food to be eaten, but for other reasons as well. Each religion bestows symbolic significance on cer-tain foods to be used in special meals or ceremonies. And in all three reli-gions, abstinence from food, whether through fasting or food prohibitions, tests and proves one's faith and capacity to sacrifice. There are significant differences as well in terms of the purpose or origins of food rituals, as well as differences that evolve over the course of time. For example, Christians do not adhere to as many dietary restrictions as Muslims or Jews. Common attitudes toward food prevail, however. Indeed, the use of food to commemorate one's faith and religious practice, significant to all three religions, links the populations of the Mediterranean together, not only on special occasions but every day.

Judaism

It is commonly said that Jewish holidays involve either fasting or feasting. Certain foods or special dishes make Jewish religious holidays and rituals significant. On so many of these holidays, food offers a way for the faithful to revisit their past; food is used in very tangible ways in Jewish rituals to explain the past and its relevance to Jews today. Thus special occasion foods are more than symbolic; they instruct the faithful. In times of fasting, the absence of food reminds people of past sufferings among Jews and brings contemporary participants closer to God through self-denial and purification. In everyday life, dietary regulations, called kashrut, reinforce the individual's faith and define the devout Jewish

A Passover Seder plate contains symbolic foods used during the Seder meal. From top center: horseradish, a shank bone, *charoset* (a mixture of fruit, wine, and nuts), lettuce, parsley, and an egg. AP Photo/Dan Goodman.

community through the practices of purchasing, preparing, and eating food. Jewish populations throughout the Mediterranean are diverse: European or Ashkenazi Jews populate the south of France, parts of Italy, Greece, and Israel. North African or Sephardic Jews live throughout North Africa and the Levant. Although they celebrate the same holidays, Sephardic and Ashkenazi Jews draw on their regional culinary heritage, and the foods served on special occasions vary in accordance with local food culture.[1]

The most obvious symbolic use of food during Jewish holidays is the Passover Seder, in particular the foods on the Seder plate, which represent different moments in the history of the Jewish people. Passover is a holiday celebrated for eight days in spring, commemorating the Jews' exodus from Egypt and the liberation of Israelites from slavery. Passover is also known as the Festival of the Unleavened Bread, because anything made with yeast is forbidden at this time. Before the Passover meal, a plate is prepared with different foods, and the head of the table explains each of the foods to the others. A roasted shank-bone recalls the paschal offerings brought to the Temple in Jerusalem in ancient times; bitter herbs such as horseradish root or lettuce remind diners of the bitterness the Jews experienced as slaves in Egypt; a green vegetable (usually parsley) represents hope and faith in the future; an egg represents the continuing cycle of life; *charoset* (a combination of apples or dried fruit, wine, walnuts, and cinnamon) stands for the mortar that Jews used to make bricks out of in Egypt; and a dish of salt water symbolizes the tears they shed in Egypt. After Passover diners receive and eat this "history-lesson-on-a-plate," there is a large meal. Because extended family gather together and because there are different Seders given for different communities and groups, preparations for the meals can be rather time-consuming and involved. Moreover, in the days leading up to Passover, all traces of *hametz* must be removed from the house in a ritual cleansing of the house of the forbidden food. *Hametz* or *chometz* translates into a food that is fermented or could cause fermentation. Bread made with yeast is strictly forbidden and so unleavened products like matzoh—a cracker-like flatbread—replace bread. Ashkenazi Jews will not eat any grains such as wheat, spelt, oats, rye, barley, rice, or legumes. Sephardic Jews of the Mediterranean region did not accept the ruling of post-Talmudic authorities on rice and legumes, given that rice and legumes formed the basis of their diet. So during Passover, Sephardic Jews eat rice and legumes, as well as some seeds or spices such as allspice, fennel, cumin, nutmeg, and sesame, and flavorings such as rose water or orange-flower water.[2] A typical Passover meal in North Africa might include a tajine made with lamb and prunes with honey, Tunisian sausage,

Moroccan carrot salad spiced with cumin, and an artichoke stew, along with the more familiar matzoh and *charoset*.

In almost every other Jewish holiday, special foods, or the lack of food, serve to remind Jews of what and why they are celebrating. On the Jewish new year, Rosh Hashanah, sweet foods are served so as to ensure that one has a sweet year; for centuries Jews have dipped pieces of challah bread, apples, grapes, and other fruits in honey. Round loaves of challah bread symbolize the cyclical nature of life, the coming back to beginnings and the hope that the coming year will be complete. In Tunisia, Jews serve a beef and bean stew with semolina bread for Rosh Hashanah. There is nothing particularly symbolic about the main course, but accompanying the food are pomegranates, whose seeds symbolize one's good deeds in the coming year; a bowl of sesame seeds to stand for virtue; and figs, quince, and dates symbolize a sweet new year. Across the Mediterranean, Jews avoid eating any foods that are black or dark on Rosh Hashanah, as the holiday is intended to be a joyful one. On the holiest day of the Jewish calendar, Yom Kippur, the day of atonement, a 25-hour fast fulfills the prophecy for one to practice self-denial, and other writings stress fasting as a reminder of repentance, in asking for God's forgiveness. For some, fasting enables the individual to ignore physical desires like hunger, concentrating instead on spiritual needs like repentance and self-improvement. The fast is broken by a simple meal, prepared in advance and quickly reheated. Five days after Yom Kippur, Sukkot (Sukkos), the Feast of Booths, commemorates the 40 years Jews lived in the wilderness before entering Israel. Coming as it does in the fall, Sukkot also celebrates the harvest, as a temporary shelter or sukkah is built in people's yards and decorated with hanging fruits and vegetables. Because all meals are supposed to be eaten in the sukkah for the seven days of the celebration, families invite friends over to dine or members of a synagogue might dine together as well. There are no specified foods that one must consume in the sukkah, so most people prepare traditional favorites or involve their children in meal preparation, as the holiday is supposed to be joyful and fun. The sukkah, however, is supposed to be decorated with *etrog* (citron) and *luvav* (palm, willow, and myrtle branches bound together). On Chanukah, fried pancakes (latkes) and donuts are served. It is not the foods but the oil that they are fried in that is significant to the holiday. Oil calls to mind the miracle of the Maccabean revolt (the candelabra in the temple burned for eight days even though there was only enough oil for one day). These special foods have become symbolic over the course of centuries, and although there may be some variation between

Sephardic and Ashkenazi traditions, or between regions depending on local traditions and available foods, Jewish communities throughout the Mediterranean use food to represent or call to mind past struggles and events in ancient Jewish life. Sometimes, symbolic food is a more contemporary creation, as on Shavuot, the holiday commemorating the giving of the Torah at Mount Sinai. Cookies are made in the shapes of mountains and Torah scrolls.

Latkes

1 pound potatoes, peeled

1 large egg, beaten

1/3 cup flour

1 teaspoon salt

Oil for frying

Use a food processor to grate potatoes, squeeze out any excess liquid and place in large mixing bowl. Add egg, flour, salt and pepper to taste. Stir well. Heat 1/2 inch of oil in large skillet. Drop potato batter into oil and fry, flattening each pancake with a spatula and cooking until golden brown. Drain on paper towels and serve immediately, either with apple sauce or sour cream or dusted with powdered sugar.

Using specific foods and preparing traditional dishes are a means to connect Jews with the symbols of their faith and to reinforce the lessons of their history. On another level, these same foods and dishes create powerful and lasting memories regarding the content and meaning of the special occasion. These include memories of sharing food at table as well as learning how to prepare a certain dish, or planning a holiday menu. Although the origin and purpose of special days like Rosh Hashanah and Chanukah are religiously inspired, foods order and define the event. Ask people what they do on a holiday like Passover and their answer will most certainly include discussion of food and food preparation.

The Jewish Sabbath, or Shabbat, is also a time for commemorating one's faith through the preparation and consumption of food. Although the Sabbath occurs every week and is therefore more frequent and less "special" than a holiday, it is nonetheless significant because families and friends gather together to eat. In more traditional Jewish communities in the Mediterranean, wives and mothers spend a lot of time preparing special foods before the Sabbath (on Friday nights and Saturday mornings) and serving food to their families on the Sabbath day. These tasks take some planning and forethought, given that the cooking must be completed before the Sabbath begins. Moreover, depending on the size of the family and the expectations of family members for a good Sabbath meal, food preparations can be quite complicated or involved, as evidenced by this description of a Middle Eastern Jewish woman's work:

For a typical Sabbath on which her children and grandchildren visit her, one woman prepares two cakes (one with cheese and one with no milk products), cookies (bagelah) for visiting grandchildren, nuts and seeds that she herself has cleaned, salted, and baked, soup, chicken stuffed with potatoes (for the recipe the chicken is first boiled, the potatoes are fried separately, and then the chicken and the potatoes are baked together—three separate processes), string beans, rice and tomato sauce, burekas (filled pastries for which a stiff dough is rolled out and then spread with margarine and folded in thirds once each day for three successive days), Sabbath stew (a bean, vegetable, and meat stew that sits in the oven from Friday afternoon until it is eaten for lunch on Saturday), two different eggplant salads (one fried and one baked), and several vegetable salads (at least one consists of tomatoes, cucumbers, and onions cut into tiny pieces).[3]

Not every Sabbath meal is so elaborate. Sometimes, a much simpler meal is served, along with kosher wine or grape juice, and two loaves of challah to remind Jews of the story of manna falling in the desert so that no Jew would have to gather food on the Sabbath. For some women, though, food preparation plays an important role in their religious life. Anthropologists who have studied traditional Jewish communities in Algeria and Israel have observed a contrast between the men of the community, who prayed together, and the women, who prepared food in order to properly maintain and nourish their families, a task they understood as central to their faith. In these communities, men celebrate or observe the Sabbath while women make or prepare the Sabbath. This does not necessarily mean, however, that women's roles are less significant because they focus so intensely on the home and the preparation of food. As one anthropologist noted, women in these communities become the ritual experts and guardians of law and tradition, with the power to make or create the Sabbath or a special occasion. For these women, cooking is a sacred activity because it "embodies, concretizes, dramatizes, and ritualizes a number of the central elements in Judaism."[4]

For observant Jews, following dietary laws, or kashrut, is a way to demonstrate one's spirituality every day. Thus the kosher kitchen is the spiritual center of the home and food preparation is a highly significant act of faith and devotion. Kosher literally means fit or proper and describes the types of foods and ways you can prepare them as specified by the Torah. These laws apply primarily to the eating of animal products (meat and dairy), as plants (fruits, vegetables, nuts, herbs, spices, and grains) are by definition kosher. All foods are then classified according to the category they fit: meat, dairy, or pareve (neither meat nor dairy, but vegetables, fruits, grains, eggs, and nondairy substitutes like margarine). Acceptable or kosher meat must come from animals that chew cud and have cloven hooves. In addition, these animals must be ritually slaughtered, and the meat must be soaked in cold water and salted to remove all blood before cooking. Kosher meats include beef, lamb, veal, and goat; pork and all carnivorous animals are forbidden. Shellfish are forbidden, as are shark, eel, squid, snails, and octopus. Dairy products must come from kosher animals and must not be cooked and served with meat or poultry. Keeping meat and dairy foods separate is an important part of keeping kosher; this means the two types of food must be consumed separately. If one eats dairy first, then one can eat meat afterward, but if one eats meat first, there is a ritual waiting period of between one and five hours to eat dairy. A kosher kitchen will have two sets of dishes, pots, pans, and utensils for preparing meat and dairy. All implements that touch the foods must be washed separately, so as to avoid any possible mixing of the foods. And there are no prepared dishes that mix meat and dairy together; thus a cheese pizza with a meat topping is not kosher.

Following the laws of kashrut is a means to link oneself to God every day through the mundane practice of preparing, eating, and thinking about food. Like dietary regulations found in other religions, kashrut becomes a distinctive way to remind the faithful of their obligations and faith. Many observant Jews do not think very much about keeping kosher because these rules become internalized, but for some Jewish populations in the Mediterranean, following the laws of kashrut can be difficult at times. For example, one can readily find kosher pizza in Israel, but grabbing a quick snack in areas where there is not a large Jewish population requires a bit more thought about what kind of food is available. Many processed foods can contain trace amounts of dairy products, so one must carefully read labels so as to avoid mixing meat and dairy products accidentally. And for Jews with limited kitchen space, maintaining and cleaning two sets of dishes can be a frustrating experience if meat and dairy are mixed. Despite such difficulties, kashrut sanctifies everyday life by providing guidelines for the faithful to express their faith and community with and through food.

Islam

For Muslims in the Mediterranean, food and eating are powerful vehicles through which people express their faith and values. In addition to reminding the individual of his or her relationship to Allah, food and food rituals emphasize the importance of community and one's obligations to others. Meals with friends, which are special occasions in themselves, are also suffused with spiritual meaning. At the beginning of the meal, the host will pronounce *"Bismillah,"* which means "in the name of Allah" and then this will be repeated by everyone present at the table. Bread is then broken and offered to each guest to scoop food from a communal dish. The way that one eats is also an expression of one's faith. In Morocco, people eat using the thumb and first two fingers of the right hand (the left hand is considered unclean), using bread as a utensil. They do this, because, in the words of Moroccan chef Hassan M'Souli, "to eat with one finger is said to have the devil's influence, eating with three fingers is a sign of the Prophet, and only gluttons eat with four or five."[5] After the meal, the host and guests thank Allah once more. Hospitality and appropriate ritualized behavior around food remind Muslims every day of their relationship with Allah. As with Judaism, fasting and feasting are special events for the Muslim communities and dietary regulations reaffirm individual and community religious obligations.

Muslims follow the tenets of the Qur'an when thinking about food and diet. Dietary rules distinguish certain foods as either allowed (halal) or forbidden (haram). Forbidden foods include pork and pork products, any meat that is not slaughtered in the prescribed Islamic way, blood, carnivorous animals or birds of prey, and alcohol and intoxicants or any food with alcohol in it. These rules should be followed at all times, whether one is at home or dining out. For example, Muslims are discouraged from eating in restaurants that serve forbidden food or alcohol. In practical terms, Muslim dietary restrictions mean that meat should never be served rare, but always well done. Cooking with wine is out of the question and chefs in four-star restaurants in Islamic countries must be creative in thinking of flavorful alternatives to cooking with wine. Some chefs combine fruit juices and vinegars to mimic the flavor of wine; others simply do not make coq au vin or a dish that calls for alcohol in the recipe. Halal meat should come from animals killed by ritual slaughter, which is governed by strict rules and, if done correctly, is intended to preserve the dignity of the animal (animals are not slaughtered in groups; the knife is not shown to the animal; before slaughter, the animal should be stroked and have its throat pointing to Mecca; the fatal cut should be a swift and clean one to the windpipe, gullet, and both jugular arteries; a prayer is recited during the slaughtering process) and death comes quickly.

Fasting or abstaining from food constitutes both a somber reflection on, and a celebration of, the Muslim faith. The fourth ritual observance in the five pillars of Islam, fasting is a complete control of one's appetite and

Egyptian Muslims wait patiently to begin eating during the holy month of Ramadan. AP Photo/Amr Nabil.

therefore one's self. Because fasting is about controlling bodily appetites, it enables the individual to pay more attention to one's spiritual nature and therefore come closer to Allah. In enabling the individual to experience hunger, fasting helps one develop compassion for the less fortunate by understanding the bodily sufferings of those who cannot afford to eat. Fasting also teaches Muslims to be thankful for what they do receive from Allah. In periods of fasting, Muslims avoid all food and drink from sunrise to sunset; people with health conditions and pregnant or nursing women are excused. Muslims spend more time fasting than Jews and most Christians do (however, the Greek Orthodox Church mandates many fasting days). There are both prescribed fasting days like the celebration of Ramadan and voluntary fasting days every Monday and Thursday.

One of the most significant events in the Muslim calendar is Ramadan, a 30-day fast. Ramadan happens on the ninth month in the Islamic calendar, the month when God revealed the holy book of Islam, the Qur'an, to the prophet Muhammad. During Ramadan, the faithful worship, read the Qur'an, give charity and perform other virtuous deeds, and fast. All Muslims at the age of puberty must fast from sunrise until sunset. A proper fast means abstaining from all food and drink, which takes a great deal of

A Turkish man tastes dates at a bazaar in Istanbul. Traditionally, Muslims break their Ramadan fast with dates and water. AP Photo/Murad Sezer.

willpower and strength when Ramadan falls in the warmer months and thirst can become intense. After sunset there are prayers and then Muslims can eat. In people's homes, a dinner is prepared to eat after prayers. In restaurants, tables are set up for the evening meal with drink, salad, and bread. Street vendors prepare all kinds of treats, like candy and pastries, for people to consume after the evening prayer; but in the meantime, everyone has to wait patiently before they can break the fast.

When the fast ends, some Muslims prefer to begin feasting straight away, but others break their fast with a few dates and some water, to prepare the stomach for the feast to come. Dates are thought to bring good luck and prosperity and are the food that the prophet Muhammad ate during his fast. When Muslims break their fast, they eat a large meal composed of favorite foods. In Morocco, the Ramadan fast is ended with *harira*, a soup made with meat, legumes, vegetables, and spices; the word *harira* means silk, as the soup is supposed to be as soft as silk and to delight the senses like silk does. Moroccans also enjoy *bisteeya*, a pigeon pie. In Egypt, a Ramadan tradition is *ful*, a seasoned bean dish, and bread. Elsewhere Muslims may break their fast with a couscous and a meat dish. Across North Africa and the Levant, Muslims break their fast with regional specialty dishes or foods they like to eat; there is no universal Ramadan dish. A typical meal during Ramadan might be fruit juice or carob drink, followed by fish soup, then a fish and potato casserole served with rice and eggplant and tomato salad. Hot soup at the beginning of the meal is supposed to stimulate the digestion after a period of fasting. Then the main courses should be filling, providing vitamins, minerals and other essential nutrients. After meals, there are sweets: puddings, cakes, pastries, and candies, to provide the body with adequate energy.[6]

Harira

1 pound cubed meat (lamb, beef, or chicken)

1 teaspoon ground turmeric

1 teaspoon pepper

1 teaspoon salt

1 teaspoon cinnamon

1/4 teaspoon hot pepper

3 tablespoons butter or margarine

2 stalks celery, chopped

2 medium onions, chopped

1/2 cup fresh chopped cilantro

3 medium tomatoes, seeded and diced, or 1 large can of chopped tomatoes

7 cups water

3/4 cup dried lentils

1 can chickpeas, rinsed and drained

1/2 pound vermicelli, broken into pieces

2 eggs, beaten

Juice of 1 lemon

In a large soup pot combine meat, spices, butter, celery, onions, and cilantro and cook over low heat, stirring frequently, for 5 minutes. Add tomatoes and cook for 15 minutes. Add water and lentils, bring mixture to a boil and reduce heat, simmer covered for 2 hours. Add chickpeas and vermicelli and cook 15 minutes or until vermicelli is tender. Stir in eggs and lemon juice and cook a few minutes more. Add salt and pepper to taste. Garnish with chopped mint leaves.

It is customary for Muslims to eat two meals during Ramadan: the first is called *iftar* and is the largest meal, eaten shortly after sunset and consisting of multiple courses. The second meal is called *suhur* and is a lighter meal, eaten just before sunrise. In some cases, people who dine out or eat at other peoples houses eat so much and stay so long at *iftar* that a host serves *suhur* just before everyone goes home. Because Ramadan involves 30 days of fasting, one might assume that the celebration emphasizes asceticism or deprivation, but this is not entirely the case. In fact, many Muslims break their fast by indulging in their favorite foods and eating more than their fill after the sun sets. Throughout the Mediterranean, Muslims actually eat more food during Ramadan because of all the feasting that occurs after the fasting.

In addition to Ramadan, the Muslim calendar includes several holidays in which food plays a central role in the celebration. After Ramadan, the day of *Eid al-Fitr* is celebrated. It is customary to eat dates and other sweets to commemorate Muhammad's consumption of only dates and camel's milk during his month of fasting. Feasting is a central part of *Eid al-Fitr*, and so preparations are made in the last days of Ramadan to ensure there will be more than enough food for family and friends to eat. Muslim families will donate foods such as rice, barley, and dates to poor families to ensure that they will have enough to eat for the celebration. On the first day of *Eid al-Fitr*, there is a mid-day feast, which is a welcome occasion after an entire month of nightly meals. The dishes served vary according to regional and individual tastes. In Algeria, Muslims start their feast with soup or stew, then eat either lamb, beef, or seafood for the main course. Egyptians make special cookies called *kahk* (spiced cookies either rolled in sesame seeds or stuffed with dates and nuts, then dusted with powdered sugar) to give to friends and family, and it is customary to enjoy fish for lunch. In Turkey, all kinds of dishes are eaten for lunch and children take special delight in going to friends and family to collect candy in a celebration similar to the American Halloween. *Eid al-Fitr* is, above all, a family holiday where the extended family gathers at the home of the most senior member.

Another significant Muslim holiday is *Eid al-Adha*, which happens 70 days after *Eid al-Fitr*, at the end of the month when Muslims make the pilgrimage to Mecca. People usually eat fish, particularly salted cod, as well as a variety of homemade biscuits. Known as the Festival of Sacrifice or the Great Festival, *Eid al-Adha* commemorates the story of Abraham, who was prepared to follow God's instructions to sacrifice his son, who was ultimately spared (a ram was sacrificed instead). Any family that can afford to pays to have a sheep slaughtered and distributes the meat among relatives and the needy. Lamb meat is prepared in many ways and forms: in soup, baked, grilled, and sautéed. And throughout the Mediterranean, some Muslims celebrate *Moulids*, which are festivals in honor of a local holy person (Christians in North Africa and the Middle East might honor a local saint with a *Moulid*). A *Moulid* lasts anywhere from a single day to a week, and food plays a special part in the celebration. Food stands and carts selling special treats are always set up close to the holy person's tomb or the site of the celebration.

Although Muslims throughout the Mediterranean cook and eat different dishes to celebrate special occasions like Ramadan or *Eid al-Adha*, they share a common belief that food, or the lack thereof, defines and commemorates the significance of the holiday. Food brings family and community together during religious holidays, and fasting draws attention to the spiritual importance of the act of food consumption. Muslims make foods with ingredients that have religious symbolic significance, like dates, or they prepare elaborate foods that they do not eat as often, like roasted lamb. In particular, sweets like candy, pastries, and cookies mark holidays as out of the usual culinary routine for most Muslims, who eat fresh fruit for dessert and snacks. Muslims are reminded of the spiritual significance of food daily, however, when they follow dietary regulations and restrictions.

Christianity

In contrast to Judaism and Islam, Christianity adheres to few dietary restrictions or regulations. Prohibitions on blood, carrion, or foods previously offered to idols fell out of practice or were not enforced over time. Those denominations that did adopt food prohibitions (Seventh-Day Adventists and Mormons) are not all that numerous in the Mediterranean region. Instead, most Christians are Catholics or members of the Greek Orthodox Church. Christians throughout the Mediterranean prepare and eat many special foods and dishes on Christmas and Easter; they also abstain from certain foods or fast to get closer to God or to practice self-denial. Fasting occupies a central place in the Greek Orthodox faith. In other parts of the European Mediterranean, however, many Christians do not consider themselves that religious, if one measures religiosity by church attendance. For example, in Italy, the seat of the Catholic Church, fewer Catholics attend mass now than they did 20 or 30 years ago. Such indicators of religiosity are troublesome, however, given that in Italy, there is a great deal of informal worship. Thus although masses seem sparsely attended, street altars to Saints or the Virgin Mary are well tended on a regular basis. The preparation and consumption of food are perhaps forms of informal worship, and

Christians throughout the Mediterranean agree that food occupies a central place in the celebration of religious holidays, both as a means of marking the event as special and as symbolic reinforcement of Christian values and community.

No food is more symbolic to Christians than bread. In a Catholic mass, for example, people consume a breadlike wafer, called the host, during Holy Communion. The host represents the body of Jesus. On major holidays such as Christmas and Easter, foods made with wheat tend to be the most popular holiday foods—not only breads of all types but also cookies, pastries, and cakes. In parts of southern Italy and in Sicily, bread dough is twisted and shaped to resemble a religious image or scene; in Greece, breads called *prosforon* (a plain, round loaf of bread made with very fine flour) are brought to the Church as offerings and breads called *artos* are made and offered to a favorite saint several times a year. Bread and other foods made with wheat are symbols of prosperity, fertility, and mercy for Christians; but perhaps most importantly, wheat symbolizes the resurrection of Jesus because in the life cycle of the grain, wheat dies and is reborn months later in the form of a spike that becomes a plant. In the Old Testament of the Bible, wheat and bread are symbols of the fertility or fecundity of the earth; in the New Testament, wheat and bread are depicted as the supreme gift from God to humankind in that they extend life by providing nourishment. In many ancient cultures, wheat, whether in the form of breads or porridges, occupied a special place in celebrations and rituals, probably because wheat contained the mysteries of life and death within the same plant.

Special breads and other foods made with wheat occupy a central place in Christian holiday celebrations. On Christmas and Easter, sweet breads, frequently studded with nuts and dried or candied fruits, are eaten in the morning or as part of the large holiday meal. At Christmas, one can find the sweet breads known as panettone all around Italy. Such breads used to be made at home or by local bakers, but they are now made industrially and sold commercially in cafés, supermarkets, and department stores. During Easter, in Greece, bread dough is wrapped around dyed eggs (at Easter, they are usually colored red) then baked. At Christmas and Easter in Greece, breads and other sweets made with honey and nuts symbolize fertility and prosperity. And on New Year's day in Greece, Christians make and eat something called St. Basil's bread (*vassilopita*), which has a coin inserted in it for good luck and prosperity in the coming year. And the French *bûche de Noël*, or Yule log, is a decorated cake roll popular not only in France, but in North African countries with a French colonial legacy. In addition to bread and other foods made with wheat, sweets such as candies abound at

Bûche de Noël. © J. Susan Cole Stone.

Christmas and Easter. Christians in the Mediterranean celebrate Epiphany, which occurs 12 days after Christmas and marks the event of the Magi giving their gifts to the baby Jesus. In the days before Epiphany, street vendors and bakeries sell all kinds of little sweets and toys for kids, who receive gifts from family or the Epiphany witch, *"la Befana,"* as she is known in Italy. Street fairs offer sweets and special foods for children and their families, who enjoy a day off from work and school.

Vassilopita

1 cup butter, softened

2 cups sugar

3 cups flour

6 eggs

2 teaspoons baking powder

1 cup warm milk

1/2 teaspoon baking soda

2 tablespoons lemon juice

1/2 cup slivered almonds

3 tablespoons sugar

Preheat oven to 350°F and butter or grease a 10–12 inch round cake pan. Cream butter and sugar, add flour and mix, then add eggs and mix well. Combine baking powder and warm milk, add to the egg mixture and mix thoroughly. Combine lemon juice and baking soda then add to batter. Pour into cake pan. Bake for 20 minutes. Remove and sprinkle nuts and sugar on top. Return to oven and bake another 30 minutes or until cake springs back when touched. Remove from oven and after a few minutes, slit the cake with a sharp knife and insert a coin. Cover slit mark with more sugar. Cool cake for 15 minutes then turn out onto serving platter. When serving, slice cake and serve pieces to guests in order from youngest to oldest. Whoever gets the coin will have good luck for the coming year.

Traditional meals for Christian holidays such as Christmas and Easter vary greatly depending on regional traditions, individual preference, and food trends. Sometimes, the meal has religious significance; for example, in Greece, a whole roasted lamb is eaten at Easter, a practice that goes back to pagan sacrificial rites or ancient Greek heroes' banquets. Today, lamb symbolizes the sacrifice God made with his son. On Christmas Eve in Italy, people eat fish or seafood, adhering to a Lenten tradition of abstaining from meat. Some families may make as many as 10, 15, or even 20 separate fish and seafood dishes for Christmas Eve. In France, a huge feast called *le Réveillon* is eaten after midnight mass on Christmas Eve. Eaten in people's homes or in restaurants and cafés that stay open all night, the feast consists of traditional Christmas foods such as oysters, escargot, seafood, smoked salmon, or caviar for starters, followed by turkey, capon, goose, or chicken for the main course. Everything is washed down with generous amounts of wine or champagne.

The food served at *le Réveillon* has little religious or symbolic significance; rather, the meal is regarded as an opportunity for friends and family to gather and eat well. Regional and family traditions tend to influence food choices more strongly than does religious symbolism for Mediterranean Catholics. For example, throughout France and Italy, Easter means lots of chocolate. In France, master chocolatiers make elaborate chocolate eggs, rabbits, and even fish (actually to celebrate the month of April, the *poisson d'Avril* is an April Fool's joke, but chocolate fish can be found throughout the entire month) for customers to admire, purchase, and eat. In Italy, hollow chocolate eggs of all sizes are filled with toys and wrapped in shiny paper. Most of the eggs are commercially made, available in supermarkets, cafés, and bars, and children look forward to the toys inside as well as the chocolate. During Christmas, special treats are also mass produced for Italian consumers. *Torrone,* a kind of nougat, is produced in northern Italy; panettone, a light cake studded with candied fruit and raisins, originally hails from Milan but is likely to be made in factories across the Italian peninsula. Panforte, a spicy, dense cake with hazelnuts, honey, and almonds, was originally a regional specialty, but thanks to industrial production and marketing, it is enjoyed by all Italians during the Christmas season.

Similarly, in Catholic Spain, the emphasis during holidays such as Christmas and Easter is on feasting at home with the family. Before Christmas, special markets are set up, filled with different foods, especially dried fruits and sweet baked goods. On Christmas Eve, menu choices vary by region, either a baked fish dish or stuffed chicken. And on Christmas day, menus vary widely, with families choosing from seafood, fish, turkey,

lamb, or pork, accompanied by wine, cider, or cava, a white or pink spar-
kling wine from Catalonia. One of the most important Christmas desserts
in Catalonia is *turrón*, or nougat. Made with honey or sugar, *turrón* is
flavored with chocolate, coconut, or orange, and it is made with either
ground or whole almonds. In Catalonia, the day after Christmas, Saint
Stephen's Day, is also a holiday. People usually consume the same dishes
that they do on Christmas, perhaps even the leftovers from Christmas
dinner.

Few of the foods that Mediterranean Christians eat for Christmas and
Easter have any obvious symbolic significance. Instead, the emphasis
during these holidays is on community and feasting. Feasting, of course,
constitutes an important counterbalance to fasting, which was more prevalent in the past for Christians observing Lent or those engaged in mo-
nastic ways of life. Historically, feasting served symbolic social functions.
For centuries, events like Carnival were rare and unique opportunities for
peasants and others to finally eat their fill. And if they could eat their fill
because their landlord provided the food, peasants were reminded of their
master's beneficence with every mouthful that they ate. Today, feasting
serves an important social function; it brings friends and family together
to enjoy many different types of dishes. It demonstrates the munificence
and hospitality of the host and/or hostess, and sometimes, if the feast is
prepared by several members of the family, it underscores the value of
hard work and cooperation in the kitchen.

Like the faithful in the other religions of the Mediterranean, Christians spend time fasting or abstaining from certain foods. For members
of the Greek Orthodox Church, fasting means total abstinence from
foods derived from animals containing red blood, dairy products, and
sometimes olive oil and wine. Strict observance to the fasting calendar
means a collective fasting period of more than 180 days in the year. The
major fast periods include Lent, Holy Week before Easter, the Fast of the
Apostles (which lasts between one and six weeks between Pentecost and
the Feast of Saints Peter and Paul), the Fast of Dormition and Theoto-
kos (August 1–14), and a fast in the two weeks before Christmas. There
are also numerous individual fast days throughout the calendar. Christians outside the Greek Orthodox Church fast during the Lenten season,
which occurs in the 40 days between Ash Wednesday and Holy Saturday, the day before Easter Sunday. Lent commemorates the 40 days that
Jesus spent in the desert being tempted by the Devil; therefore fasting
for 40 days (not including Sundays) symbolizes the triumph of the spirit
over the temptations of the body. Historically, Christians were forbidden from eating any animal products and had to fast every day of Lent,

which meant they could consume only one meal later in the day. The rules of abstinence relaxed and meat, eggs, and dairy products were the only foods forbidden because they afforded greater pleasure than other foods. Dairy products and eggs were eventually allowed, and, today, abstinence rules have relaxed considerably. Catholics should fast and abstain from eating meat on Ash Wednesday; yet there is considerable variation among Catholics regarding food restrictions on Fridays during Lent. Some Catholics abstain from meat and/or fast on the Fridays during Lent, but others may give up a favorite food or drink during Lent to remind themselves of the temptation of Jesus Christ. Others may give up something besides food.

Given the scarcity of food in the region of the Mediterranean in the past, the practice of fasting for such a long period in the early spring makes sense, as it would stretch out the remainder of the harvest. Before such lengthy fasts, Christians would feast for a period before Lent, known in many areas as Carnival, once considered a time for feasting and mischief. Right before the Lenten fast began, a family or community might kill a pig and eat just about every part, or on Fat Tuesday (Shrove Tuesday), southern Italians would eat a meal of pasta and sausage. This meal may sound simple by today's standards, but hundreds of years ago, this would have been an incredible feast. In this world of abundance and overproduction, it is difficult to imagine the circumstances of poverty and want, where Carnival meant the opportunity to finally eat one's fill of food. Today, Carnival is not about eating enough, but it is devoted to parties, parades, and other special events. Food plays a prominent role in some of the festivities; for example in Sicily it is traditional to eat pastries called cannoli, fried pastry tubes filled with a sweet ricotta cheese and cream mixture. On the island of Sardinia, children wear costumes and masks, and their parents take them around town to visit friends and family. Every house offers pastries or candies, or perhaps a glass of new wine for the adults. *Orillettas,* fried pastry braids dripping with powdered sugar or honey, are one of the favorite treats for Sardinian carnival.[7] If Christians are about to participate in fasting or abstaining from a particular food during Lent, they may indulge a little bit in some extra meat or sweets in the weeks or days before Lent.

Special foods frequently figure prominently in Christian traditions known as Saint's days. Throughout Italy and Greece, Saints are commemorated and celebrated for their virtues or for the community they protect. Many villages, towns, and cities have a particular, or patron, saint that protects the citizens and is therefore honored with a celebration or event. Thus many communities "personalize" the saint and the way he or she is celebrated, and so there is great variety in terms of what the celebration actually looks like. For many saint's days, food constitutes an important part of the commemoration and celebration. One of the most popular Saint's days, celebrated by many Italians, is the day of St. Joseph (the father of Jesus), or San Giuseppe, on March 19. Usually, the celebration of St. Joseph happens right in the middle of Lent and thus comes as welcome relief to the austerity of the season. Italians make bread of all types; sweet fried breads made with rice or wheat flour are popular in the form of *zeppole, fritelle,* or *bigné* di San Giuseppe. Pastries feature prominently on this day because Saint Joseph is the patron saint of pastry chefs. In other places, bakers shape bread to resemble carpenter's tools to bring to mind Joseph's profession, or the bread is shaped to resemble Jesus, or elements of the Crucifixion like a crown of thorns. In Sicily, ritual banquets were, and still are, staged. Called *altare di San Giuseppe* (the altar of St. Joseph), these banquets may be organized by a single family or an entire community. The meal is simple and consists of some variation of bread and legumes: sometimes a soup served with bread or the stew of *pasta e fagioli,* or pasta and beans. The meal is supposed to be a ritual offering of a family or group whose prayers have been answered and can be prepared for only a few people or an entire town, as this account of an *altare* describes: "In the mountain towns east of Palermo, the banquet is a fairly simple meal prepared in enormous quantity and served to all and anyone, friend or stranger, who passes by. At the one I attended in Làscari we ate in four shifts of at least sixty people each, including all the members of the town band."[8] In other towns west of Palermo, teams of women would construct elaborate bread sculptures, literally creating a large altar out of bread, decorated with oranges, lemons, and hung with smaller bread sculptures. It was not unusual for teams of women to use hundreds of pounds of flour and to work in shifts for a week or two to create these culinary tributes to Saint Joseph.

Other Saint's days involve food, but the historical connections between a particular saint and the symbolism of the food consumed are not always clear. In Palermo, Sicily, for example, the patron saint of the city is Saint Rosalia, who intervened to save the city from plague in 1624. The Festival of Saint Rosalia, celebrated on July 13, used to be one of the most elaborate events in all of nineteenth-century Europe, stretching out to eight days of celebration with parades, church services, and fireworks. The highlight of the festival was a giant decorated cart, which would be hauled through the streets of Palermo. Feasting played an important role in the festival as well, with banquets and food tributes throughout the city. Today, Saint Rosalia is celebrated with a smaller version of the triumphal cart and with fireworks. Instead of banquets, celebrants might watch the fireworks while eating a variety of snacks purchased on the streets: ice cream or a paper cone filled with some type of seed or nut (pumpkin seeds, toasted chickpeas, hazelnuts, peanuts, and chestnuts are the most popular). Watermelon pudding (*gelo di melone*), made from watermelon, cornstarch, and sugar, is also popular for Saint Rosalia day. Another popular food is sautéed snails (*babbaluci*) with parsley and garlic. These foods are not tied specifically to Saint Rosalia's life or memory, but because they are popular summertime snacks, Palermo's street vendors made them popular items to consume during the festival. Sometimes, a saint is not connected to a particular town or city, but symbolizes a particular wish or emotion. Greeks make a cake called *fanouropita* at the end of the summer to honor St. Famourios, the patron saint of lost or unrevealed fortunes. Folk beliefs maintain that if an unmarried woman places a piece of this cake under her pillow at night, she'll dream of her future husband. For many of the Saint's days, participants create a special sweet or dish to honor the Saint. In so doing, Christians make or prepare a holiday, as opposed to merely observing it. Food provides them with an opportunity to become more involved in celebrating the community and their faith.

Watermelon Pudding

1 small seedless watermelon

1 cup sugar

3/4 cup cornstarch

1/4 teaspoon vanilla

semisweet chocolate chips

Cut watermelon into chunks and then run through a food mill, collecting enough juice to make about 5–6 cups. Pour juice into large saucepan containing the sugar and cornstarch, stirring until the cornstarch is dissolved. Cook mixture of medium heat until it begins to boil, stirring constantly. Remove from heat and add vanilla. Allow to cool. When the mixture is partially cooled, add chocolate chips to resemble watermelon seeds and pour into serving bowl or dishes. Chopped nuts like almonds or pistachios may also be added to the pudding. Chill in the refrigerator for several hours before serving.

Although all three religions honor the dead in funeral ceremonies and rituals, Christians reserve a special day in the year (All Soul's Day, which, depending on the location, is celebrated from the end of October through November 2) to honor the dead and celebrate the bonds between the living and the dead. In Sicily, bakers used to make special breads to symbolize these bonds, usually breads in the shape of a dead person or breads called *armuzzi*, shaped to resemble two hands crossed on the breast with the fingers spread wide. Today, one is more likely to find vendors selling candy and toys to children on All Soul's Day. Especially popular are sweets: *torrone* (a nougat made with nuts) and *cubaita* (a nougat made with sesame seeds, from the Arabic *qubhayt*) are sold on the streets and in shops; street vendors and bakeries carry little marzipan or sugar statues for children to eat. One might expect these little sculpted treats to serve as grim reminders of everyone's fate, but children are more likely to find a little marzipan Mickey Mouse or soccer ball than a skeleton or skull. The exception, however, is the Sicilian cookie known as *osso di morto*, or bones of the dead, hard cookies with lumps of meringue that are supposed to resemble cartilage. Historically, Greeks and Italians have associated fava beans with the dead. Ancient Greeks saw black spots on the petals of the fava plant as a stain of death, whereas others believe the hollow stems of the plant connected the dead with the living. Greeks did not eat fava beans but used them in funeral ceremonies. Ancient Romans prepared and consumed fava beans as the most sacred dish at funeral banquets. In parts of Italy today, some bakeries make little cookies shaped like fava beans and flavored with almonds or pine nuts, for All Soul's Day.

OTHER CELEBRATIONS

In addition to the religious celebrations that use food to define and commemorate the occasion, people throughout the Mediterranean celebrate a number of holidays that are not necessarily religious, but are significant for the meaningful place that food occupies in the celebration. Life events such as birth, death, and marriage can be either religious or secular in terms of the celebratory rituals marking the occasions. Yet many of the special foods served at these occasions have their origins in folk practice or ritual. Thus people in Turkey have soup for weddings instead of cake, but neither cake nor soup has any overt religious connotations. In Libya, mothers who have just given birth are fed a paste made from dates and camel's milk, foods that symbolically link back to Muhammad's fast, but they are also given chicken soup, perhaps to rebuild their strength and to fortify them for the childcare duties to come. Throughout the Levant, men who have just become fathers are offered cinnamon tea with grated coconut, whereas in Syria, they are given a kind of trail mix comprised of almonds, pistachios, walnuts, and grated coconut. In addition to a particularly significant food (a nut mixture or soup) given to individuals, celebrants are frequently treated to a meal or a feast in honor of the occasion.

Sometimes the occasion has clear religious connections, as in the case of a light meal provided for celebrants at a baptism in the Catholic Church, or a variety of dishes offered to those who sit shiva for the recently deceased in the Jewish faith.

Turkish Wedding Soup

2 medium onions, chopped

2 medium carrots, peeled and chopped

4 tablespoons butter or margarine

1/2 cup bulgur

3/4 cup dried lentils

3 tablespoons tomato paste

3 tablespoons fresh chopped mint

1 teaspoon sweet paprika

8 cups water

Salt and pepper

Cook the onions and carrot in butter until soft, about 15–20 minutes. Add bulgur and lentils and stir well. Cook for a few minutes. Add the tomato paste, mint, and paprika, plus salt and pepper. Add water and bring to a boil. Reduce heat, cover, and cook for about an hour or until lentils are soft. Serve with wedges of lemon.

Weddings are frequently the cause for much celebration with food. After the wedding ceremony, guests are invited to a wedding banquet, held for lunch or dinner, either at someone's home or in a restaurant. In Catalonia, wedding banquets usually have four courses, a starter, soup, the main course, and dessert, in many cases an elaborate wedding cake cut by the bride and groom. A wedding banquet might be a simple affair, lunch for only a few people, or it might be an elaborate feast for hundreds of guests. Food memoirist Colette Rosant, who was born in France but grew up in Egypt during and just after World War II, recalled a particularly sumptuous wedding banquet held for her aunt:

On the table were the little dishes, the mezze: vine leaves stuffed with saffron rice, tomatoes, parsley and onion; eggplant purée mixed with yogurt with tiny meatballs floating in it; fried eggplant with garlic; eggplant caviar; lamb's brain salad prepared with scallions, garlic, lemon and cumin; fried ground chicken balls; and artichoke hearts stewed in olive oil. Thick slices of batarekh (pressed smoked fish roe) were set on toast rounds and topped with crème fraîche and lemon zest. There were fried mussels, slices of French pâté; baskets of thinly slices Italian salami; *loubiya*, a salad of black-eyed peas, one of my favorite dishes; and a celeriac and fennel salad with lemony vinaigrette. Ahmet (the cook) had slaved the entire night before the wedding making hundreds of tiny hot *sambousaks*.

A second table held meats, fish, and vegetables. I stared at the huge roast legs of lamb; Ahmet's famous duck ballottine; tiny squabs stuffed with rice and roasted almonds (a famous dish made especially for young couples to wish them a sweet life full of love); *kofta*, small meatballs in apricot sauce; and countless other delicacies. Dessert included not only the wedding cake but ice cream made from buffalo milk, pyramids of apricot pudding, and Middle Eastern pastries such as *kunafa*, stuffed with pistachios; *zalabia*, tiny, light, crisp deep-fried dough soaked in honey and orange blossoms; and paper thin filo stuffed with chopped walnuts. I ate until I could no longer move.[9]

The dishes offered in this feast are a mix of French and Middle Eastern specialties, with some other foods of different ethnic origins (Italian salami, for example) mixed in. This cosmopolitan mix of dishes demonstrates clearly not only the sophistication of the upper-class palate in mid-twentieth century Egypt but also the varied and integrated nature of Mediterranean cuisine.

Today, Israel is home to Jews from more than 70 countries. Food at wedding banquets clearly reflects the diversity of population and the cross-cultural influences found in Israeli cuisine. First, a rabbi will bless the traditional challah and will cut the first slice, signaling the guests to eat. A typical banquet might include Eastern European specialties like Polish *piroschki* (a filled noodle turnover), Russian-style sautéed mushrooms, eggplant caviar and eggplant salad from the Middle East, and chicken soup with kreplach (dumplings). The appetizers are accompanied by lots of different breads. Main dishes might include a North African couscous dish, an Eastern European roast brisket with vegetables, and *pashtida*, Israeli vegetable casserole. Cookies, candy, and honey cake are offered for dessert.[10]

In addition to the traditional banquet and the traditional cake, weddings are also a time for sweets. Guests might receive a party favor of candied almonds or other nuts, along with marzipan or sugar sweets, wrapped up in a commemorative container. Or, according to Middle Eastern traditions, the bride and groom might shower their guests with little candies to spread love and good prospects to their guests, especially the single ones. Candied nuts and sweets are also popular in Italy and Greece, where they are distributed to wedding guests as party favors. Italians in particular make a wide variety of wedding cookies out of nuts. These are to be eaten at the wedding banquet but frequently, they will be taken home by guests as well.

Parties and ceremonies associated with childbirth and new family members are also a memorable time for food. In rural areas of the Mediterranean, nourishing foods are given to the new mother to replenish her energy and prepare her for the work to come. Such foods include soups, stews, eggs, and dairy products like milk. In Syria, the "completion of birth" banquet was a popular event. Women related to the new mother would gather at the house to wait while the midwife delivered the baby. As soon as the baby arrived, the young women of the household would get to work in the kitchen, preparing a lot of dishes for the banquet. A birth banquet can be as elaborate as a wedding banquet. Siham Tergeman, a young Syrian woman who wrote extensively about her life in Damascus, recalled her first completion of a birth banquet, where the women ate "boiled white cheese, cheese in oil, cheese balls in oil with zatar spice (thyme), green and black olives, large limed olives, jams of native apricots, plums, green plums, kabad, cherries, cream, honey, cottage cheese, sesame seed sweets, molasses, tahina, milk, tea, tanur bread, stuffed pastries and fruit."[11] The meal is accompanied by lots of tea with milk, and friends and neighbors are invited to share the feast. Later, treats were prepared and sent around to family and friends to announce the birth of the child and the cutting of the first teeth. In Libya, a goat or lamb is sacrificed during the naming ceremony for the baby. And in Syria, Tergeman remembered receiving a large bowl of sliqa, a boiled corn dish made with sugar, pomegranate seeds, walnuts, and pistachios, when a baby first cut teeth. Her family immediately devoured it and her mother returned the bowl filled with sugared nuts. In Greece, relatives and friends pay their respects at the birth of a baby by dropping off gifts and money at the house. Coffee and sweets are set out for the visitors, who are also given wrapped candies, usually at the baptism of the baby. Italians also give out candy at baptisms, either wrapped in pink or blue netting or placed in an elaborate box called a bomboniera.

Childhood celebrations include birthdays, frequently celebrated throughout the region with parties and cake, and coming-of-age ceremonies, the most common of which is circumcision for boys as a way of representing his passage into adulthood or into a religious community. For Jewish boys and girls, the bar mitzvah and the bat mitzvah are celebrated with parties, banquets, and special meals. And in Turkey, Muslim boys are circumcised between ages 7 and 14; the sunnet (circumcision) heralds the introduction of the child into his religious community. A large banquet is held is a ceremonial hall, restaurant, hotel, or in the home. The centerpiece dish for the occasion is roast baby lamb or spiced leg of lamb, in addition to many side dishes and lots of sweets and desserts.

Death is another event that is commemorated with food. Many Christians in the Mediterranean used to have wakes at the house of the bereaved family. Friends, neighbors, and relatives would bring food and drink for the family and join them in mourning. Today, wakes still exist in rural areas, but it is increasingly uncommon for wakes to be held in someone's house; rather, funeral homes make the arrangements for paying last respects, or a service or mass is held for the deceased. Sometimes there is a small reception at the house, but this is becoming less and less common in countries such as Spain, France, and Italy. Similar to the wake is the Jewish shiva, where friends, neighbors, and family come to sit with the bereaved family at the house. They bring food of all kinds, not only to eat in the house at that time, but for the family to have in the future, so they will not have to worry about preparing meals. For Muslims, a simple dinner is offered after the funeral at the house of the deceased, although wealthier families might offer more; each family offers what they can afford. After dinner, everyone is served a bitter cup of coffee.

There are also celebrations involving food that have nothing to do with religious ceremonies or life cycle celebrations. Instead, they honor a type of food itself, or celebrate the good fortune of the harvest. Agricultural festivals or celebrations of the harvest do not necessarily fall under the domain of any one religion, given their roots in older pagan traditions. Moreover, any formal rituals or celebrations of the harvest have become rare in this day of mechanized and industrialized agriculture. In some regions, however, the celebration of the harvest has made a comeback, thanks to organizations like Slow Food International, which promote local agriculture and seek to resurrect and preserve older rituals and traditions associated with the harvest. In Italy, for example, local communities have held something called a *sagra*, a festival or banquet honoring a specific food or dish, usually something that has just been harvested. A *sagra* can celebrate grapes, or wild boar, or porcini mushrooms, or chestnuts, by having participants cook, display, and eat dishes made with that particular food. Thanks to the Internet, today many tourists are likely to attend in addition to members of the local community. Artichokes, available in Italy from mid-November through April, are venerated among Italians and prepared in many different ways, either raw or cooked. In the town of Cerda, near Palermo, Sicily, the artichoke *sagra* means that the restaurants of the towns fill their menu with artichoke offerings. Author Clarissa Hyman, who visited Cerda during the *sagra*, observed that in one trattoria:

There was no choice, simply an array of little dishes that covered the entire surface of the table—artichokes stewed in oil and vinegar, braised with tomato and garlic or with lemon and oil, whole roasted artichokes the size of oranges, artichoke frittata, deep-fried artichokes, caponata made with artichokes, grilled artichokes, raw baby artichoke salad dressed with oil, lemon, peperoncino and breadcrumbs, homemade *casareccia* (a short, twisted pasta) with artichoke and wild fennel sauce.[12]

Diners would finish their artichoke meal with a pastry and a glass of artichoke liqueur, called *Cynar*. Celebrations of the harvest used to be, and still are, times when the community comes together to enjoy themselves and eat to their heart's content after weeks or months of hard work and worry. Today, events like the *sagra* provide an important economic boost for small farmers and businessmen, bringing tourists into rural areas and small towns and promoting a greater sense of civic engagement and commitment.

Special occasions are all about food in the Mediterranean region. From religious holidays to weddings to celebrations of the harvest, people are constantly thinking about food preparation as it relates to the solemnity or joyousness of the occasion. There is no doubt that people in the Mediterranean love to celebrate. This is the case in Egypt, where rising levels of obesity among the population have been blamed, in part, on overindulgence on holidays and at parties. And, as this chapter has pointed out, food consumption levels actually go up during the fasting of Ramadan, because people are so committed to celebrating the end of the fast. It seems clear, then, that food does more than mark the symbolic significance of a special occasion. Parties, banquets, and meals provide an opportunity for cooks and chefs to make unusual dishes or to splurge on extravagant ingredients. Friends and family gather together to eat their fill, and bonds of community are strengthened.

NOTES

1. Ashkenazi Jews are from Central and Eastern Europe and Sephardic Jews come from Spain, although the term *Sephardic* is used more broadly today. Some Jewish communities are neither Ashkenazi nor Sephardic; for example, the Roman Jewish community goes back to ancient Roman origins, not Spain or Eastern Europe. In Israel today, the Ashkenazi Jews are recent immigrants from Russia.

2. Joyce Goldstein, *Saffron Shores: Jewish Cooking of the Southern Mediterranean* (San Francisco: Chronicle Books, 2002), p. 22.

3. Susan Starr Sered, "Food and Holiness: Cooking as a Sacred Act among Middle-Eastern Jewish Women," *Anthropological Quarterly* 61 (1988): 134–135.

4. See Willy Jansen, "French Bread and Algerian Wine: Conflicting Identities in French Algeria" in Peter Scholliers, ed. *Food, Drink and Identity. Cooking, Eating and Drinking in Europe Since the Middle Ages* (Oxford: Berg, 2001), pp. 195–218; and Susan Sered, "Food and Holiness," p. 136.

5. Hassan M'Souli, *Moroccan Modern* (Northampton, MA: Interlink, 2005), p. 10.

6. Magda Mehdawy, *My Egyptian Grandmother's Kitchen* (Cairo: American University Press in Cairo, 2006), p. 353.

7. Efisio Farris, *Sweet Myrtle and Bitter Honey* (New York: Rizzoli, 2007), pp. 232–233.

8. Mary Taylor Simeti, *Pomp and Sustenance. Twenty-Five Centuries of Sicilian Food* (Hopewell NJ: The Ecco Press, 1989), p. 135.

9. Colette Rosant, *Memories of a Lost Egypt. A Memoir with Recipes* (New York: Clarkson Potter, 1999), pp. 79–81.

10. See Lois Sinaiko Webb, *Multicultural Cookbook of Life-Cycle Celebrations* (Westport, CT: Oryx Press, 2000), p. 108, for a full description of an elaborate Israeli wedding banquet.

11. Siham Tergeman, *Daughter of Damascus,* taken from *Ya Mal al-Sham,* English version and introduction by Andrea Rugh (Austin: Center for Middle Eastern Studies, 1994), p. 90.

12. Clarissa Hyman, *Cucina Siciliana* (Northampton, MA: Interlink, 2002), p. 146.

7

Diet and Health

Today, people in the Mediterranean are universally known for eating healthy diets that contribute to a long lifespan. They are also known for what they *do not* have: heart disease and poor health conditions usually associated with populations in the United States and parts of northern Europe. The now favorable reputation of the Mediterranean diet is ironic, of course, given that for much of the modern era (the eighteenth and nineteenth centuries and a good part of the twentieth century), popular diet was less than adequate and so poor in some regions that it became the object of government study and a symbol of economic backwardness for the region. Although dietary habits contributed to poor health when people were poorly nourished, many populations throughout the Mediterranean developed certain habits that, decades later, helped them avoid certain diseases and live longer, healthier lives. These habits included eating more legumes and fish instead of red meat, using local oils like olive oil for cooking and seasoning food, and relying mostly on cereals as a main source of nutrition. Historians believe that people ate this way out of economic necessity: they lacked the money to buy more expensive foods (like red meat or canned goods), or if they were farmers they preferred to sell the costlier foods they produced rather than consume them. In the decades after World War II (1939–1945), the economies of the Mediterranean region improved, sometimes dramatically, but many people did not change their dietary habits, even when they could afford to buy more meat, processed foods, or fats. Their abstemious habits and dietary traditions have served them well: by the 1980s, a growing number of doctors and nutritional experts around the world noticed that people in the Mediterranean regions seemed healthier; they suffered from lower incidence of heart problems and high blood pressure (diseases associated with affluence and a rich diet), and they also appeared to have lower incidence of certain cancers. Could their diet have contributed to their general state of health?

For the last few decades, scientists have been studying the so-called Mediterranean diet to see whether a diet high in carbohydrates, low in protein, high in olive and fish oils, and high in fresh vegetables and fruits contributes to a longer life because it reduces the risks of certain cancers and heart disease.[1] This chapter examines the history of these kinds of studies and their findings. It also describes how the Mediterranean diet has become one of the most popular dietary regimens in the world, as more and more people from affluent cultures try to reform their eating habits in order to live longer and healthier lives. By focusing on the physiological impact of the Mediterranean diet, this chapter explains exactly how the food choices of Mediterranean people affect their health and why so many doctors think this is significant. Because this type of diet has been so closely studied by the medical and nutritional profession, we now have many variations on the Mediterranean diet (for example, the "Miami Mediterranean Diet"), and there are scores of printed cookbooks, magazine articles, and nutritional advice literature encouraging the use of the Mediterranean diet as a cure for certain illnesses. The chapter sorts out the many claims being made about the Mediterranean diet, some of which appear confusing and contradictory to the average reader who does not know a great deal about medical research or nutrition. For example, the healthy dietary habits of Mediterranean populations can be offset by other unhealthy lifestyle choices; or medical findings can sometimes reverse previous findings about the role of certain foods in fighting diseases such as cancer. Last, this chapter examines some of the most recent changes in eating habits throughout the Mediterranean region. At the same time that the Mediterranean diet is being championed around the world for its healthful characteristics, people in the region are adopting less healthy eating habits, such as consuming more meat and eating more processed foods. Doctors, nutritional experts, and ordinary people are alarmed by these recent changes, so much so that various organizations now attempt to halt or even reverse these less healthy habits. There is no doubt that lifestyles and eating habits around the Mediterranean are changing, but experts disagree about the scope and impact of these changes.

THE MEDITERRANEAN DIET AND HEALTH

Popular diet is one of the most studied aspects of health in the Mediterranean region. The Mediterranean diet has been adopted around the world by individuals who wish to guard against potentially unhealthful conditions, combat certain diseases, and prolong life. Physicians and other medical experts have used the Mediterranean diet as a form of medical intervention since 1975, when American doctor Ancel Keys published *How to Eat Well and Stay Well: The Mediterranean Way*, proposing a relationship between the eating habits of populations within the Mediterranean region and the distribution of morbidity and mortality rates (Keys based his 1975 book on a previous study, *Eat Well and Stay Well*, revised throughout the 1950s and 1960s). The Mediterranean diet is most frequently prescribed for patients with heart disease, high blood pressure, and high cholesterol, although it can also be used as a weight reduction regimen, and it is thought by some to prevent certain forms of cancer. It is now firmly established as a model of healthful eating habits, and it has been adapted to suit many regional food tastes.

Doctors may understand which foods constitute the Mediterranean diet, but the general public has differing opinions about what this diet consists of and how it is used to improve one's health. The words "Mediterranean diet" were first used by Keys, who referred to a general model of dietary behavior he found in southern Italy in the 1960s and 1970s. As medical experts are quick to point out, however, there are *many* types of diets throughout the Mediterranean region. For example, the typical diet of someone from North Africa would be different from that of a southern Italian consumer. Each would eat different foods and therefore would take in a different combination of carbohydrates, fats, protein, vitamins, and minerals. When Keys defined the term, he referred to a general set of habits and patterns that characterized healthful eating in southern Italy as being distinct from the dietary habits he saw in other parts of the world, in particular, northern European countries and the United States. First, the Mediterranean diet made use of olive oil instead of animal fat (butter, lard, fat in meat) and was therefore lower in saturated fats and cholesterol. Although there weren't large differences between the Mediterranean diet and other diets in terms of overall fat consumption, there was a difference in the proportion of saturated fat intake. Put a different way, Mediterranean peoples may consume as much fat as some American consumers, but there is a significant difference in the type of fat they eat. Keys also noted that Mediterranean consumers ate a lot of cereals, between 30 and 60 percent of their total caloric intake. Mediterranean consumers ate more legumes and more fresh produce than their counterparts in northern Europe and the United States. Overall, their diet was rich in complex carbohydrates and vegetable and leguminous fiber; it was lower in the amount of animal fat and animal protein consumed. This very general definition of the Mediterranean diet has changed little over the decades since Keys first published his book. Doctors and others think of a diet where cereals, fresh produce, legumes, and olive oil figure more prominently than do red meat, processed foods, and animal fat. The Mediterranean diet also entails a low to moderate consumption of dairy products, fish, poultry, eggs, and red wine.

Although there are many Mediterranean diets, Keys and others found that throughout the Mediterranean, diet seemed to play a key role in contributing to lower mortality rates and lower incidences of certain diseases such as heart disease, certain cancers, and diabetes. Initially, Keys recommended the Mediterranean diet to improve cardiac health and to control and combat obesity (which is connected to heart health). He first grew interested in this issue when he worked on the epidemiology of coronary heart disease in Italy and Spain in the 1950s. He then went on to publish dietary advice books such as *Eat Well and Stay Well*; and in 1980, Keys and others published a study called *Seven Countries. A Multivariate Analysis of Death and Coronary Heart Disease*, which found lower rates of cardiovascular disease and mortality and lower serum cholesterol levels in Greece and Italy, in comparison with northern European countries (Finland, the Netherlands) and the United States (Yugoslavia and Japan were also included in this study). The study of 12,763 men began in 1958 and continued through 1974, allowing for a 10-year follow-up period among the various populations studied. The general death rates varied considerably among the nations, but the national comparison of coronary death rates was thought to be a significant finding. In the United States and in northern European countries, coronary death rates were much higher than they were in Greece and Italy. Keys and other doctors now had more evidence from this large-scale study to suggest that dietary habits were related to incidence of, and mortality from, heart disease.

The authors of the *Seven Countries* study also found that in Italy and Greece, cigarette smoking was a relatively minor risk factor in the overall death rate; Greek and Italian smokers died of various diseases only at slightly higher levels than did nonsmokers. By contrast, in the United States and in northern Europe, smokers died of various diseases at much greater levels than did nonsmokers. This finding has led to much speculation, and a few published studies, about the relationship between dietary habits and the effects of tobacco. The authors of the *Seven Countries* study found a high incidence of tobacco use in some Mediterranean countries but a lower-than-expected incidence of lung cancer. At the time of the publication of this study, many doctors had already begun to examine the Mediterranean diet to understand how it worked and the impact it could have on the body. These efforts included studies of groups and individuals and laboratory analyses of the various foods that composed the Mediterranean diet. Published articles have noted that the Mediterranean diet can help people control and even reduce weight, but there are other reducing diets that work more quickly. Therefore, the Mediterranean diet is less popular as a reducing diet and more popular as a regimen for people with heart disease, diabetes, high blood pressure, and metabolic syndrome. Not surprisingly, scientific inquiry has focused on efforts to understand the relationships between the consumption of certain Mediterranean foods, disease prevention, and general health. Medical researchers have been interested in understanding how and why this particular kind of diet helps people throughout the Mediterranean region to stay healthy.

Perhaps one of the most important characteristics of the Mediterranean diet is that it relies on fresh food rather than processed and packaged foods; therefore it is not as high in saturated fats, salt, sugar, and other foods that can lead to weight gain and health complications. As the previous chapters have explained (chapters 3 and 5), Mediterranean consumers prefer fresh food. Local produce from outdoor markets is considered superior to that purchased at supermarkets. Frozen food reheated in the microwave is to be avoided if possible. Fresh fruit is the preferred dessert after lunch or dinner. It may seem obvious to some, but a diet based on fresh ingredients contributes to overall well-being and health. The Mediterranean diet also relies on lots of vegetables, legumes, and cereals, all of which are high in soluble fiber. Studies have shown that soluble fiber slows the rate of digestion, and a slower rate of digestion reduces any blood glucose increases and the need to secrete insulin.[2] Foods like pasta, bulgur, oats, barley, coarse cornmeal (the kind used to make polenta), and legumes have been found to slow the absorption of nutrients in the digestive tract. Eating lots of these cereals keeps blood sugar and metabolism in check, and this in turn combats both obesity and diabetes. In fact, many plant foods have the effect of reducing the rate of carbohydrate absorption. Slower digestion rates are now advised and being practiced as forms of therapeutic treatment for some chronic diseases. Patients can follow the Mediterranean diet, add more soluble fiber to their diets, or eat smaller meals more frequently. Overall, the consumption of legumes, cereals, and fresh produce provides a high level of energy from carbohydrates and protein without a lot of fat. This stands in contrast to diets where lots of meat and other animal proteins are consumed.

One of the chief benefits of the Mediterranean diet is its effect on heart disease and high blood pressure. The diet is low in saturated and hydroge-nated oils, both of which have been found to contribute to heart disease, and high in fiber and potassium, both of which reduce blood pressure.[3] The use of olive oil in Mediterranean cooking is associated with a lower risk of coronary disease, given that olive oil contains linolenic acid, a type of omega-3 fatty acid found also in canola oil and nuts. Moderate amounts of fish consumed in the Mediterranean diet also supply omega-3 fatty acids, which lower triglycerides and have an anti-inflammatory effect on the lining of blood vessels. Residents of the Mediterranean eat very little red meat and average nine servings a day of fruits of vegetables, which are rich in antioxidants. This contributes to a lower level of low-density lipoprotein cholesterol (the bad cholesterol) that might contribute to the buildup of deposits in the arteries.

The main purpose of the diet is to help people keep their hearts healthy, to lower blood pressure, to regulate blood sugar, and to control obesity. Some medical evidence suggests that the antioxidant properties of the Mediterranean diet can help those suffering from degenerative diseases such as cancer, whereas other studies have found that the oleic acid in olives can alleviate the symptoms of rheumatoid arthritis. The health-ful properties of the Mediterranean diet have meant that an increasing number of doctors outside the Mediterranean have started to prescribe the diet for their patients with heart disease, high blood pressure, or diabe-tes. The published results of several clinical tests seem promising. In one trial conducted in the United States between 1995 and 2005, 380,296 men and women between 50 and 71 years old tried the Mediterranean diet. Doctors optimistically concluded "the risk of death from any cause over the five-year follow-up period was lower for those with the most Mediterranean-like diets. Deaths from cancer or cardiovascular disease were also significantly lower in this group." Results were especially signifi-cant among smokers who were not overweight; they halved their risk of death if they followed the basic guidelines of the Mediterranean diet.[4] The majority of clinical studies, conducted on patients who are older and/or face certain diseases, have found that the Mediterranean diet effectively combats metabolic syndrome, a condition characterized by obesity, hyper-tension, and increased levels of blood sugar. Eating the Mediterranean way can lower blood pressure, help people lose weight, and decrease total lev-els of glucose and insulin in the body. Moreover, several studies indicate that it is never too late to start eating right; in clinical trials with elderly patients, doctors have found that following the Mediterranean diet can decrease mortality among elderly persons.[5]

All of the recently published studies on the effects of the Mediterranean diet confirmed what Keys argued decades ago: eating the Mediterranean way is good for one's health and longevity. Hundreds of medical studies were conducted and published throughout the 1980s and 1990s; this in turn led to a boom in publications about the benefits of the Mediterranean diet, as well as an increase in cookbooks and other informational literature about how to cook healthy Mediterranean dishes. Scientific findings have influenced medical advice: the American Heart Association borrows heavily from the Mediterranean diet in making suggestions for people facing certain types of heart disease or high blood pressure. Even people who do not have high blood pressure or other illnesses have adjusted their diets to conform more with Mediterranean habits—perhaps by eating less red meat or by substituting olive oil for other cooking oils—so that they can feel better and live longer. Because few medical professionals contest the healthful benefits of the Mediterranean diet, the scientific debates have tended to focus on just how far-reaching an impact the Mediterranean diet has on one's health and health risk. There is no end in sight to studies linking the diet to some type of medical cure or disease prevention. The omega-B fatty acids prevalent in the diet may lower the risk of Alzheimer's disease; the diet itself may help patients with Alzheimer's disease live longer. For pregnant women, the diet may help prevent asthma and allergies for her baby; in children, it may protect against childhood respiratory allergies. And the Mediterranean diet may reduce the risk of progressive lung diseases such as chronic obstructive pulmonary disease.

The medical profession, however, is far from certain that the Mediterranean diet constitutes a cure-all for certain chronic conditions or diseases. Put another way, it may seem obvious that a diet low in animal fat and high in fruits and vegetables is a healthy one, but can the Mediterranean diet perform miracles? Doctors still do not have sufficient information about all of the medical effects of the Mediterranean diet, given that so much research has been conducted in so many different locations within a relatively short period (a few decades). A 2007 review of 489 published articles on the Mediterranean diet argued that although the evidence regarding the impact of dietary intervention was reasonable, there is still much to be done in terms of more research and more systematic reviews of current projects. There has been little coordinated effort to share information and some of the published studies were found lacking in scientific rigor. Instead, as the authors concluded, "one of the most immediate conclusions obtained from this review is that the scientific evidence for the Mediterranean diet is mostly sustained by observational studies and personal reviews."[6] This is not to say that much of the published data on the Mediterranean diet is unreliable. Rather, there is considerable variation in the ways in which studies have been conducted; therefore not all the claims about the Mediterranean diet are well supported or evidenced. Moreover, the Mediterranean diet will not protect its consumers from other potentially life-threatening diseases. According to epidemiological studies, the death rate from stroke is higher in Mediterranean countries than in other parts of the world, and in Italy, there is an elevated rate of mortality from gastric cancer. This is not to say that the Mediterranean diet necessarily *causes* these medical problems, but these findings would indicate that the Mediterranean diet cannot *guarantee* greater health and an increased lifespan.

Although it is clear that following the general principles of the Mediterranean diet will not harm one's health, it is also evident that too many hopes have been placed in the potentially curative effects of this dietary regimen. And, as experimental and clinical studies continue to produce more and more evidence about the relationship between diet and health, some of this evidence appears contradictory or at least confusing, as it is read and interpreted by the general public. Consumers interested in their health read advice from a variety of sources, not from medical journals necessarily, but from printed sources on nutrition (newsletters or magazines), articles in non-health-related magazines, or Web sites on the Internet. The variety of information provided about the Mediterranean diet can be confusing and even overwhelming to the average consumer who wants to live a healthier lifestyle. For example, several studies point to the potentially beneficial effects of red wine consumption in lowering cholesterol levels, but some people can become addicted to alcohol, and recent studies also indicate that alcohol consumption can be a factor in increased risk of breast cancer. Thus a female who wants to lower her cholesterol level would have to think twice before drinking an alcoholic beverage such as red wine and, at the very least, ensure that she drinks red wine in moderation.

The average consumer may find it difficult to understand and process what appears to be contradictory advice from a broad range of media. After all, dietary habits are complex phenomena, and to isolate such a complex dietary pattern and relate to the prevention of a certain disease or medical condition with any degree of certainty is sometimes problematic. First, there are many factors that contribute to an individual's general well-being. An individual may smoke, drink alcohol to excess, or not exercise enough. Some of the published medical studies on the Mediterranean diet isolate foods or certain elements within the diet (fat, sodium, calcium) in order to study their relationship to a specific disease. Thus individuals without a background in experimental nutritional science can become confused by, or possibly misinterpret, published findings. Or they may follow the Mediterranean diet but neglect other aspects of their health and overall well-being.

What does seem clear is that the international medical and scientific profession has "discovered" what people in the Mediterranean have known for a long time—that a diet low in animal fats, protein, and high in carbohydrates, fresh produce, and olive oil is a healthy one. One of the chief reasons that medical professionals and consumers endorse the Mediterranean diet is that it serves as an alternative or antidote to the unhealthful effects of the modern diet consumed by many Europeans and Americans and a growing number of populations throughout the world. This diet consists of many processed foods, is high in animal foods, and high in salt and fat, with few fresh foods such as fruits or vegetables. This diet was forged out of convenience and the tremendous changes in food production and the food processing industries. It first gained popularity in the United States but has now spread to many parts of the world and recently, has made inroads among the younger generations in the Mediterranean region. Thus populations in the Mediterranean face an interesting and potentially alarming predicament. As their diet becomes the standard for a "healthy" diet around the world, how do they manage dietary changes and influences from outside the Mediterranean? Are people in the region still healthy and do they themselves still follow the general dietary contours of the Mediterranean diet?

A CHANGING DIET: AMERICANIZATION?

Even though people living around the Mediterranean Sea have been eating some of the same foods for thousands of years, the region is not immune to changes in dietary habits. Contemporary eating practices—fast foods sold through franchises like McDonald's and Pizza Hut, convenience foods, processed foods, the standardization of tastes—have found their way to Mediterranean region. Thus the more traditional ways of preparing and eating food now have to compete with supermarkets, snack foods, and American fast food chains. Within the last two or three decades, dietary habits across the Mediterranean region have changed, and many experts would argue that the changes have been detrimental to popular health. Ironically, at the same time that the Mediterranean diet is being prescribed for many non-Mediterranean populations who have the desire to become and remain healthy, Mediterranean populations have been trading some of their eating habits for less healthy habits found in other countries like the United States. The nature of these dietary changes, however, is highly uneven and dependent on regional and demographic factors. Moreover, there are few clinical or epidemiological studies examining these recent dietary changes in any great detail, although several clinical studies now being published indicate that those individuals who exchange the Mediterranean diet for a diet higher in fat, salt, and red meat become less healthy and more prone to heart disease, diabetes, and high blood pressure. This information should come as no surprise, but questions remain as to the pace and scope of these recent dietary changes and their short-term and long-term impact on popular health in the region.

The development of industrialized agricultural production, changes in food distribution systems (the growth of supermarkets and chain restaurants), and the globalization of food markets have meant that people in the Mediterranean (and all over the world) now have access to more red meat and more processed foods, such as frozen convenience foods, "fast" foods from restaurant franchises, and snack foods. The availability of these types of foods was not an immediate consequence of the larger structural changes in food production and distribution; rather, these changes occurred over several decades, roughly from the end of World War II to the present day. One should be careful, then, before assuming that the Mediterranean diet changed rapidly in response to the onslaught of supermarkets and fast food chains.

First, there is some evidence to suggest that populations across the Mediterranean adjusted their diets throughout this time period as their incomes rose and they began to reallocate the amounts spent on different kinds of food. Before and immediately after World War II, poor economic conditions necessitated less expensive food substitutions like legumes in place of meat or more bread instead of fresh vegetables and fruits. In the decades after World War II, European nations witnessed a steady and impressive rise in income, which meant consumers could spend more money on more expensive food items. Thus in areas like France and Italy, people ate fewer legumes. Once the mainstay of diet in France, legume consumption decreased from 16 pounds (7.3 kilograms) per person in 1925 to 3 pounds (1.4 kilograms) per person by 1980; in Italy, consumers averaged 32.8 pounds (14.9 kilograms) per person in 1925 and 8 pounds (3.6 kilograms) per person, per year for the period 1981–1985.[7] The so-called meat of the poor became less popular when consumers could actually afford more meat. Another big dietary change that occurred in the postwar period was the increase in consumption of fresh fruits and vegetables, foods considered too expensive before World War II and scarce during and immediately after the war. In France, consumers went from consuming 370 pounds (168 kilograms), per person, per year in the period 1955–1960 to consuming 381 pounds (173 kilograms) per person, per year, in the period 1984–1985. In Italy, consumers ate an average of 364 pounds (165 kilograms) per person, per year in the period 1955–1960, and they ate 564 pounds (256 kilograms) per person, per year in the period 1984–1985.[8]

Historically, some of the foods that many people in the Mediterranean region could *not* afford easily were meat and dairy products. Before World War II, populations throughout the region consumed less than 2 ounces (50 grams) per day of meat or meat products. And in many areas, consumers ate meat only on holidays, special occasions, or when they were sick. In the postwar era, little changed in North African and Middle Eastern regions; meat consumption remained at or around 2 to 2.5 ounces (50–70 grams) per person per day throughout the 1990s. In the European regions of the Mediterranean, however, consumers ate more meat. In Greece, Italy, Spain, and France, for example, meat consumption increased from around 2 ounces (60 grams) per person per day in 1961 to between 9 and 12 ounces (250–325 grams) per person per day, in 2001. A similar increase in consumption took place with regard to milk and dairy products. The regions that consumed the most milk and dairy products—Italy, Turkey, France, and Greece—continued to increase their consumption levels. In 1961, consumers in these regions ate or drank between 14 and 21 ounces (400–600 grams) of milk and dairy products per person per day; they increased their consumption of dairy products to between 25 and 30 ounces (700–800 grams) per person per day in the 1990s.[9] The increase in consumption of meat and dairy products on the European side of the Mediterranean has been so dramatic that by the 1990s, consumers in Italy, Greece, and Spain received about a quarter of their energy intake from animal products; in France, the amount is even higher, at 37 percent.

Across the Mediterranean region, the traditional use of olive oil has been supplemented by oils extracted from various seeds that can be cultivated in the region's soil (cottonseed, sunflower, rapeseed, sesame seeds, and grape seeds). Given the growing worldwide demand for olive oil, Mediterranean farmers have found it profitable to export their olive crops, and because of this, olive oil is sometimes more expensive than other oils, even when it is locally grown and produced. Another common substitution for olive oil is soy bean oil; soy beans were introduced to the region about 50 years ago, as animal feed. Today, soy beans are grown in Italy, Turkey, Egypt, and Spain, and the oil extracted from them has become an alternative to olive oil. Given the long-term changes discussed, it seems clear that the traditional Mediterranean diet has shifted even in the years since Keys first observed southern Italians in the 1950s and 1960s. For one, legumes play a much less important role in everyday diet and olive oil plays a somewhat less important role than it used to. Fresh fruits and vegetables appear to be increasing in popularity, and in some areas of the region, consumption of meat and dairy products has increased. More animal fat and less soluble fiber is present in contemporary Mediterranean eating habits. Because olive oil consumption patterns vary a great deal by region and demographics, it is difficult to generalize about changes in olive oil consumption in the region.

Another big change in dietary habits in the Mediterranean region is the increased consumption of prepared and processed foods, which frequently translates into the increased consumption of salt and saturated fats. Since the late 1990s, a great deal has been published about the "Americanization" of Mediterranean eating habits; scientific papers question whether the Mediterranean diet is in decline while the popular press cites the prevalence of fast food in the region and predicts poor health will accompany these explicitly "American" foods like hamburgers, soda, potato chips, and coffee drinks. Alarming reports from Italy suggest that the childhood obesity rate in the country is 25 percent. Scientific publications suggest that consumers are eating prepared and processed foods at a very early age, even as young as six months.[10] Doctors and nutritional experts have long compared the benefits of the Mediterranean diet with drawbacks of the so-called Western diet (the diet prevalent in northern Europe and the United States). Now experts and consumers alike are concerned that the Western or American diet is fast replacing the Mediterranean diet in countries such as France, Spain, Italy, and Greece.

Frequently, these changing dietary trends are grouped together as evidence of the "Americanization" of Mediterranean eating habits. When critics use the terms *Western diet* or *American diet*, they usually mean a diet that is high in animal fat and protein and high in fast food and convenience snack foods. The result is a high-fat, high-sodium, high-sugar diet that doctors believe contributes to obesity, heart disease, diabetes, and high blood pressure. A major vehicle of this trend is the corporate fast food franchises like McDonald's and Pizza Hut, which have thousands of outlets worldwide and several hundred scattered throughout the Mediterranean region. People also associate the Americanization of diet with intensive marketing efforts to produce new convenience foods and sell them to individuals of all ages and social status via different advertising media. Critics of the American diet not only contend that such a diet is unhealthy, they object to the onslaught of retail, merchandising, and marketing practices, many of which are aimed at young consumers. The term *Americanization* as applied to eating habits, however, is misleading and confusing because it tends to group together and generalize about some complex and interrelated trends that are not always directly related to the growth of fast food franchises or food-marketing practices. Nor can these changes be attributed exclusively to the United States.

For example, it is clear that several long-term historical transformations affected many regions throughout the Mediterranean after World War II, and some of these changes had an impact on eating patterns and habits. More people moved from rural to urban areas in the decades after the war. There was then an increased need for more retail food outlets in urban and suburban areas. Urbanization also leads to more stressful living conditions (traffic, pollution, and affordable housing seem beyond an individual's control), which may lead to eating more or reducing exercise levels. More women were incorporated into the workforce, even married women with children, resulting in greater reliance on prepared or convenience foods as a solution to family meal preparations. More men and women shifted work from manual labor to desk jobs, thereby adopting a more sedentary lifestyle. People walked less and adopted public or private forms of transportation to meet their daily needs. And per capita income rose, along with family incomes and standards of living, which meant greater value was placed on the consumption of certain goods, including foods that symbolized affluence, leisure, and cosmopolitanism. Consumers purchased more expensive food items and more non-necessity foods such as snacks and desserts; they also consumed more meals, beverages, and snacks outside the home. All of these economic and social changes had clear implications for the type of foods consumed, as well as the way in which these foods were consumed. Although similar changes were also going on in the United States after World War II, it would be difficult to call these trends Americanization because the term implies a concerted effort by Americans to influence non-Americans and to change their behavior accordingly. Although some American food companies (e.g., Coca-Cola) set up production centers in the Mediterranean, it is difficult to speak of an ongoing and concerted effort by Americans to change the behavior of people in this region.

Moreover, it is difficult to separate out what constitutes "American" influence on the Mediterranean diet from outside influences more generally. For example, it is reasonable to assume that tourism has had some impact on changing Mediterranean eating habits. In Crete and Cyprus, British-style pubs have become popular among tourists and natives alike.

Studies of populations in popular tourist areas such as the Balearic Islands show that rising tourist demand for foods like red meat and soft drinks has led to increased consumption by local populations, simply because the food is now more available. Dietary change is most evident among younger generations who have frequent contact with tourists and other foreign visitors.[11] Similarly, immigration has had some impact on changing dietary habits, particularly in European countries with growing populations of North Africans and peoples from the Middle East. Virtually unheard of 20 or even 10 years ago, fast food stands selling kebab, falafel, and pizza are sprouting up in France, Italy, and Greece. Americans may actually be some of the tourists or immigrants in these areas, but it is difficult to classify these types of dietary changes as "Americanization."

Popular health might be declining in the Mediterranean region for reasons other than dietary ones. Some people may be living an unhealthy lifestyle and never set foot in an American fast food restaurant. For example, they may smoke, drink too much alcohol, or not get enough exercise. Thus it is difficult to blame American foods for the rising levels of obesity in the Mediterranean when several studies have found that people get a lot less physical exercise than they did 10 or 20 years ago. According to one study, middle-age men in Crete walked an average of eight miles a day in the 1960s, and today they walk less than 1.5 miles per day. Among children as well, physical activity is less popular and less available: some high-rise apartment complexes in Italian cities prohibit children from playing in the courtyards, and schools throughout the region are requiring less physical education in favor of more academic work.[12] Again, it is difficult to think declining levels of physical exercise as "Americanization" even though these trends are occurring in the United States as well. When people opt to take scooters, cars, or trams instead of walking, or when schools decide to cut physical education from the curriculum, are they necessarily under the influence of an American institution, ideology, or organization? The term *Americanization* is not useful to describe what is happening throughout the Mediterranean, especially when one examines the complex interplay of behaviors and trends relating to diet and health.

MEDITERRANEAN HEALTH IN CRISIS: AN OBESITY EPIDEMIC?

Although it may be incorrect or inaccurate to categorize all these general trends and changes throughout the Mediterranean as Americanization, doctors and nutritionists still have to confront a growing body of evidence that waistlines are expanding throughout the region, and in some places, certain diseases caused by diet are on the rise. There is also evidence that among certain populations, weight gain and obesity are on the rise and a growing number of doctors and nutritionists are worried about the long-term impact of this shift in eating habits. One of the most visible signs that diet is changing in the Mediterranean is the ubiquity of processed foods: American fast food restaurants and packaged, processed snacks. In many major cities and towns, supermarkets and fast food outlets are commonplace; there are a number of alternatives to traditional Mediterranean foods and meals. Although the term *Americanization* may be misleading when it comes to thinking about how dietary change takes place, American-style foods are readily available for Mediterranean consumers. And over the last three decades, a growing number of people have criticized the availability or presence of foods such as hamburgers, soft drinks, packaged snacks, and corporate fast food. Government officials have debated whether to levy a kind of "fat tax" on processed foods for sale; on the island of Corsica, natives launched "Corsican Cola" in opposition to the American brand Coca-Cola. Differing responses to food trends from the United States indicate that there is growing opposition to an American-style diet, and thus the term *Americanization* might be useful, in that it gives populations outside the United States a set of principles and ideas to consider when it comes to food habits and traditions. In many Mediterranean countries, critics of American trends in food production, distribution, and consumption now fight to preserve their own ways of eating and living. For example, several Mediterranean countries have requested that the Mediterranean diet be placed on UNESCO's world heritage list, as a cultural practice worth preserving and defending. And, as chapter 3 describes, several organizations and individuals have worked actively to oppose Americanization and globalization while upholding local food production and cooking traditions.

There is some concern, however, that all of this activity might be too little, too late. In the summer of 2008, Josef Schmidhuber, a senior economist with the United Nations Food and Agriculture Organization, presented a paper on the impact the European Union's Common Agricultural Policy (CAP) on popular diet in Europe. His findings indicated that from 1962 to 2002, daily caloric intake throughout Europe increased about 20 percent; but in Greece, Italy, Spain, Cyprus, and Malta, all countries that started out poorer than their northern European neighbors, caloric intake increased by 30 percent. Greece now has the highest prevalence of overweight and obesity in Europe; an estimated three-quarters of the Greek population are classified as either overweight or obese. An estimated half of the Italian and Spanish populations are either overweight or obese.

Why? According to Schmidhuber, Spain, Greece, and Italy are the European Union's biggest "fat guzzlers"; fat now accounts for 40 percent of the Spanish dietary intake and in absolute terms, fat consumption has literally doubled over the last 40 years, from 2.5 ounces (72 grams) per day to 5 ounces (154 grams) per day.[13] Similar shifts in consumption patterns occurred in Italy and Greece. Although European populations throughout the Mediterranean also increased their intake of olive oil, they increased more dramatically their consumption of meat, milk, and dairy products, all sources of fat. There is reason to believe, according to the latest findings, that the Mediterranean diet as practiced by Greeks, Italians, and Spaniards is not all that different from the average European diet, at least not in terms of dietary intake.

Why is the popular diet in the Mediterranean deteriorating so rapidly? There has been much speculation that this is due to European agricultural policies, in particular subsidies paid to farmers that drive down the prices of certain foods, making them more available to consumers at cheaper prices. For the European countries of the Mediterranean, the CAP of the European Union was found by some experts to have minimal impact on rising levels of obesity. Although these policies have subsidized butter prices and made milk more available in public schools, thereby increasing fat consumption levels for some consumers, their overall effect on popular diet has not been that dramatic. Instead, economists and nutritional experts blame the rising standard of living, which has led to the increased purchase of more meat, especially beef, and fats. The increased use of supermarkets has also meant the increased consumption of prepared foods, another contributing factor to the deterioration of diet. Women working outside the home has meant families eat out more often; eating out means less healthy choices and larger portions, particularly if families are eating in fast food restaurants. Also, people exercise less, leading more sedentary lifestyles in front of televisions and computers, without, of course, adjusting their caloric intake to accommodate their lifestyle changes.

It seems clear that on the European side of the Mediterranean, an improved economy and living standard are contributing to less healthy lifestyles in the form of poor diet and incidence of overweight and obesity. European experts argue that government policies have little to do with rising obesity, which, they argue, is caused more by economic conditions and lifestyle choices. Throughout the rest of the Mediterranean, particularly in North Africa, obesity is also on the rise. In Egypt, where the standard of living is not very high and indeed, much of the population struggles to get by, obesity has also reached epidemic proportions. In 1998, the World Bank estimated that 70 percent of Egyptian women and 48 percent of Egyptian men were either overweight or obese. Experts were initially quick to blame changing dietary habits, but they frequently overlooked the Egyptian government's policy of subsidizing key foods like bread, wheat flour, sugar, and cooking oil. All of these foods are energy dense and nutrient poor. They may help poor consumers stretch their family food budget, but they do so at the expense of proper nutrition and health. Indeed, several experts have recommended that the Egyptian government subsidize healthy foods such as fruit and vegetables, as well as the basic foods such as bread, sugar, and oil.[14]

Comparing the North African side with the European side of the Mediterranean, one sees that there are multiple causes for the obesity problem on both sides of the sea. It seems clear, then, that obesity, as a measure of public health, can be caused by a complex interplay of factors and by extension, fighting obesity will be neither quick nor easy. Certainly, official policies regarding agricultural and consumer subsidies have to be reviewed and evaluated, not just for their immediate impact but also for their global influence. Although Schmidhuber noted that the European Union's subsidies did little to affect obesity rates among Europeans, he was careful to note that, in driving agricultural prices down generally, they could have impact on public health in developing countries such as those in North Africa. Put simply, certain European policies (high tariffs, export surpluses, and export subsidies) led to lower world food prices, thereby aggravating domestic economies in developing nations. In countries such as Egypt, where the government stepped in to ensure adequate supplies of basic foods in difficult economic times (to avert food riots), artificially low food prices may have contributed to excess consumption of certain foods and obesity.

Fighting obesity also requires some resolve from public officials to educate the consuming public about healthy habits. Throughout the Mediterranean, there is a considerable range of government intervention, from a willingness to debate a possible "fat tax" on unhealthy food to taking no action at all. State intervention in personal choices like consumption is controversial. Consumers, especially young consumers, may need to be educated about what food choices are good for them, but there is no guarantee that they will listen to the voice of public authority. A less sedentary lifestyle should be encouraged, but how far will authorities go to make it easier, or desirable, for citizens to get more exercise? And local producers should be supported so they can continue to grow fresh produce at affordable prices. So far, local farmers and food producers receive a combination of public and private support, as consumers have banded together in organizations like Slow Food (see chapter 3) to ensure that their products continue to find markets. Certainly, however, there are limits to what any authority, public or private, can do to combat obesity. For example, what can be done about American-style fast food? It is popular among young consumers, and it frequently comes from American-based corporations that have significant resources to spend on plans for international expansion. Local governments have been successful at fighting the expansion of McDonald's into historic city centers, but what can be done about the expansion of the same franchise throughout suburbs and even into rural areas of the Mediterranean? Although the alarm has been sounded about a current, and future, obesity crisis in the region, policymakers, doctors, and other experts have yet to agree on the best course of action to combat the problem.

More worrisome to some is the idea that the Mediterranean diet is no longer being practiced that much in the Mediterranean region, as growing

In southern France, the farmer's union dumped fruits and vegetables in a McDonald's parking lot in 1999. Farmers and others target McDonald's restaurants as a symbol of Americanization. AP Photo/Claude Paris.

numbers of consumers replace a low-fat, high-carbohydrate, and produce-rich diet with a high-fat, animal-based one. In terms of sugar, salt, and fat intake, the difference between Mediterranean consumers and American and northern European consumers is shrinking. Ironically, the Mediterranean diet is internationally famous as a curative or preventive diet, but its very existence in the region is being threatened. As this book has demonstrated, food means a great deal to the populations throughout the Mediterranean. Will this continue to be the case in the future? In other words, will Mediterranean food culture survive? It seems clear that hospitality—demonstrated through preparing, cooking, and serving food—is still very much a part of Mediterranean society. Hungry customers can still find a variety of traditional street food alongside American-style fast food. Small farmers are supported, albeit unevenly, through a combination of public and private initiatives. And technology has worked to encourage popular interest in Mediterranean cuisine, bringing information and advice about cooking techniques and special dishes to a broader audience, as well as connecting Mediterranean people to their culinary roots. There appears to be much evidence to suggest that many of the special characteristics of Mediterranean food culture will indeed survive.

Mediterranean cuisine has been in a state of change, or flux, for hundreds and even thousands of years, as populations mixed together and shared information about cooking and eating. Cookbook authors and other experts on Mediterranean life and culture have not always understood this fact, or if they have understood it, they have downplayed it in favor of highlighting a more timeless or unchanging aspect of Mediterranean cuisine. Yet an essential part of Mediterranean food culture is adaptability. It stands to reason, then, that the recent influx of food habits and culinary styles will eventually be reshaped by Mediterranean consumers, many of whom are now living in a world of abundance, not poverty and want. Mediterranean consumers will eventually adapt to these relatively new circumstances and perhaps hold on to the characteristics of the Mediterranean diet that have served them well for hundreds of years.

NOTES

1. The Mediterranean diet sometimes includes red wine, but wine consumption is sometimes studied separately.

2. Thomas M. S. Wolever, Alexandra L. Jenkins, Peter J. Spadafora, and David J. A. Jenkins, "Grains, Legumes, Fruits, and Vegetables: Lente Carbohydrate Sources in the Mediterranean Diet," in Gene A. Spiller, ed., *The Mediterranean Diets in Health and Disease* (New York: Van Nostrand, 1991), pp. 160–181.

3. Pasquale Strazzullo and Alfonso Siani, "Hypertension" in Spiller, ed., *The Mediterranean Diets in Health and Disease*, pp. 221–222.

4. "Mediterranean diet lengthens Americans' Lives," Yahoo News, December 12, 2007, http://news.yahoo.com. The article is based on medical literature from the *Archives of Internal Medicine* in December 2007.

5. One review of literature with positive results is Antonia Trichopoulou, "Traditional Mediterranean Diet and Longevity in the Elderly: A Review," *Public Health Nutrition* (2004) 7: 943–947.

6. Lluís Serra-Majen, et al. "Scientific Evidence of Interventions Using the Mediterranean Diet: A Systematic Review," *Nutrition Reviews* 64 (2007): S29.

7. Flaminia Fidanza, "Legumes," in Spiller, *The Mediterranean Diets in Health and Disease*, p. 105, Table 4–2.

8. Thomas Braun, "Ancient Mediterranean Food," in Spiller, *The Mediterranean Diets in Health and Disease*, p. 11, Table 5–1.

9. Reina Garcia-Closas, Antoni Berenguer, and Carlos A. González, "Changes in Food Supply in Mediterranean Countries from 1961 to 2001," *Public Health Nutrition* 9 (2007): 53–60.

10. L. Greco, et al., "Early childhood feeding practices in southern Italy: Is the Mediterranean diet becoming obsolete? Study of 450 children aged 6–32 months in Campania Italy," *Acta Paediatrica* 87 (1998): 250–256.

11. Josep A Tur, Dora Romaguera, and Antoni Pons, "Food Consumption Patterns in a Mediterranean Region: Does the Mediterranean Diet Still Exist?" *Annals of Nutrition and Metabolism* 48 (2004): 193–201.

12. Ellen Hale, "Junk Food Super-sizing Europeans" *USA Today*, 11/18/2003, p. 13a.

13. See the summary article, "Med People Shun Med Diet," July 29, 2008: http://www.fao.org.newsroom and see Josef Schmidhuber's report, "The EU Diet: Evolution, Evaluation and Impacts of the CAP," http://www.fao.org/es/ESD/Montreal-JS.pdf.

14. See, for example, Abay Asfaw, "The Role of Food Price Policy in Determining the Prevalence of Obesity: Evidence from Egypt," *Review of Agricultural Economics* 28 (2006): 305–312.

Glossary

bouillabaisse   Fish stew made in Marseille, France, flavored with saffron.

bûche de Noël   French Christmas cake that resembles a Yule log.

bulgur   Parboiled wheat that has had wheat bran removed, used in salads and stuffed foods, especially in the eastern Mediterranean.

chometz (*hametz*)   Food that is fermented or could cause fermentation; it must be ritually cleansed from the Jewish household before the holiday of Passover.

couscous   Tiny nuggets of semolina flour that are steamed over broth and served as an accompaniment to meat, fish, or vegetables.

doner kebab   Meat that is grilled on a vertical spit and sliced off for customers, served in Turkey.

emmer   Ancient grain used to make bread and beer in Egypt and Greece.

ful medames   Popular Egyptian dish made with fava beans, olive oil, parsley, onion, and lemon juice.

garum   Liquid seasoning made by fermenting fish or fish innards, used in ancient societies.

halal   Foods that are allowed for Muslims following Islamic dietary regulations.

haram   Foods that are forbidden for Muslims following Islamic dietary regulations.

harira   Soup made in North Africa from chickpeas, beef, onion, tomatoes, rice, lentils, and spices, eaten to break the fast during Ramadan, the Muslim holiday.

harissa   Food paste made from hot peppers and seasonings, used to season dishes in Morocco.

kashrut   Jewish dietary rules and regulations.

kibbeh   Lebanese dish made from ground raw lamb, bulgur, and spices.

kofta   Egyptian meatballs, made from lamb or beef.

koshari   Egyptian street food made of pasta, rice, legumes, tomatoes, onions, and seasonings.

leb-lebi   Tunisian chickpea soup, popular as street food, eaten with raw egg, olive oil, lemon juice, and *harissa*.

maccu   Sicilian fava bean soup seasoned with fennel, olive oil, salt, and pepper.

melokiyah   A plant that is a member of the mallow family. It resembles spinach and was used in ancient Egypt to thicken soup. Still used in Egypt and Tunisia in soups and stews.

meze   Little dishes of food served in the eastern Mediterranean as appetizers or as a meal.

paella   Rice dish made with chicken, sausage, shellfish, fish, artichokes, tomatoes, peppers, peas, garlic and seasonings; popular in Catalonian region of Spain. It is also the name of the iron skillet in which the rice is cooked.

pareve   Containing no animal ingredients, in accordance with Jewish dietary law.

pilav   Seasoned rice or bulgur dish that accompanies meat; popular in Turkey and in the eastern Mediterranean.

sagra   A festival or banquet in Italy honoring a specific food or dish, usually something that has just been harvested.

shawarma   A large kebab of meat (lamb or chicken) threaded on a skewer and grilled on a vertical grill. Served in Lebanon, Syria, and Israel.

souk   Outdoor market in which stalls are grouped together so that a particular good or trade is offered in one central location.

stifado   Greek style of cooking where meats and vegetables are stewed together.

tahini   Paste made of ground sesame seeds, used in Mediterranean dishes such as hummus or baba ghanouj.

tajine   A special pot used in Morocco to cook stew; also called tagine. The pot has a wide bottom and narrow neck, which allows for steam to condense and slide down to bottom of pot, tenderizing legumes and meat. In Tunisia, a tajine is a baked stew.

tapas   Little snacks or plates of food, eaten in Spain as appetizers or as an accompaniment with wine or alcohol.

tgilla   Ash bread made by baking dough in heated covered hole in the desert by nomadic Tuareg of Algeria.

tripe   Stomach lining of a cow, used in stews, soups, and casseroles.

Resource Guide

HISTORY AND CULTURE

Historians have long respected Fernand Braudel's magisterial history of the Mediterranean, *The Mediterranean and the Mediterranean World in the Age of Philip II* (New York: Harper and Row, 1972–1973, 2 volumes) for the way it presents the history, geography, and culture of the region. More recently, Robert Fox in *The Inner Sea. The Mediterranean and Its People* (New York: Knopf, 1993) takes a contemporary perspective on population, politics, society, and the environment; and Iain Chambers, *Mediterranean Crossings: The Politics of an Interrupted Modernity* (Durham: Duke University Press, 2008) focuses on politics today in the region. Students interested in the impact of historical change or modernization on people's eating habits may wish to look at anthropologist Carole Counihan's *Around the Tuscan Table. Food, Family and Gender in Twentieth Century Florence* (New York: Routledge, 2004). The book describes several families in Tuscany and looks in detail at their food habits, as well as their attitudes toward food. An excellent environmental history of the region is J. Donald Hughes, *The Mediterranean. An Environmental History* (Santa Barbara: ABC-CLIO, 2005).

COOKBOOKS

There are many excellent cookbooks detailing the history of Mediterranean cuisine. Cookbooks are invaluable resources for historians and anyone interested in understanding how food is prepared and described at a particular moment in time. Elizabeth David was one of the first cookbook authors who popularized Mediterranean cooking for a British and American audience. David, who spent a great deal of time in the Mediterranean region, wrote *A Book of Mediterranean Food* (London: Lehman, 1950) as an introduction to the many foods of the region. Her book is full of interesting descriptions and recipes. Today, Paula Wolfert is known as an authority on Mediterranean food. Her Web site, www.paulawolfert.com, is an excellent resource for readers curious about Mediterranean food and cooking techniques. Wolfert's *Mediterranean Cooking* (New York: Harper Perennial, 1994) is authoritative and informative. Cookbooks have more recently combined personal stories or journalistic accounts of the Mediterranean with recipes and cooking tips. Fiona Dunlop's book, *The North African Kitchen. Regional Recipes and Stories* (Northampton, MA: Interlink, 2008) follows ordinary women around their kitchens and their home cities to understand how and why they prepare food. Florian Harms and Lutz Jäkel, *The Flavours of Arabia* (London: Thames and Hudson, 2007), discusses many aspects of food culture in North Africa and the Middle East. In between the many recipes from this region are forays into history and contemporary culture, as they relate to food, its preparation, and consumption. Anissa Helou traveled around the Mediterranean region, sampling all kinds of street foods and writing about them. Her experiences and the recipes she collected are in her book, *Mediterranean Street Food* (New York: HarperCollins, 2002). And Mary Taylor Simeti, who has lived on the island of Sicily for a number of years, wrote *Pomp and Sustenance. Twenty-Five Centuries of Sicilian Food* (Hopewell, NJ: Ecco Press, 1989) as a tribute to the rich culinary history of the island.

Selected Bibliography

Andrews, Colman. *Catalan Cuisine*. New York: Atheneum, 1988.

Counihan, Carole. *Around the Tuscan Table*. *Food, Family and Gender in Twentieth Century Florence*. New York: Routledge, 2004.

Counihan, Carole. "Bread as World: Food Habits and Social Relations in Modernizing Sardinia." In Counihan, Carole and Van Esterik, Penny, eds. *Food and Culture*. *A Reader*. New York: Routledge, 1997.

Dalby, Andrew. *Siren Feasts*. *A History of Food and Gastronomy in Greece*. New York: Routledge, 1996.

Dunlop, Fiona. *The North African Kitchen*. *Regional Recipes and Stories*. Northampton, MA: Interlink, 2008.

Faas, Patrick. *Around the Roman Table: Food and Feasting in Ancient Rome*. New York: Palgrave Macmillan, 2003.

Farris, Efisio. *Sweet Myrtle and Bitter Honey*. *The Mediterranean Flavors of Sardinia*. New York: Rizzoli, 2007.

Fox, Robert. *The Inner Sea*. *The Mediterranean and Its People*. New York: Knopf, 1993.

Harms, Florian and Jäkel, Lutz. *The Flavours of Arabia*. *Cookery and Food in the Middle East*, trans. Andrew Cowin. London: Thames and Hudson, 2007.

Heine, Peter. *Food Culture in the Near East, Middle East, and North Africa*. Westport, CT: Greenwood Press, 2004.

Helou, Anissa. *Mediterranean Street Food*. New York: HarperCollins, 2002.

Hyman, Clarissa. *Cucina Siciliana*. Northampton, MA: Interlink, 2002.

Jansen, Willy. "French Bread and Algerian Wine: Conflicting Identities in French Algeria." In Peter Scholliers, ed. *Food, Drink and Identity*. *Cooking, Eating and Drinking in Europe Since the Middle Ages*. Oxford: Berg, 2001.

Keys, Ancel. *How to Eat Well and Stay Well the Mediterranean Way*. Garden City, NY: Doubleday, 1975.

Keys, Ancel. *Seven Countries. A Multivariate Analysis of Death and Coronary Heart Disease*. Cambridge, MA: Harvard University Press, 1980.

Kochilas, Diane. *The Glorious Foods of Greece: Traditional Recipes from the Islands, Cities, and Villages*. New York: HarperCollins, 2001.

Medina, Xavier. *Food Culture in Spain*. Westport, CT: Greenwood Press, 2005.

M'souli, Hassan. *Moroccan Modern*. Northampton, MA: Interlink, 2005.

Nathan, Joan. *The Foods of Israel Today*. New York: Alfred A. Knopf, 2001.

Ricotti, Eugenia Salza Prina. *Meals and Recipes from Ancient Greece*. Los Angeles: J. Paul Getty Museum, 2005.

Rivera, Oswald. *The Pharaoh's Feast: From Pit-Boiled Roots to Pickled Herring. Cooking Through the Ages with 110 Simple Recipes*. New York: Four Walls Eight Windows, 2003.

Rosant, Colette. *Memories of a Lost Egypt: A Memoir with Recipes*. New York: Clarkson Potter, 1999.

Simeti, Mary Taylor. *Pomp and Sustenance: Twenty-Five Centuries of Sicilian Food*. Hopewell, NJ: Ecco Press, 1989.

Torres, Marimar. *The Catalan Country Kitchen*. New York: Aris Books, 1992.

Wolfert, Paula. *Mediterranean Cooking*. New York: Harper Perennial, 1994.

Woodward, Sarah. *The Ottoman Kitchen*. Northampton, MA: Interlink, 2001.

Young, Daniel. *Made in Marseille*. New York: HarperCollins, 2002.

WEB SITES

www.chowhound.com: a Web site for food fans, also known as "chowhounds," started by a group of food editors and fans to provide news, information, recipes, and tips. Contains information about eating out or finding food in Mediterranean countries, as well as recipes and travel tips.

www.faithandfood.com: The faith and food initiative is part of Global Tolerance Limited, a United Kingdom based company that seeks to promote inter-faith understanding. Contains information, recipes, and ideas for celebrations and holidays, covering all aspects of interfaith eating.

www.mediterranean-food.net: A Web site that contains many recipes for Mediterranean dishes as well as some information about the Mediterranean diet as a health or weight reduction regimen.

www.paula-wolfert.com: Cookbook author Paula Wolfert's Web site, with lots of information, recipes, and tips about Mediterranean cooking and cuisine. Especially strong on Moroccan food.

www.slowfood.com: The official Web site of the Slow Food movement, this site contains information about the organization in the United States as well as around the world. Recipes, news stories, and a calendar of events are featured and updated daily.

Index

About the Author

CAROL HELSTOSKY is Associate Professor of History at the University of Denver. She is the author of *Pizza* (2008) and *Garlic and Oil: Politics and Food in Italy* (2004).

641.59 Helstosky, Carol
HEL   Food culture in the
         Mediterranean   (Greenwood)
MYN   10-09

DISCARD

MAYNARDVILLE PUBLIC LIBRARY
MAYNARDVILLE, TENNESSEE 37807